HOW TO SURVIVE
(and Even Excel in)
GENERAL CHEMISTRY

ELIZABETH KEAN
University of Nebraska–Lincoln

CATHERINE MIDDLECAMP
University of Wisconsin–Madison

McGraw-Hill, Inc.

New York   St. Louis   San Francisco   Auckland   Bogotá
Caracas   Lisbon   London   Madrid   Mexico City
Milan   Montreal   New Delhi   San Juan
Singapore   Sydney   Tokyo   Toronto

To our students
and
to Marion

Copyright © 1986 by Random House, Inc. under the title The Success Manual for General Chemistry. All rights reserved.

HOW TO SURVIVE (AND EVEN EXCEL IN) GENERAL CHEMISTRY

Copyright © 1994 by McGraw-Hill, Inc. All rights reserved. Printed in the United States of America. Except as permitted under the Copyright Act of 1976, no part of this publication may be reproduced or distributed in any form or by any means, or stored in a data base or retrieval system, without the prior written permission of the publisher.

3 4 5 6 7 8 9 10 11 12 13 14 15 16 17 18 19 20 SEM SEM 9 8 7 6 5 4

ISBN 0-07-034033-1

Library of Congress Cataloging-in-Publication Data

Kean, Elizabeth.
    How to survive (and even excel in) general chemistry / Elizabeth Kean, Catherine Middlecamp.
        p.   cm.
    Updated ed. of: The success manual for general chemistry. 1st ed. c1986.
    Includes index.
    ISBN 0-07-034033-1
    1. Chemistry—Study and teaching (Higher)   2. Study skills.
I. Middlecamp, Catherine.   II. Kean, Elizabeth.   Success manual for general chemistry.   III. Title.
QD40.K3935   1994
540'.71—dc20   93–50200
                                                              CIP

Manufactured in the United States of America

How to Use this Book

This book is about the *process* of learning chemistry. It contains information that will help you design the personal strategies you will need for success in your general chemistry course.

This book does *not* teach the specific topics needed for success in your chemistry course. Nor should it. Other resources exist for this purpose: your instructor, your textbook, other printed materials, and computer software.

Over the years, as we have watched our students learn, we have become learners along with them. They have allowed us to see chemistry through their eyes and have taught us study approaches that lead to successful and efficient learning. In this book, we now pass them on to you.

How you might best use this book depends on who you are:

If you have never studied chemistry before, you may want to read carefully Chapter One, A General Approach to Learning Chemistry and Chapter Two, Planning Your Personal Approach to Learning Chemistry. Then read quickly through Chapters Six through Eleven, which introduce you to the different types of chemical content. Use this book to get a general idea of what the subject will be like and how you might go about learning it.

If you have had a high school chemistry course and will soon be taking college chemistry, you may want to read the book straight through. You will probably be able to relate the points in each chapter to your previous experiences of learning chemistry. When your course begins, you will need to discover how it differs from your previous learning experiences. Let this book be your guide to mapping out the differences and planning new strategies.

If your chemistry course is under way (and things are going reasonably well), focus on Part Two, Mastering the Content of Chemistry. Once you can identify the types of chemical content described in Chapter Five, assess the content demands of your own course. Find the most prevalent type of content and go directly to the chapters in Part Two that describe what you can do to master it. Refer also to the chapters that may meet your immediate needs, such as the one about laboratory or on taking chemistry exams.

If your chemistry course is under way (and things aren't going so well), start with Chapter Two. You may find that you are able to map out some new strategies that will increase your ability to succeed. Look also at Chapter Four on chemistry tests. Also be sure to consider the question, "Am I in the Right Course at the Right Time?" (see page 34). We have known many capable students who were unable to succeed until they first improved their math or chemistry background. Lots of smart students drop their chemistry courses in order to retake them under more favorable circumstances.

At any time, should you have a specific question about a chemical topic, check out the Chemical Content Index, which will refer you to pages in the book where that topic is mentioned. If you want specific information about study activities such as summarizing or classifying concepts, check out the Learning Skill Index.

Finally, we point out that we have never met anybody who knew all there was to know. Learning doesn't stop unless you die—or act as if you were dead! In this book, we invite you to work toward mastery of the process of learning chemistry. Once you have good control of the process, you can apply it to learn what you wish. We wouldn't be surprised if some of the information in this book were to be of use in your other subjects as well.

Good luck, and we wish you well as you meet the challenges that lie ahead.

Acknowledgments

This book has come into being with the help and inspiration of many people. We are deeply grateful to all of them.

Our students have been our finest resource, bringing to us their willingness to teach us what the subject of chemistry is all about. Over the past 20 years, their successes, failures, frustrations, and joys have made the writing of this book possible.

Marion O'Leary, now professor of biochemistry at the University of Nebraska–Lincoln, has been with us in the writing of this book since its earliest days. His abilities to cajole, inspire, laugh, and encourage, as well as his flawless writing and editing skills, have helped keep us at the task. Husband to one of us, and friend to both, he has been an unflagging supporter. Maybe the fact that he has a grand piano named Max is also of note.

Sr. Marion Hosinski, S.S.M., Ph.D., and Br. Marion Belka, S.M., Ph.D., counseling psychologists, helped us to see the many dimensions that are part of our students' lives and of our own. Their insights into human behavior and development, as well as their vision for growth and wholeness, are woven into every chapter of this book.

Colleagues from around the country and around the world have assisted us in refining and clarifying our perception of the demands of chemistry courses. In particular, we would like to thank Derry Scott and the other members of the Department of Chemistry at the Australian National University for their helpful comments during the early stages of the book.

At the University of Wisconsin–Madison, we are grateful for the input and support of Paul Treichel, Glen Dirreen, and Fred Juergens, all of the Department of Chemistry. Jim Stewart and Michael Streibel of the Department of Curriculum and Instruction likewise helped us clarify what the learning process is all about. Within the Chemistry Learning Center, we are happy to acknowledge the contributions of many of the talented tutors who have engaged students in the process of learning. Nina Nethercote, Kathleen Plute, Gary Wesenberg, Selene Nikaido, Emily Jones, and Laura Rahn stand out as contributors.

Colleagues at other institutions who have given us comments, criticisms, and encouragement include Wesley Smith (Ricks College), Gary Wulfsburg (Middle Tennessee State University), J. Dudley Herron (Purdue University), and Janie Copes (now, alas, lost from chemistry to computer science). To these, and to others who have written their encouragement and suggestions, we extend our thanks.

We also acknowledge those who have supported and funded the Chemistry Learning Center, making it possible for us to work these many years with our students. Specifically, Dean E. David Cronon (now retired) and Dean Judy Craig of the College of Letters and Science, University of Wisconsin–Madison, have been supporters in times of plenty and in times of want. We are most grateful to them both.

Lastly, this book would not have been possible without a grant from the Fund for the Improvement of Postsecondary Education, Department of Education. A Mina Shaughnessy Scholar's grant gave us the space and time to create a manuscript from which this book evolved.

Contents

PART TWO   MASTERING THE CONTENT OF CHEMISTRY   83

Chapter Five   Identifying Types of Chemical Content   85

Chapter Six   Memorizing Chemical Information   116

Chapter Seven **Mastering Chemical Concepts** **133**

Chapter Eight **Mastering Chemical Rules** **158**

Chapter Eleven **Solving Chemical Problems: Harder Problems**   **240**

Appendix **Basic Chemical and Mathematical Knowledge**   **260**

PART ONE

GETTING THE MOST FROM YOUR CHEMISTRY COURSE

In the first part of this book, we focus on you: your interaction with your chemistry course, your study schedule, and your ability to take tests.

In Chapter One, A General Approach to Learning Chemistry, we introduce you to the many dimensions of your chemistry course, pointing out what you can expect to encounter. In Chapter Two, Planning for Success, we next invite you to see yourself as an active participant in your course. Here, we encourage you to make a personal study plan that will help you to meet the demands of your course.

Chapter Three, The Laboratory, prepares you for the interactions and learning experiences that your laboratory work offers. There are few experiences that rival the excitement—and frustration—of working in the laboratory. We do not want you to miss the opportunities that the laboratory presents!

Finally, in Chapter Four, we focus on tests and your ability to show what you know on them. Here, we draw from the wisdom of what many students have taught us about taking chemistry exams.

You may find it helpful to refer to these chapters in Part One throughout your study of chemistry. As you progress through your chemistry course, we encourage you to use these chapters to develop your personal skills for success.

CHAPTER ONE

A General Approach to Learning Chemistry

If you want to do well in your introductory chemistry course, this book is for you. People have different reasons for wanting to succeed in chemistry. You may want to master the subject because chemistry or biochemistry is your major. Perhaps you need a good chemistry grade in order to be admitted to a profession like medicine, nursing, pharmacy, or engineering. You may simply be frustrated and want to do better because you are not learning as well as you would like. No matter what your reason, this book is designed to help you become a better student in chemistry.

You may have heard other students complaining of the stress they felt while enrolled in chemistry. Chemistry courses do have a reputation for being difficult. On many campuses, students fail or drop chemistry courses in large numbers. The students we have known who have had a hard time with chemistry frequently have told us that they have felt stupid, inadequate, or incompetent while taking chemistry. And yet, we know that these people are not stupid, nor are they inadequate or incompetent when armed with the appropriate learning skills. These students have been able to acquire stronger learning skills, and so can you.

This book will teach you the skills that you need for learning chemistry. We promise no miracles. We offer no easy shortcuts to success. We do promise, however, to help you understand how you are being taught, what you are being asked to learn, and how you will be tested. We will show you ways to meet the demands of your course, helping you learn how to learn chemistry.

Think of these skills as stepping stones to increased mastery of chemistry. At first, they will help you enter the realm of chemical knowledge. As your skills become stronger, you will be able to step confidently into the more difficult areas of chemical problem solving. Finally, when you master these skills, you will be free to enter areas requiring creative thinking and chemical intuition.

STUDENT FEARS ABOUT LEARNING CHEMISTRY

Over the last 10 years we have asked many students why learning chemistry was hard for them. In this section we examine some of their responses. Do any of the following statements sound familiar? Which of them might you make?

I'm Just Not Smart Enough to Learn Chemistry

Do you believe that you have to be extraordinarily smart to learn chemistry? Many chemistry students worry that they are not smart enough to learn the subject. Put this fear aside. People of normal intelligence can learn chemistry.

You must become competent to receive an A in chemistry, but you need not be a genius. Yes, chemical concepts are complex and you need a facility in mathematics in order to work chemical problems. But more important, you need certain learning skills to be able to process the information, recall it without error, and use it in new situations. Genius or not, you can learn these skills. This book will assist you.

I Just Can't Think Like a Chemist

Do you believe that chemists think differently from other human beings? Not so! The "chemical mind" is a myth. It is not an inborn characteristic like the color of your eyes or hair.

Some students appear to know intuitively how to learn chemistry. They need no help in picking out essential information, fitting ideas together, or solving chemical problems. In actuality, those students have already learned skills such as structuring information, analytical reasoning, and problem solving. You can learn these skills as well.

I Can't Keep Up with the Work in My Chemistry Course

Do you fear that you will not have time to learn all the required information in your chemistry course? Depending on your current commitments, this may be true. This chapter will help you assess the demands that your course will make on your time. Whether or not to allot the time to meet these demands is your choice.

If you are already having trouble keeping up, ask yourself whether you are prepared to take the course. Is your math adequate? Is your background in chemistry similar to that of other students? Do you know how to study efficiently to make the best use of your study time? Can you memorize effectively? Do you know how to master a concept? You will need answers to questions like these in order to assess your chances for success.

I'm Afraid I Will Fail Chemistry

Do you believe that you will fail chemistry no matter how hard you try? Few students will come right out and say this. However, their actions may show that they believe it. In other words, they may not try terribly hard. After all, why try hard when you are going to fail anyhow?

Trying your best involves a risk. If you fail in spite of your best efforts, you cannot rationalize your failure by saying, "Oh, I could have passed if I'd really tried." However, to succeed in chemistry you must be willing to take the risk of trying your best. In this book we will suggest active strategies for study that can result in powerful learning. We will try to enable you to make your risk pay off.

I Don't Like the Material and I Don't Want to Study It

Does studying chemistry give you a headache? Do you put off working on your chemistry problems? What we question here is your motivation. If you do not particularly like chemistry, you may need to become aware of your reasons for working at it. Some reasons are immediate ("I don't want to fail tomorrow's quiz"). Others involve future rewards ("I want to become a pharmacist, and I'm willing to do whatever it takes").

Can your teachers, parents, or friends motivate you to study chemistry? Perhaps, but they are not responsible for your learning; you are. You must be willing to work because it is in your best interest. In short, your motivation must come from yourself.

By picking up this book you have already shown motivation for success. We will help you face the challenges of your course and provide you with ways to improve your performance. As you become more successful, studying will become more pleasurable and satisfying.

My Memory Isn't Good Enough to Handle All the Information

Do you mix up sulfide and sulfite? Molality and molarity? Does what you have learned seem to slip out of your head? If the answer to any of these questions is yes, don't panic. It is quite normal to forget. Otherwise, your brain would quickly overload.

Although it is normal to forget, for success in chemistry you need the ability to learn rapidly and to retain what you have learned. At the outset you will have to memorize certain basic facts and vocabulary. Later on, you will learn important chemical information by successfully integrating chemical ideas and using them repeatedly.

Part Two of this book will teach you skills for meaningful learning. As you discover the appropriate techniques for learning each type of chemical material, your learning will become more powerful and complete. You will move beyond surviving your chemistry course to mastering it.

HOW THIS BOOK WILL HELP YOU LEARN CHEMISTRY

By now, you should have a good idea of what successful chemistry students are like:

• They believe that they are capable of learning chemistry.
• They are confident enough to risk trying hard.

· They work to develop their thinking and reasoning skills.

· They are motivated to do the required work, even in the absence of immediate rewards.

· They look for ways to improve the efficiency of their studying.

· They analyze the demands of their course and develop study patterns that can meet these demands.

As you work through this book, you will encounter some descriptions of constructive attitudes—those that make learning more enjoyable or productive. However, the emphasis in this book is on **skills**—what you need to be able to do in order to master chemistry.

Not every skill will be covered. For example, we will not attempt to teach you how to take notes, how to read at the college level, or how to do algebra. We will tell you, however, when such skills are important and will provide references to other books that can help you develop these skills.

HELPFUL STUDY APPROACHES FOR CHEMISTRY

We now turn our attention to the subject itself: *chemistry*. We will look at five important characteristics of the subject and detail some study approaches to help you deal with each.

Characteristic 1: Much of Chemistry Is Abstract

Atoms, molecules, electrons, chemical bonds—these typify the invisible world of chemistry that you must imagine rather than experience directly. Because atoms are so incredibly small, they are not visible. When chemists talk about atoms and molecules, they are referring to the molecular (or microscopic) level of matter. Much of your thinking in a chemistry course will be on this abstract molecular level.

Study Approach 1: Create Mental Pictures of the Abstract World You Study

A picture can help you both conceptualize and remember essential information. For example, the atom is at the heart of chemistry. You cannot see an atom, but you can form a mental picture to represent one. You might picture a nitrogen atom as:

This representation reminds you that a nitrogen atom is different from other kinds of atoms and that it is a real object with a definite shape and size.

Figures 1–1 and 1–2 show how you can imagine a water molecule and the ionic solid KBr.

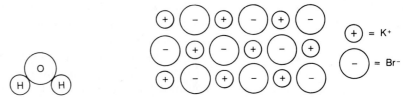

FIGURE 1–1 *Water molecule*   **FIGURE 1–2** *Ionic solid KBr*

In reality, atoms and molecules are three dimensional and are in constant motion. Does it matter that your pictures do not represent atoms and molecules as they truly are? Not really. Your schematic drawings are still a powerful tool to help you develop a mental picture of the microscopic world. Just keep in mind that they are a simplification.

Throughout this book we will ask you to answer questions and work exercises. Do not skip these. They will provide you with experience and practice. Get a pen or pencil and work Exercise 1 in the space below. Answers will be found at the end of this chapter.

EXERCISE 1   Imagining Atoms and Molecules

1. The molecule CO_2 contains one atom of carbon and two atoms of oxygen arranged in a straight line, with carbon in the middle. Draw a schematic picture of a molecule of CO_2:

2. Figure 1–1 depicts a water molecule. What do you think this would look like in three dimensions?

Characteristic 2: The Chemistry You Study Is a Simplified Version of the Real World

All matter in the world is made up of chemicals—air, trees, rocks, pesticides, polyester socks. Since you are surrounded by chemicals, you have had many first-hand experiences with them. You see, touch, smell, taste, and play with chemicals. One goal of your chemistry class is to help you understand how the world around you is organized. Many of the principles taught in your chemistry class will help to explain how the world works.

The problem is that most objects in the world are complex, hard-to-study mixtures of chemicals. To make things more manageable, the study of chemistry begins with a simplified picture, looking at substances that are pure or contain only two or three chemicals mixed together. However, the behavior of these simple systems is often quite different from that of the more complex, naturally occurring systems. As a result, you sometimes get into trouble when you try to relate what you have experienced to what you are studying in class.

Study Approach 2: Use Care as You Relate Everyday Experiences to Your Chemistry Class

A powerful way to understand what you have learned in the classroom is to relate it to what you have experienced in your life. We encourage you to seek connections between the knowledge presented in your chemistry course and your life outside the classroom. For example, most people have made orange juice from the frozen concentrate: add three cans of water to one can concentrate, and mix. If by mistake you add four cans of water, the juice is more watery (less concentrated). If you add two cans of water, the juice is stronger (more concentrated). These experiences give you some notion of solution concentrations, a topic studied in most chemistry courses.

As you look for similarities between classroom knowledge and your real-life experiences, look for differences as well. For example, you cannot apply all of your experiences with orange juice to your study of solutions. If orange juice is left standing for a time, it will become more concentrated at the bottom. You may be tempted to believe all solutions behave in this way, but they do not. In actuality, orange juice is not a solution, but rather a suspension. It contains orange particles that can be suspended temporarily in the juice but settle to the bottom upon standing.

Characteristic 3: All Matter Can Be Viewed Microscopically and Macroscopically

Table salt is an inexpensive, white crystalline solid that you sprinkle on your hamburger. Table salt is also a chemical composed of sodium and chloride ions, with the formula NaCl. Which of these descriptions is the "correct" way to describe this well-known chemical? They both are! At the atomic (or microscopic) level we describe the substance in terms of the relative numbers of atoms of each type that are present in the substance. At the macroscopic level, we encounter billions upon billions of these atomic-sized particles. Even though individual atoms cannot be seen, extremely large collections of these atoms can be seen, observed, weighed, measured, and so on. Your job is to learn to view matter and its properties from both perspectives.

Study Approach 3: Connect the Macroscopic and Microscopic Views of Matter

Many chemical ideas can be viewed on both macroscopic and microscopic levels. The microscopic level is often used to rationalize or explain macroscopic phenomena. For example, you may have encountered the phenomenon of *air pressure* when you inflated a bicycle tire. On the macroscopic level you observe that your tire becomes harder as you inflate it. You can explain this macroscopic behavior by picturing the tire filled with gas molecules, all of which are banging against each other and against the walls of the tire. It is the collision of gas molecules with the tire walls that gives rise to the pressure (force per area of tire wall). The more you inflate your tire, the more gas molecules are hitting the tire walls and the harder the tire becomes.

To help you connect the two levels, you can make use of schematic pictures that combine elements of each level. For example, in Figure 1–3 we have drawn a picture of a beaker filled with water. Inside the beaker we have represented the water by drawing several "molecules" of water.

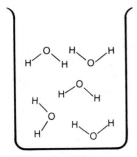

FIGURE 1–3 *Schematic representation of water molecules in a beaker*

Your understanding of the macroscopic and microscopic aspects of water is complete when you can connect such schematic pictures with real samples of water. The next time you encounter a glass of water, imagine the molecules that are there. A glass of water contains billions upon billions of three-dimensional water molecules. Each molecule is in contact with its neighbors. All are in constant motion, jostling each other, rolling around, and shifting position. Can you "see" those molecules with your imagination?

EXERCISE 2   Drawing Macroscopic-Microscopic Pictures of Objects

There are three states of matter: solid, liquid, and gas. Each may be described macroscopically and microscopically.

SOLID

Macroscopic: Matter with a definite shape and volume
Microscopic: Matter that has its atoms, molecules, or ions held rigidly to one another so that they do not change positions

A schematic drawing of a solid piece of matter might be represented as follows:

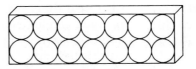

LIQUID

Macroscopic: Matter that has a definite volume, but that takes the shape of its container
Microscopic: Matter that has its atoms or molecules fairly close to one another, but still able to move freely over one another, constantly changing position

Here is a picture of an empty container. Imagine that it contains a sample of liquid and draw a schematic picture to represent this. (Answers to this exercise may be found at the end of the chapter.)

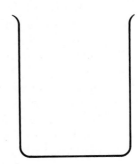

GAS

Macroscopic: Matter that has no definite shape or volume and that takes the shape and volume of its container.

Microscopic: Matter that has its atoms or molecules relatively far apart and able to freely collide with each other and with the walls of the container.

Here is another container. Imagine that it contains a sample of gas and draw a schematic picture to represent this.

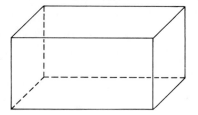

Characteristic 4: Chemical Content Is Sequential and Builds Rapidly

Chemical topics must often be learned in a particular order. For example, you cannot mentally put atoms together to make molecules unless you first learn what atoms are. Your ability to understand what you are currently being taught may depend on your already having mastered earlier material. Since information is presented at so rapid a pace, getting everything learned at the appropriate time may be no easy task.

Study Approach 4: Study Chemistry Every Day and Correct Your Mistakes as They Occur

Keep up with your studies! Many students find that they learn chemistry best when they study it every day, although skipping a day now and then usually does no harm. It is not possible to learn chemistry well by studying it only once or twice a week. The cumulative nature of the material as well as the sheer amount to be learned make occasional studying ineffective.

Pay attention to the mistakes you make. For example, if you get questions wrong on an exam, take the time to find and learn the correct answer. If you do not, you will make the same mistakes on subsequent exams and lose additional points for them.

Characteristic 5: There is More to Chemistry Than Solving Problems

Solving numerical problems is such an important part of learning chemistry that we have devoted two chapters of this book to the subject. However, do not focus your attention solely on problems. The subject of chemistry contains much descriptive material—chemical facts, specialized vocabulary and the ideas underlying it, and chemical rules that relate these ideas to one another. You will be tested directly on this descriptive material. You will also need to understand this material in order to work the problems.

Study Approach 5: Use Appropriate Learning Techniques for Each Type of Chemical Material

As you work through Chapters 6 through 11, you will learn effective study techniques for different types of chemical content:

- Chapter Six   Memorizing chemical facts
- Chapter Seven   Forming and using chemical concepts
- Chapter Eight   Forming and using chemical rules
- Chapter Nine   Presenting rules in special formats: mathematical formulas and graphs
- Chapter Ten   Solving routine chemical problems
- Chapter Eleven   Solving harder chemical problems

Each type of material requires different actions for mastery. You do not study factual material in the same manner as you study conceptual material.

Not only must you use the appropriate learning techniques for different types of material, but you must learn that material in the appropriate order. For example, certain facts are necessary in order to understand a given concept. Concepts are necessary for understanding rules. Fact, concept, and rule information is essential for the solution of chemical problems. Therefore, fundamental material (facts, concepts, and rules) must be learned before you attempt to solve problems related to it.

Chapters Six through Eleven present topics in order of increasing complexity. Problem solving will be the most difficult and complex of all your work in general chemistry. Memorization is the easiest. All types of skills covered in these chapters are necessary for mastery of the subject.

HOW CHEMISTRY COURSES TEACH CHEMISTRY

In this chapter we first looked at you, the student, and the characteristics that you bring to your studies. We then examined the subject of chemistry and how its nature requires certain study patterns. We will now consider your chemistry course—the activities that bring you and the subject matter together.

There are four characteristics of chemistry courses that affect how you conduct your study.

Chemistry Courses Require You to Learn Much in a Short Time

Students often complain that their chemistry course requires more study than any of their other subjects. It's true that chemistry courses require a lot of work. A large amount of information will be presented in your course and must be rapidly mastered. Thus, students who hope to do well in chemistry must plan their studying carefully so as to use the available time most efficiently.

Because of the heavy load, you cannot afford to spend time learning much material that is not required by your course. Nor can you afford to waste time by studying the required material inefficiently. An efficient study plan does not just happen; it must be carefully planned. In the next chapter we will describe in detail how to develop a study plan that works for you.

Chemistry Courses Teach Chemistry, *Not* the Skills Necessary to Learn Chemical Content

In presenting large amounts of information to you, your instructor will not tell you how best to go about learning the information. For example, you will learn about acids such as HCl, H_2SO_4, and HF. However, you will probably not be taught how to master the concept of an acid (see page 135), how to visualize acids on the molecular level (see page 7), or how to memorize efficiently the names of the strong and weak acids (see page 117).

In not telling you these things, faculty members are not trying to hide something. Most professors assume that you have either learned these skills or will pick them up on your own. Furthermore, professors do not have time to spell out to you all that you need to know. You are responsible for identifying the learning skills you are missing and for developing them.

Chemistry Courses Contain Many Sources of Information

Most college chemistry courses present information to you in many ways. Place a check before the sources of information available in your course:

( ) Lectures
( ) Textbook readings
( ) Textbook problems
( ) Discussion classes
( ) Laboratory write-ups
( ) Laboratory observations
( ) Handouts
( ) Computer programs
( ) Textbook study guides
( ) Films
( ) Other _____ .

Next, ask yourself some questions about the sources of information you have checked. For example, are there one or two sources on which you should focus? Which sources tend to add "extra" information? Which sources are at a level closest to the level on which you will be tested?

These may not be easy questions to answer, but your success in chemistry may be related to your ability to find answers to them.

Usually, more information is available to you in your course than you can possibly learn. To make the best use of your time and energy, you should focus your studying on the most important sources of information. Chapter Two will help you with this skill.

Chemistry Courses Tend to Be Well Structured, Giving You Ample Feedback on Your Progress

An important feature of any course is its **structure**: the activities (such as assignments or weekly quizzes) that determine in what ways and how often you must study.

Chemistry courses are usually highly structured. In addition to attending lectures during the week, you may be required to attend laboratory sessions, write lab reports, attend discussion classes, take weekly quizzes, and/or work assigned problems. Although this may look like a lot of work, these activities are beneficial. They encourage you to keep up and give you opportunities to find out how well you are doing.

How is your course structured?

(   ) Quizzes are given.

(   ) Lab reports are collected and evaluated.

(   ) Answers are provided for assigned problems.

(   ) Detailed solutions are given for assigned problems.

(   ) Homework problems are graded.

(   ) Instructors have office hours to give you help.

(   ) Other _____.

Each part of your course gives you feedback on your progress. Are you using the feedback? Do you know how you are doing in the course? If you have not yet begun your course, how will you use the available feedback? We encourage you to ask your instructor for help in interpreting your progress if you are unsure of where you stand.

These four characteristics of chemistry courses can help you learn, but only if you are aware of them and make them work for you. Expect to be taught the subject of chemistry, but recognize that you must acquire the learning skills to master it by yourself. Expect to be presented with a lot of information, but be aware that you will have to focus more on some parts than on others. Expect to engage in many different learning activities and look for ways to monitor your own progress.

SUMMARY

This chapter has explained how you, the subject matter, and the course organization work together to determine the effective study approaches for your chemistry course.

As a student, work to develop the following attitudes:

· I'm smart enough to learn chemistry (and if I'm having trouble, this does not mean that I am stupid).

- I am willing to risk an all-out effort to learn chemistry.
- I can learn the skills I need to process chemical information.
- I will provide my own motivation to work hard in the course.
- I will improve my learning efficiency.
- I will develop strong study habits.

The subject matter of chemistry has the following important characteristics:

- Chemistry is abstract, dealing with atoms and molecules that you cannot see.
- Chemistry is taught as a simplified version of the real world.
- Chemistry provides microscopic and macroscopic descriptions of the world.
- The material is sequential and builds rapidly.
- The subject matter involves more than just solving problems.

Organize your studying to accommodate the nature of chemical content by acquiring these useful study approaches:

- Create mental pictures of the abstract (microscopic) world you study.
- Relate everyday (macroscopic) experiences to your chemistry class knowledge, but do so with care.
- Learn to make connections between the macroscopic and microscopic versions of the world.
- Study chemistry daily; do not fall behind.
- Correct mistakes as they occur.
- Determine which learning techniques are appropriate for each type of chemical material, and use them.

The characteristics of your chemistry course affect how you conduct your study:

- The course will teach large amounts of material very rapidly.
- Your professor will teach chemistry, not how to learn chemistry.
- The course will contain many sources of information; you must choose the most appropriate ones to use.
- The course is probably well structured, giving you ample feedback on your progress.

SELF-ASSESSMENT

At the end of each chapter of this book we will give you an opportunity to assess your position with respect to the information provided in the chapter.

Mark an X on the line in the position that describes your response to the following statements.

1. My attitudes toward the study of chemistry are primarily

HELPFUL ————————————————————————————— NOT
                                                    HELPFUL

Your attitude toward studying chemistry can make a difference in whether or not you succeed. In the preceding summary, we listed attitudes that are helpful for many students. If you are not satisfied with your approach to your chemistry course, you may want to work on changing how you look at things related to chemistry. It takes effort, but over time you can change your attitude.

Is there an attitude that you would like to work on changing? Write it below. As you work through this book, keep in mind the attitude that you would like to change. Also jot down below any insights you have into your present attitude and how you could change it.

2. I accept the need to organize my studying to accommodate the nature of the subject of chemistry.

YES ————————————————————————————— NO

Few students succeed in chemistry if their study habits are not compatible with the nature of chemical subject matter. You can begin to use some of the habits recommended in this chapter immediately in your course. The need to use others will become more clear as you progress through this book. Plan to review this chapter after a month has passed to see how well your study approaches match those we suggest.

ANSWERS TO EXERCISES

EXERCISE 1

1.

2.

EXERCISE 2

Microscopic "picture" of a liquid:

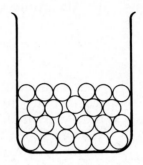

Microscopic "picture" of a gas:

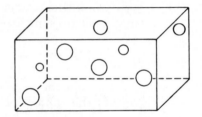

CHAPTER TWO

Planning Your Personal Approach to Learning Chemistry

Most people find it necessary to plan their strategy for studying chemistry. Devising a strategy is usually not difficult, but it does require decisions on your part. What might you need to decide? Here are some examples.

- What material is important for me to learn? What material is not?
- What ways of studying work best for me?
- How much time should I spend studying?
- How do I tell if I know the material well enough to stop studying it?
- What options do I have if I am not doing as well as I would like?

Since no two students are alike and no two courses are alike, we cannot give you definitive answers to these questions. We can, however, give you some guidelines for developing your own answers. After reading this chapter you will be better equipped to make your own decisions about your course and will be able to set up a study plan that works for you.

DECISION 1: WHAT MATERIAL AM I EXPECTED TO LEARN?

Your professor has expectations about what you are to learn in the course. Figure 2–1 shows the relationship between what you are expected to learn and the whole realm of chemistry.

The amount you are expected to learn is considerably less than the total of chemical knowledge. Indeed, it is probably also much less than the amount of chemical information contained in your textbook. However, this amount is still sufficiently large to be challenging, given the amount of time that you have available for studying chemistry.

Realistically, you will have to decide what material is most necessary to learn. To meet the challenge of learning what is expected of you, you must be able to direct your effort to the most important material.

We have seen many students misjudge what they are expected to learn. Some students struggle to learn an impossibly large amount of material; others do not learn enough. Still others learn much information that is not required while missing some that is. Figure 2–2 diagrams these situations.

Students who struggle to learn impossibly large amounts of material may do well in chemistry. But if they are spending an unreasonably large amount of time on the course, other courses or their personal lives may suffer. Students who learn too little or who fail to learn required material are at risk of believing that they are doing well when such is not the case. When they take the first exam, they may receive a much lower score than they expect.

In order to know what is expected of you as you study chemistry, you may need to play detective. We already have described the major sources of information in your course (see page 12). You need to sift through these sources, seeking clues that tell you what you are expected to learn from each. Let's look at these sources more closely. As we do, keep in mind your purpose in reading this discussion: to learn to identify within each source the precise information that you must know.

Sources of Information

Lecture

Lecturing gives your professor the chance to tell you what she or he considers to be important. Since lecture time is limited, your professor

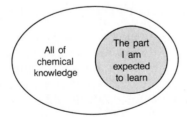

FIGURE 2–1 *Chemical knowledge to be learned*

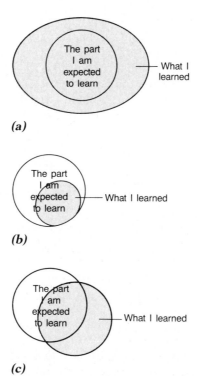

(a)

(b)

(c)

FIGURE 2–2 *Ways of misjudging material to be learned: (a) learning an amount of material that may be impossibly large; (b) not learning enough; (c) missing some required material*

will not have time to teach you everything. And since your capacity to absorb information is limited, you will not absorb everything that is presented.

To use the lecture appropriately, you must identify the role it plays in your course. Does the lecture content include most of the important information you need? How clearly is this information presented? Are you able to capture the essentials in your lecture notes? What are you expected to do with this information when you leave the lecture hall? By knowing how your professor views the lecture, you will have some idea of how you are expected to learn.

Sometimes you will receive hints in lecture about how to focus your study. For example, your professor may say, "If I don't talk about it in lecture, you are not required to learn it," or "I didn't have time to talk about this in lecture, but go learn it on your own." Use these hints to determine the boundaries of the chemistry you are expected to master.

Also look for clues in lecture as to the level of problem you are expected to work. Does your professor say that the problem he is working is a "hard one to solve"? Does she say: "This is the level of problem I expect you to solve"? If you are unsure of what level of difficulty is expected, ask for clarification.

At many schools, you experience chemistry by observing **lecture demonstrations.** Unless told otherwise, assume that demonstrations convey important information to you, just as does material written on the chalkboard. The demonstration may be used to illustrate rules or principles, to provide factual information, or both. For example, your lecturer may mix two clear, colorless liquids to produce an opaque yellow solution. What must you learn from this demonstration?

· That there are classes of compounds that do not dissolve in water?
· That the substance formed is lead chromate?
· Both of the above?

Furthermore, are you expected to be able to describe from memory the demonstrations performed in your class? If so, you may need to learn what conditions or chemicals were initially present, what changes occurred, and how to account for the results observed. By knowing how your instructor uses demonstrations, you are able to decide which questions about demonstrations you should be prepared to answer.

Textbook

Most chemistry courses require a **textbook,** but its use varies considerably from professor to professor. For example, your professor may use the text to provide you with a more complete explanation of topics discussed in class, but you may not be expected to master all the material in the book. Alternatively, your text may treat some topics incompletely, and you will need to supplement its information with information from lecture or other sources. How is the textbook used in your course?

Assigned Problems

Assigned problems can serve many different purposes. Some problems give you practice in using a particular process. Others teach new content by presenting subtle points or details. Still others are intended to extend what you know into new areas. The assigned problems are often clues as to what your professor thinks is important. Compare these problems with other clues. How does the difficulty of assigned problems compare with those worked in lecture or on last year's exams? Must you discover new information on your own in order to do the assigned problems?

Occasionally, professors assign problems that are harder than they intend. This can happen when problem sets are used year after year, even though the problems no longer match the content taught in lecture or other parts of the course. If the assigned problems seem inconsistent with the type or level of material presented elsewhere, this is your cue to ask for clarification of what is expected of you.

Do not assume that the level of assigned problems will automatically match those you are expected to do on exams. Sometimes they are much harder, or easier! Your assignments provide a clue as to what level of problems you must master, but seek confirmation by considering other clues as well.

Laboratory Experiments

In some courses **laboratory experiments** illustrate what has been taught. In others, the lab allows you to discover "new" information for yourself. In still others, the laboratory is based on information that will be taught at a later date or will never be formally taught. How is the laboratory experience used in your course? How does laboratory connect with the textbook and the lecture? How do you cope if the laboratory is unrelated to what you are learning from text or lecture?

Most professors convey the message to students that the laboratory experience is important. However, there is a large variability in the extent to which they expect laboratory material to be learned. Look for clues that tell you which laboratory information is important and how the laboratory material integrates with information from the rest of the course.

Handouts

Handouts are used in many ways: to provide new information, to clarify current information, or to present material merely for your enjoyment. Some handouts are discussed at great length; others are ignored. How are handouts used in your course?

Audiovisual Materials

Cassette recordings, videotapes, and films may be used as **audiovisual materials** to enhance your learning experience. Which ones are used in your course? What are you expected to learn from them? Do they contain information presented in no other place in your course? Are they merely a means of mastering material taught in other places?

Computers

Computers are everywhere: look for them in the lecture hall, classroom, laboratory and library. You may be given computer assignments for the purpose of teaching you new material or reviewing basic chemical concepts. You may manipulate experimental data on the computer, using graphing or spreadsheet software. In the library, you may search chemical databases via computer. The list of possibilities is constantly growing.

Some computer programs are written by your instructor; others are purchased from a software vendor. In the latter case, note whether the material on the program matches what your course is requiring you to learn. For example, a program might provide drill on the names and corresponding chemical symbols of some elements. If you are required to learn 36 names and symbols and the program covers 50 (or 20), you may be doing more (or less) work than is required.

Many students enjoy learning on a computer. The computer is infinitely patient and gives corrective feedback in nonthreatening ways. Other students are frustrated by the inflexibility of the computer in accepting alternative, reasonable answers. Whether you are pleased or frustrated by computers, the important question to answer is what role the computer is to play in your mastery of chemistry.

Deciding What to Learn

Are you feeling overwhelmed? Do you wonder how you will ever be able to sort through all this information and decide what is important to learn? First, notice that not all sources are equally important in giving you information to learn. In general, we have found that most professors expect you to learn somewhat more than they cover in lecture, but quite a bit less than is contained in the textbook. The other sources of information serve the function of completing the basic information that you have pieced together from the lecture and text. These last bits of information are important to good performance, but in most courses they are of secondary importance to the major learning that you are expected to accomplish.

To a certain extent you are left to your own resources in the task of deciding exactly what information you are expected to learn. To make the best possible decisions about what to learn and where to find the required information, seek information about course requirements from as many sources as possible, including:

· Direct statements from instructors about course requirements
· Exams given in previous terms
· Quiz questions
· Written statements of learning objectives
· Study lists handed out by instructors
· Handouts of sample test questions
· Experiences of past students in course

Any of these sources may at times be misleading. For example, courses may change over time, making old exams a poor guide to topic importance. Previous students may not accurately recall what and how they studied that brought them success in the course. Thus, to minimize the risk of totally misjudging what you are expected to know, use as many sources of information as possible. If you have trouble when you take the first exam (many students do!), use this experience to redirect your efforts for subsequent exams. See page 78 on how to use tests to reorganize your studying.

EXERCISE 1   Identifying What I Am Expected to Know in My Chemistry Course

For each category below, write whether each is a *major, minor,* or *not important* source of required information in your chemistry course. For each category, use the questions asked in the discussion above as your guide to determining how you will use this source to identify required information. Include also the evidence (e.g., old exams, statements from professors) that led to your assessments.

LECTURE

LECTURE DEMONSTRATIONS

TEXTBOOK

ASSIGNED PROBLEMS

LABORATORY EXPERIMENTS

HANDOUTS

AUDIOVISUAL MATERIALS

COMPUTER PROGRAMS

OTHER

If you are doing this exercise near the beginning of your course, you may not be able to complete it with certainty. If so, wait a week or two and then come back and redo this exercise. Select a date now for this review and post it where you will find it at the appropriate time. Selecting the appropriate topics for study is critical to your ultimate success in your chemistry course.

Expecting Some Uncertainty

We have stressed that you need to know what is expected of you and to focus your studying accordingly. For emphasis we have drawn pictures that suggest sharp boundaries between what you do and do not need to know. However, the boundaries are seldom this clear. Figure 2–3 gives a more realistic picture. The fuzziness of the boundary is due in part to the complexity of the subject matter. Chemical content does not always fall neatly into categories. The fuzziness may also arise from the way in which you are taught. No matter what the origin, be prepared for a certain amount of ambiguity in what you are to learn. Expect that at times you may find it difficult to determine how far in depth to study a topic.

It is usually acceptable for students to request clarification from their professors of what major points are to be learned. However, professors sometimes resent your asking detailed questions about what you should learn. They interpret such questions as attempts by students to study only for exams, at the expense of a broad understanding of chemical topics. In this section we have given you guidelines for making your own judgments about what you must learn. Seek additional information about limits only when you are unable to make reasonable judgments on your own.

Finally, by encouraging you to focus your studying on required material, we do not mean to discourage you from learning nonrequired content. The subject of chemistry can be captivating. By making your study as focused as possible, you may have some time to explore other areas of interest.

DECISION 2: HOW SHOULD I GO ABOUT STUDYING?

With so many sources of information available, you must decide when and how to use each. Rather than leaving open an infinite number of

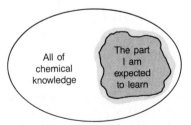

FIGURE 2–3 *A more realistic representation of the boundaries of chemical knowledge to be learned*

possible approaches, consider the following study plan as a model. This study plan has worked for many students in general chemistry courses. How might you modify it to fit your own particular needs?

Step 1: Skim the Text Before the Lecture

Where is your course going next? A course syllabus usually provides this information. If none is available, request this information from your instructor. Before a new topic is introduced in lecture, skim through the text chapter covering that subject. This overview provides a topic framework and helps you to understand the flow of information in the lecture. With increased understanding you will find it easier to take useful notes from the lecture.

To skim a text chapter, read through the chapter quickly, looking for the major points and the relationship among them. Skimming should not take much time—usually less than an hour for a typical chemistry text chapter. Begin skimming by reading the introduction and summary of the chapter. Then read quickly through the chapter, paying attention to the titles and subtitles of sections, as these give you an outline of the topic. Look for the meaning of new words. For more help in skimming techniques, see references such as:

Walter Pauk, *How to Study in College*, 5th Ed. (Boston: Houghton Mifflin Company, 1993).
James F. Shepherd, *College Study Skills*, 3rd Ed. (Boston: Houghton Mifflin Company, 1986).
James Deese and Ellin K. Deese, *How to Study and Other Skills for Success in College*, 4th Ed. (New York: McGraw-Hill, Inc., 1994).

Step 2: Attend the Lecture and Take Notes

Taking notes in lecture is hard work. In order to obtain a useful set of notes, you must maintain a high level of concentration over an extended period of time. You also need the discipline to write rapidly and accurately, copying what was written on the blackboard as well as writing down what was said aloud. We believe that the ability to take careful accurate lecture notes has a powerful payoff: You obtain a clear record of the required material.

Lecture demonstrations present specific difficulties in note taking. For example, you may be asked to write chemical formulas or equations (e.g., microscopic descriptions) to correspond with the phenomena you observed (macroscopic descriptions). You may have difficulty taking notes from the strictly visual and oral presentation, without written chalkboard notes or a handout. You may not be able to see clearly what happens during the demonstration. If the demonstration does not work as intended, you may become confused as to the points it was intended to make. If you are unsure about what is important to learn from a demonstration, do not hesitate to ask your instructor or a fellow student.

Some people believe that you can understand and mentally organize what is being presented as you take notes during the lecture. Our experience, however, suggests that student concentration spans are considerably shorter than the length of the lecture periods. While it is desirable to understand the material as you hear it, be realistic about your ability to do so for an entire period. During lecture, do your best to figure out what is going on. Skimming the text before lecture (Step 1) should help you in this. However, if you are not able to understand everything, strive to provide yourself with a detailed set of notes so that you can make sense out of the material at a later time.

If possible, structure your notes as you take them. For example, you might write down major points close to the left margin, with minor points indented underneath. Use a large notebook and don't cram together what you are writing. Leave lots of space to add comments later.

If your professor lectures at a furious pace, forget most of this and simply write madly. In this case, you will have little time to organize your thoughts as you listen. Although we do not routinely advise the taping of lectures, rapidly paced lectures may warrant this. It may not be necessary to listen to the entire tape. Rather, replay only the parts of the lecture that you missed. Most lecturers will permit you to tape their lectures. It is a simple, but required courtesy that you ask their permission before doing so.

Most people learn best from their own set of notes. If your note-taking skills do not enable you to record the information you need, you can work to improve them. There may be resources on your campus that teach note-taking skills. Also, both of the general study skills books noted on page 25 contain chapters on note-taking techniques.

Step 3: Organize Your Notes, Relating and Structuring the Information

The sooner you work through your notes after lecture, the easier the job of filling in missing information will be. When scheduling classes, consider keeping the hour after your chemistry lecture open for immediate work on your notes. This allows you to fill in what you heard in lecture but did not have time to write down.

Even more important than completing your notes is actively working on them. Organize them and fill them in, looking for relationships and meaning. To illustrate how this might be done, we have reproduced in Figure 2–4 a portion of class notes from a general chemistry course.

The information written at the left margin was added after the lecture as part of the lecture note analysis. One purpose of the analysis is to obtain an outline of the major topics and subtopics. You may find that reading the corresponding sections of your text makes the outline of the topic clearer.

In addition, your analysis identifies the specific information to be learned from that lecture, including the following:

· New words and their meaning
· Facts and rules to be learned
· Examples of facts, rules, and concepts
· Typical problems to be solved

The activities you might use to learn each of the major types of content are detailed in Chapters Six through Eleven.

Define atomic number	The number of protons is the atomic number. The number of protons determines the type of element.
	For example,
Atomic No. Type of element	Carbon has 6 protons always. " can have 6, 7 or 8 neutrons.
Define Mass number	The sum of the number of protons and neutrons is the mass number.
Define isotope Isotope examp. How to write Isotope Symbols	$^{12}_{6}C$ $^{13}_{6}C$ $^{14}_{6}C$ } Isotopes of carbon. Isotopes are atoms of the same element that have different numbers of neutrons.
Standard for atomic masses	The standard for the atomic masses of the elements is chosen to be $^{12}_{6}C$
Define a.m.u.	1 atomic mass unit (a.m.u.) is defined as $\frac{1}{12}$ (mass of $^{12}_{6}C$).

Subatomic particles; properties		mass (a.m.u.)	electrical charge*
	proton	1.0073	+ 1
	neutron	1.0081	0
	electron	0.00055	− 1

How electrical charges act Neutrons as nuclear glue	*Created to explain why some particles repel and attract each other. Similarly charged particles repel. Oppositely charged particles attract. Neutrons serve as a "glue" for the protons that repel each other in the nucleus.

FIGURE 2–4 *Example of lecture notes from a general chemistry course*

A second technique for abstracting meaning from your notes (or from a text passage, for that matter) is to pretend that each section of notes is the answer to a test question.[1] Your job is to write the test question. For example, the information in the lecture notes shown in Figure 2–4 might be used to answer the following questions:

[1] The technique of making up questions from lectures is one promoted by Marcia Heiman, Learning Skills Consultants, Cambridge, Massachusetts. The technique has been used successfully to teach students in any course how to find meaning in their lecture notes.

> Discriminate between atomic number and atomic mass number. Tell what information may be obtained from each.
>
> Illustrate with symbols the difference between isotopes of an element.
>
> What does an amu measure? On what is it based?
>
> What are the mass and charge properties of the subnuclear particles?

Notice that we have avoided "simple" questions such as, "What is an amu?" or "Define mass." The emphasis is on how information in the notes can be used.

EXERCISE 2 Lecture Note Analysis

Take your lecture notes from an entire lecture and analyze them. Develop an outline of the major topics and subtopics. Identify specific terms defined, rules and facts to be learned, typical problems, and so on. Write your analysis in the margin.

After this analysis has been completed, write a series of questions that you could answer with the information in this lecture.

We believe that the struggle to summarize, outline, or organize the information in your lecture notes is a key element in mastering chemistry. Through these efforts you will succeed in learning much of the material. To be effective, your work must include writing down such analyses. Note how different this work is from simply trying to memorize information from your notes or book. Passive memorization is ineffective in mastering the complex material of chemistry.

Many students do not come to their course appreciating the skill needed to take and work on a set of lecture notes. Working on your notes is difficult! If you cannot yet analyze your notes as proficiently as you would like, don't give up. Most students improve their skills with practice.

Step 4: After the Lecture, Read the Assigned Parts of the Text

After working through your lecture notes, read the assigned textbook chapters. Pay particular attention to those parts that cover material presented in lecture. Assume that you will need text information to clarify the lecture material. You are looking specifically for information to help you organize lecture content and to place it in the proper context. It may help you to insert relevant information from the text right into your notes.

Read all assigned parts of chapters, even those that contain material not presented in lecture. However, do not spend a lot of time on this new material unless your instructor has specifically directed you to do so.

We do not recommend that you outline or take notes from entire text chapters. There are two exceptions to this rule. First, make text notes when your instructor has told you that you are responsible for an entire section in the text. Second, make text notes or outlines if your lecture notes on that material are incomprehensible and cannot be used for learning.

See the two books mentioned on page 25 for further advice on how to use texts appropriately. Note, however, that these books are written by nonscientists. In nonscience courses the text usually plays a more central role than it does in chemistry courses. Thus, these books place more emphasis on text learning than is probably wise in your chemistry course.

Step 5: Study Your Notes and the Text, Then Work the Problems

We recommend that you complete your lecture note analysis and text reading before working your assignments. The order of activity is important here. Some students are tempted to start working problems immediately as their first study task on new material. However, solving problems is an inefficient way to develop an initial understanding of a topic. Learn the material before attempting to use it.

Attempt all assigned problems, even if they are not collected and graded. How else will you know how well you are learning? Confirm your mastery of each process by checking your answers. Many texts give answers at the back of the book. If answers are not provided, check your answers with an instructor or a fellow student. Once you have solved a problem, take the time to go back through it and review why and how you performed each step. Chapters 10 and 11 will provide more information on developing strong problem-solving techniques.

Is it wise to try to work all end-of-the-chapter problems in the text, even the unassigned ones? Perhaps, but do so with caution. You may not be expected to know how to solve many of these. Later, as time permits, you may choose to work on unassigned problems that are similar to the assigned ones or that you think will increase your understanding of the topic.

It is not safe to assume that the assigned problems will be similar to those on the tests. Check out all your assumptions. If text problems are consistently easier or harder than test problems, you may want to ask your instructor for some problems at the appropriate level.

Step 6: Complete Your Learning, Then Review and Self-Test

Complete the picture of what you are to learn by gathering information from the other sources in your course. These sources may include computer programs, films, and audiotape material. At first, you may want to try using all of these in order to assess their relative importance. Thereafter, continue to use only the helpful ones.

As you study the material you have gathered, assume that over time you will forget it. You therefore need to build time for review into your study schedule. See Chapter Six for information on how your memory works and the need for timely reviews.

As you review, also design ways of testing yourself. The better able you are to anticipate test questions, the better you can test yourself before an exam. In Part Two of this book, examples of test questions are provided at the end of each chapter to help you envision how you will be tested. Chapter Four, Chemistry Tests, also contains helpful information on self-testing.

This six-step process for studying has proven effective for many students, and we urge you to give it a try. However, we expect that you will want to modify the procedure to fit the needs of your particular course. For example, if your lecture notes are complete and well organized, you may not need to supplement them from your textbook. Similarly, if you find that some assigned problems are much more difficult than you are expected to solve, you may want to spend little time on them. Use your own judgment.

Finally, we have talked of a study plan in this chapter as if you would be studying all by yourself. If you like, you can work alone. However, many of the learning activities described here can be done efficiently and enjoyably with others. Consider forming a study group to share with others in your course the joys and pains of learning chemistry.

EXERCISE 3   My Provisional Study Plan

In the space below, describe your general approach to studying chemistry. Compare your current plan to the six-step plan described above. Note particularly areas in which your plan is different from the above plan because of characteristics of your course.

DECISION 3: HOW MUCH TIME SHOULD I SPEND LEARNING CHEMISTRY?

In general, your chemistry course will require considerable study time. You can expect to succeed only if you are able to give it the time it demands. To begin, write down the total hours that you spend in class or lab each week:

Total class hours = _____ (per week)

What is a reasonable amount of time to spend working on chemistry outside of these class hours? One rule of thumb is that the "average" student will spend approximately two hours working outside of class for each hour in class. For example, to prepare for and write up a three-hour lab experiment would require six hours. Thus, the total time commitment each week for laboratory would be three in-class hours plus six out-of-class hours, for a total commitment of nine hours. To determine an approximate time commitment for your study time outside of class hours, multiply your *total class hours* by 2:

Total class hours $\times$ 2 = _____ Estimated hours outside class
(per week)

These hours outside of class may be spent in a variety of ways. Here are some of the possibilities:

· Working on lecture notes
· Reading the textbook
· Studying the required material
· Doing assigned problems
· Preparing for and writing up labs
· Working computer assignments
· Studying for quizzes or exams
· Other

Keeping these possibilities in mind, now write down your estimate as to how many hours you actually spend studying chemistry outside of class:

My time spent outside of class = _____ hours (per week)

How does this number compare with your earlier estimate of the number of hours that you would have to spend outside of class? You may find yourself spending more than the estimate if:

· Your math skills are below the expected level.
· You took a prerequisite high school chemistry course more than a few years ago.
· You took a prerequisite college chemistry course more than a year ago.
· English is not your native language.
· More than one professor is teaching the course, and you must take time to figure out the demands of each professor.

Is your study-time assessment reasonably accurate? Some students overestimate the time they spend studying by including those hours spent worrying about the course rather than actually working on it. If you are not sure how much you are actually studying, keep a study log for a week or two. Every time you work on chemistry, write down the time spent and the general activity (e.g., working on lecture notes). This will help you estimate more accurately how much time you are spending on learning chemistry.

Finally, not only the amount of study time but its quality is important. Are you likely to make any of the following statements?

(   ) I don't know where to start, so I put off studying.
(   ) I get very sleepy whenever I try to study chemistry.
(   ) I have trouble concentrating; I seem to daydream a lot.
(   ) I get angry and frustrated when I work chemistry problems.
(   ) I try but seem to forget everything I've learned.
(   ) I mix everything up when I study chemistry.

Responses such as these can indicate ineffective studying. Some of the difficulties can be solved by finding better ways to study chemistry. Others, however, are symptomatic of an anxiety level high enough to prevent effective studying. See page 74 for suggestions on where to seek help for such barriers to learning.

Our purpose in having you examine the hours you spend studying is not to tell you that a certain amount of time is right or wrong. Rather, we hope to bring to your attention the factors affecting the amount of time you spend and to encourage you to make decisions based on these factors.

DECISION 4: AM I LEARNING WELL ENOUGH?

Your exam scores will tell you how well you are doing in your course. However, an exam is not the ideal place to find out that you do not know something. You will want to know where you stand before the exam, while there's still a chance to learn the missing information.

Fortunately, many chemistry courses provide you with ample opportunities to assess your progress prior to exams. On page 13 you identified the feedback mechanisms (such as quizzes) available in your course. But you need to use these mechanisms properly to obtain helpful information. For example, what does a grade of 10 out of 15 on a quiz mean? Are you doing well or poorly? If your course is graded on a curve, you will need to know the average score in order to interpret your score. Thus, if the average was 10, your score of 10 means that you are doing average work. If you will be satisfied with an average grade, often a C, you are doing fine. However, if you want a higher-than-average grade, you need to modify your method of studying for quizzes. In Chapter Four, Chemistry Tests, we will discuss how to use the results of your tests to improve your studying process. You can use the same techniques to improve your quiz performance as well.

Be cautious about assessing your progress in the course, particularly if you are competing for grades on a curve. A few points below the class average on a particular quiz or lab may seem unimportant. However, if you are continually a few points below average, your final grade is also likely to be lower than average.

Before you take your instructor's quizzes, you can use a self-testing process to check your progress in the course. For example, suppose you have been told to memorize a list of chemical formulas. After studying, test yourself to see if you know them. The following day, retest yourself to see which ones you have forgotten. Plan your studying according to what you still need to learn. Chapters Six through Ten contain suggestions for self-testing on different types of chemical content.

Self-testing may be formal, such as writing yourself a quiz and correcting it. It also may be informal, such as mentally reviewing the information you have learned. You may self-test totally by yourself, or you may work with other students in your class. Together, you can work homework assignments and quiz each other. No matter how you do it, keep asking yourself the questions: How am I doing? What do I know? What do I still have to learn? Use your answers to help plan your study.

DECISION 5: WHAT DO I DO IF I CAN'T SEEM TO LEARN WELL ENOUGH?

Some Final Questions to Consider

Even with decisive action on your part (such as forming an effective study plan, making a reasonable time commitment, and self-testing), success in chemistry may still elude you. If you are still struggling with the chemical content, here are some final questions to consider:

Am I Expecting Too Much Too Soon?

Weak learning skills, the result of your old, ineffective study habits, cannot be improved overnight. Are you giving yourself time to develop your skills? As you work on improving your ability to learn, be alert for signs of improvement. When you see progress, don't forget to acknowledge it!

Am I Making Appropriate Use of My Instructor for Help?

If you are having trouble understanding the material, ask your instructor for help. Needing help doesn't mean that you are stupid. The willingness to seek help is the mark of a mature, serious student. Also, it is possible that your difficulties may be in part due to your teacher's inability to teach well under certain circumstances. For example, the instructor's nervousness in the lecture hall may result in an incoherent presentation. In this case, you may want to seek him or her out on a one-to-one basis.

Before you do see the instructor, first make sure that you have done some work on your own. Specific questions ("I don't understand why you did this step in that pH problem") are more effective than general ones ("I don't understand pH"). Specific questions show that you have tried to work on your own. Professors are usually willing to help, but they may resent being asked for help by students who apparently have not attempted to understand the material on their own.

Finally, don't wait until just before an exam to seek help. It is your responsibility to ask for help when you first encounter difficulties.

Are There Personal Reasons Why I'm Not Working Effectively?

Chemistry courses are demanding. They cannot be approached half-heartedly or with minimum time and attention. If you experience personal problems such as a death or divorce in your family, money problems, the beginning or end of a love affair, or chaotic living arrangements, you may not be able to pay attention to the subject. Unless the crises in your life are at a manageable level, you may not be able to attend to your coursework.

Is the Stress of the Course Too Much for Me to Manage?

You can get "psyched out" by a chemistry course, especially if you find the subject hard and the work load heavy. Many students feel pressure to get a good grade. Other circumstances may add stress as well. For example, you may be carrying a heavy course load this term. You may have scheduling difficulties such that chemistry exams fall at the same time as other exams or papers. Or you may be repeating chemistry after having previously dropped or failed it.

There are times when it is wise to get help in handling stress. Rather than assuming you always have to "go it alone," you might want to seek help at your local campus health center, counseling center, dean of students' office, or wherever assistance is offered on your campus. Skilled people may be able to help you find new ways of looking at your situation and help you to keep difficulties in perspective. In the process you may be relieved to discover that you are not the only one to have encountered difficulties.

Am I in the Right Course at the Right Time?

If you do not have the prerequisites for the chemistry course, acquire them before you sign up for the course. In saying this we recognize that it is not always easy to decide if you are adequately prepared for a particular course. Some courses have functional but unwritten prerequisites. For example, a single year of college algebra may be required for a chemistry course. Yet, when you enroll, you may find that this level of proficiency does not enable you to solve the required chemistry problems.

Thus, there are many valid reasons for having difficulty in a chemistry course. Some of the factors that cause difficulty you can control;

others you cannot. At some point, you may realize that you are unable to learn at a sufficient pace to earn a reasonable grade. In this case, dropping the course may be the most constructive action you can take. If you are past the date for dropping courses without penalty, check with your advisor or dean for help as to how to proceed.

If you do drop the course, yet wish to retake it later, consider attending as long as possible. As you sit in, learn as much as you can. Also, learn as much about the process of learning as you can. Try to work directly on the causes of your difficulty before you enroll again.

SUMMARY

In this chapter we have identified some of the critical decisions you make as you plan your chemistry studying.

First, you must determine what you are expected to learn. Ask yourself:

- What are the major sources of information to be used in this course? Lecture notes? Textbook and handouts? Assigned problems? Laboratory experiments? Computer programs and audiovisual materials?
- What clues tell me how to use them?
- How can I recognize the important information?

Second, decide on the study process that is best for you. Many students find the following suggested process useful:

- Skim the text before the lecture.
- Attend the lecture and take complete notes.
- Organize your notes, structuring information.
- Read assigned parts of the textbook.
- Study your notes and the text; do the problems.
- Self-test and review.

How might you modify this plan? Would studying with others be useful?

Third, determine how much time learning chemistry will take. Ask yourself:

- What is my estimated time commitment?
- Is the recommended time commitment (two hours of study for each hour of class) adequate for me?
- Is my study time well spent or can I improve its quality?

Fourth, decide if you are learning well enough. Consider these questions:

- How can I use course feedback to judge my progress?
- How can I generate my own feedback?

Finally, decide what you will do if you are not learning well enough. Ask yourself:

· Are my expectations of progress realistic?
· How can I use my instructor for help?
· Are personal distractions interfering with my success?
· If anxiety is hampering me, how can I reduce it?
· Is dropping the course a constructive alternative at this time?

SELF-ASSESSMENT

Respond to the following statements to assess the effectiveness of your chemistry study process.

1. I know what my professor wants me to learn.

YES _____ NO

If you need to improve your ability to discriminate the important information from that which you are not required to learn, check out the suggestions on page 22.

2. My current approach to studying chemistry is:

WOEFULLY _____ DECIDEDLY
WEAK   STRONG

In order to improve my performance in chemistry, I need to:

(   ) Increase my time commitment to the course.
(   ) Improve the quality of my study time.
(   ) Change my study process.
(   ) Other: _____

If you are not satisfied with the effectiveness of your approach, use the suggested study process beginning on page 25 to plan some specific changes.

MY NEW STUDY PLAN

3. I am getting the grade I want in chemistry.

YES _____ NO

If you are not satisfied with your grade, you must take action in order to change your performance. Simply wishing for a better grade will not work. Copy your new study plan onto a small note card and keep it with your chemistry study materials. Remind yourself daily of the study changes you need to make. Find ways to reward yourself when you make these changes.

4. I am realistic about factors in my life that affect my ability to study.

YES ——————————————————————————————— NO

Wisdom starts when you can distinguish those things that you control from those that you do not control. Expect the best possible effort from yourself, but acknowledge the realities of your life situation. What factors in your life affect your ability to study? Which of these can you work to control? Which are "givens" that you must work around?

CHAPTER THREE

The Laboratory

Few students feel indifferent about working in a chemical laboratory: Most either love it or hate it. Those who like working there are quick to point out that the laboratory has many things going for it. In the lab you can discover things for yourself. You can be actively involved, seeing, touching, smelling, and perhaps even hearing chemicals. Laboratory can bring alive the symbolic chemical world that you have spent countless hours hearing about in lecture.

Laboratory also offers an opportunity to develop personal relationships. You work closely with other students in the course, sharing both good moments and bad. Having shared these experiences, you are likely to form close friendships that will continue after the course is over. In addition, you will be able to talk with your instructor during lab, giving you the opportunity to build a good working relationship.

However, some students find laboratory to be a trying experience. They are likely to say things such as:

· Half the time I have no idea of what I'm doing.
· I stand around a lot.
· Everything I touch seems to break.
· I am afraid of the dangerous chemicals.
· The safety glasses give me a headache.
· It's hard to find a good lab partner.

Such difficulties are as real as the positive aspects of laboratory. Do you anticipate facing any of these situations in lab? Are any of these frustrations already part of your lab experience? If so, you may need a way of coping with them.

Just about everyone encounters some difficulties in lab. It may help you to know that you are not alone in your frustrations. Moreover, many problems are more manageable if you can anticipate them. Let's look at some lab problems that you can expect to encounter:

- *Things go wrong in lab:* A flask breaks while you are heating it. Your filter paper plugs up. Your Bunsen burner will not light. If you encounter such problems, don't jump to the conclusion that you are clumsy or that *you* did something wrong; the equipment may be at fault. Expect that apparatus and equipment will not always work properly.

- *The experiment may deal with material that you haven't been taught:* At some schools laboratory exercises are used to illustrate material discussed in lecture. Ideally, the lab experiment will follow the lecture presentation. However, if the lecturer falls behind in presenting a topic, you may be expected to conduct a lab experiment without having had an introduction to the material. This happens so regularly in laboratory courses that you can expect it will happen to you.

- *Laboratory skills are difficult to teach and learn:* Your instructor may want you to observe a properly executed lab technique such as weighing a substance or using a pipet. It is difficult, however, to demonstrate a laboratory skill so that every student can see every detail of the procedure. Furthermore, watching someone else demonstrate a technique does not necessarily prepare you to do it for yourself. Expect that your first tries at equipment manipulation will feel awkward. They will become more comfortable only with practice.

- *Some laboratory operations are boring:* You will often have to wait in line for a balance, spend time washing a pile of glassware, or stir a solution for ten minutes. If you find yourself getting bored at such times, learn to anticipate the moments when boredom will strike. Then think up some ways to get through this time. For example, you might use these moments to get some mental rest, to think over what you have done, or to plan what you will do next.

- *Laboratory write-ups may have "bugs" in them:* It is difficult to write good directions for an experiment, and most experiments need to be written several times before all the bugs disappear. Experiments also may change from year to year, and if the write-ups do not change quite so often, you may find contradictions or misdirections. Thus, you may have questions about how to proceed with an experiment. Ask for clarification if the lab directions are not clear.

Why are there so many difficulties with lab work? Are professors deliberately trying to make things hard for you? No. In defense of most schools, running a laboratory is extremely expensive—in both time and money. Few professors can devote the resources to doing the job as well as they would like. However, it is the responsibility of your school to design a good laboratory experience for you. Give your instructor constructive feedback if you think there are ways that the laboratory experience could be improved.

You also have responsibilities. One of them is to show up for lab. When you miss a lab, you miss out on a learning experience. You may also not be able to make up the experiment without inconveniencing someone. So, as much as you are able, try to get to lab. If you must be absent, send word to your instructor so he or she will know that you are concerned about your absence.

You have other responsibilities as well. These include:

· Preparing for the experiment
· Acquiring correct laboratory skills
· Clearly communicating your results
· Working safely in the laboratory so as not to endanger yourself or others

We will discuss these responsibilities in the remainder of the chapter.

PREPARING FOR AN EXPERIMENT

Do you go into lab fully prepared? Many students feel the need to improve their ability to prepare for lab. In this section, we will discuss two areas of preparation: your emotional and your intellectual preparation for the experiment.

Emotional Preparation

Your emotional preparation involves your feelings about the laboratory. Your feelings are important. As we pointed out earlier, most students react strongly to the laboratory experience. How do you react? Are you anxious about going to lab? Do you delight in the chance to perform experiments? Do you feel uncomfortable working with chemicals?

Whatever your feelings are, they are a part of you. We encourage you to acknowledge their existence. What should you do about your feelings? That depends on what they are and how they are affecting you. For example, if your anxiety about the laboratory is interfering with your work, it may help to talk about your "lab anxieties" with a friend. In the process of talking you may discover that you are not alone with your dislikes and fears. Another way to lessen your anxiety about laboratory is to have a systematic way to prepare for it. In the next section we will discuss a method of preparation that has lessened the uncertainty about upcoming labs for many students.

Negative feelings about laboratory may arise from what happens to you there. Do the chemicals give you a headache? Do your measurements always seem to come out wrong? With situations like these, it may help if you can pinpoint the sources of your irritation. Then examine these sources and decide whether or not you can change them. Suppose, for example, that wearing safety glasses gives you a headache. However, since state law requires that you wear safety glasses, you recognize that you cannot change this, and mentally prepare yourself to accept the aggravation. Or, a different type of approved safety glasses might be less irritating. You might look into buying a better pair, perhaps one with prescription lenses.

In short, in asking you to give thought to your feelings, we are acknowledging that they are real and will not go away. Try to keep the inconveniences of lab work in proportion, and do not waste valuable energy complaining about realities that you cannot change.

Intellectual Preparation

Preparing for laboratory also means becoming knowledgeable about the chemistry involved. Specifically, this means that you must understand what you are told in the laboratory write-up. At first reading, the experiment may seem overwhelming. It helps to have a systematic way to approach an experiment. For this purpose we have provided a worksheet (see Figure 3–1).

The laboratory worksheet is divided into five sections. By completing each part before you go to lab, you arm yourself with the material you need in order to complete the experiment successfully. All five sections may not be applicable to a given experiment. Use the sheet accordingly, letting it guide you in thinking about what is important. Do not hesitate to modify it to fit your own needs.

Let's look at some points to keep in mind as you answer each section.

Vocabulary

We suggest that you begin any experiment by looking closely at the vocabulary in the write-up. Are there any unfamiliar terms? New chemicals? If you want to feel at ease with the experiment, you should learn this vocabulary before you go to the lab. Consult your textbook or instructor if you need help with new material.

Equations: Chemical and Mathematical

This section of the worksheet helps you to summarize all of the chemical reactions involved in your experiment. Once you have a list, ask yourself some questions. Do you need to memorize these equations? How do these equations relate to what you have been taught in lecture? Will you be tested on them? You may not be able to answer these questions right away, but if you keep them in mind, you may find answers to them as you work through the experiment.

Many labs require calculations. It is also helpful to list the mathematical equations that you will need for these calculations. Again, ask yourself questions. Are there any equations you will need that are not listed in your write-up? Where can you find them? For each equation, do you know what each symbol stands for? What the units of each variable are? Which values you will measure in lab? Which values are given to you?

1. VOCABULARY
   Names and chemical formulas for all chemicals that are new to me:

   Words or phrases whose meanings are new or unclear to me:

2. EQUATIONS: Chemical and mathematical
   Chemical equations relevant to this experiment:

   Mathematical equations used in this experiment:

3. SUMMARY

4. PLAN OF ACTION FOR LAB
   What will I do first? Second?

5. SPECIAL THINGS TO REMEMBER
   a. Any calculations to be done before lab? Any values to be looked up?

   b. Do any parts of the experiment need special attention? Are there any I want to be careful
      not to mix up?

   c. Is there anything I should remember to bring to lab?

FIGURE 3–1 *Laboratory worksheet*

Summary

Many labs for introductory chemistry courses tell you exactly what to do and when to do it. It is good practice to read through the entire set of directions *before* you start work in lab. As you read through each section, underline or highlight the important parts. Then, write on your Laboratory Worksheet a brief summary of what you will do in the experiment. Refer to this summary at the beginning of the laboratory period.

If the lab write-up directions are not complete, you have more work to do. It may not be easy for you to figure out the missing information. Still, you need to know exactly what to do when you get to lab. Work out as much of the procedure as you can, and do not hesitate to ask for help if you get stuck. In most cases, your instructor would prefer that you think and ask questions before lab rather than come to lab baffled by the experiment. When you have figured out what is to be done, again write yourself a summary of the procedure so that you can refer to it right before lab.

Plan of Action for Lab

The directions in your write-up may not always be given in the most useful order. For example, some activities should be carried out earlier than others in order to minimize the time that you spend standing around. What should you do right away? Weigh out chemicals? Set up apparatus? Warm up an instrument? Here are some suggestions:

· Some activities in your experiment require time. Identify them and start these first. For example, if you need a boiling water bath, start the water boiling at the beginning of the period.
· Lines form quickly at the balances. If you need to weigh out something, plan to go straight to the balance when you arrive in order to avoid the rush. Do calculations for the amounts to weigh out before you get to the lab.
· Washing glassware is a poor way to start any lab. If you form the habit of washing your dishes at the end of each lab, they will be clean and dry for the next period.
· There will be some "dead time" in lab—time when you have to stand around waiting for something to heat, to cool, and so on. Plan to use this time for other tasks. Can glassware be cleaned? Calculations done? Observations written down? Avoid the temptation to spend the time chatting with friends.

Special Things to Remember

While working your way through the write-up, you may come across things that must be remembered before you get to the lab. For example, are there calculations that you must do beforehand? Are there some constants that you need to look up before lab?

You are also likely to come across lab procedures that require special precautions. Mark these in your lab book as you come across them. Then list them on your Laboratory Worksheet. Such precautions might include:

· Tips on running reactions (mix *well*, heat *gently*)
· Safety precautions (no *flames* permitted)
· Chemicals that are easily confused (HNO_2 and HNO_3)
· When to use distilled water rather than tap water
· How to safely dispose of hazardous chemicals

Finally, jot down the things that you need to bring to the lab. These might include:

· Calculator
· Safety goggles
· A watch with a second hand

Allotting Time for Preparation

How long will it take you to prepare for laboratory? There is no hard-and-fast answer to this question.

Some lab experiments require many decisions on your part. For example, you may be required to design your own procedures, decide what data you need to acquire, and determine how to acquire them. This type of experiment may require hours of preparation. It is, however, relatively uncommon.

Other lab experiments are more clearly defined; some even resemble cookbook recipes. For these experiments you may need only an hour or so for preparation. However, even "cookbook" experiments may require additional preparation time if you need to learn some prerequisite background information.

The quality of the time you spend preparing for lab is as important as the quantity. In the preceding section we have given you questions to ask yourself as you read through the laboratory write-up. The more effectively you can use these questions to pick out what the lab is about, the more efficiently you can use your time to prepare for the experiment.

ACQUIRING CORRECT LABORATORY SKILLS

Learning Good Laboratory Techniques

One of your laboratory goals is to learn correct techniques for carrying out laboratory operations. Your approach toward learning these techniques can make a difference in how well you master them. We recommend that you enter the lab with the following mind set as you work toward acquiring good laboratory techniques:

- There is a right way to carry out each laboratory procedure. There are also many wrong ways.
- It is hard to learn the right way by watching somebody else demonstrate it. However, you will often be taught in this manner. Mastering the skill comes by doing it yourself.
- Performing a lab operation the right way may feel awkward at first. You might need to remind yourself constantly to do it the correct way.
- Performing procedures the right way will make a difference in the quality of your lab work.

You may be assuming that somebody will explain the right way to perform most lab operations. In fact, you may never be told or shown that there is a right way to do certain procedures. For example, is there a "right way" to boil water over a Bunsen burner? You could set up your apparatus to boil water in two ways, as shown in Figure 3–2. If you unknowingly choose the setup on the right, you will stand around a long time waiting for the water to boil. You can heat the water more quickly if you put the hottest part of the flame directly under the beaker.

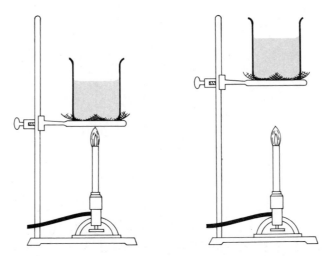

FIGURE 3–2 *Which is the "right way" to boil water over a Bunsen burner?*

Your instructor cannot tell you how to do everything in the lab, nor can we. You can pick up many of the correct techniques for yourself by noticing details of operations that are demonstrated to you and reasoning about why actions are done in particular ways. You may need to ask for clarification from an instructor when the purpose of an action is not obvious.

To give you some idea of what details you might watch for, we will describe one laboratory operation: the correct use of a buret. Our purpose here is not to make you a buret "expert" but to illustrate some typical aspects of using lab equipment to which you can become sensitive.

Using a Buret

Knowing the Purpose of the Equipment

A buret is a long glass tube with a stopcock (i.e., a valve) at the bottom. The buret is used to deliver an exact volume of liquid. Figure 3–3 gives a diagram of a buret. Its correct use requires manual dexterity, attention to detail, and patience.

Cleaning the Equipment

A buret cannot deliver a precise volume of liquid if it is dirty. To check whether a buret is clean, fill it with water, open the stopcock, and let the water drain completely. If you see water beading up on the inside wall, the buret is dirty. To clean a buret, scrub the inside with a dilute (weak) soap solution, using a long-handled "buret" brush. Don't use abrasive cleansers—they may scratch the glass. If soapy water does not clean the buret well, your instructor may provide you with a more powerful cleaning solution. Rinse the cleaning solution from the buret by filling it several times with water, draining it each time through the tip.

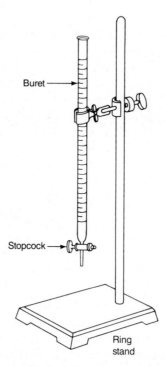

FIGURE 3–3 *Buret and ringstand*

Preparing the Equipment for Use

There is a correct way to fill your buret. Take your wet, clean buret and close its stopcock. Place a clean funnel in the top of the buret and pour through the funnel about 5 ml of your liquid. Remove the funnel and take the buret loosely in your fingers. Tilt and rotate the buret so as to wet all the inside wall surfaces with the liquid. Then drain the liquid through the tip. Reclose the stopcock and repeat this entire rinsing procedure one or more times. This process washes out any water that would alter the composition of your liquid.

Now attach your buret to its stand and fill it, using the same funnel. Be careful not to pour more liquid into the funnel than the buret will hold! After the buret is filled, drain a small quantity of liquid through the tip to remove any air bubbles trapped there.

Note: Don't reach high over your head to fill a buret. If you pour with your arms over your head, you run the risk of having the liquid run down your arms. If you cannot comfortably reach the top of your buret, place the buret stand apparatus on the floor and fill the buret from there.

Using the Equipment

To use the buret, you must read and record the beginning level of liquid in the buret. As you view the level of the liquid in the buret, you will notice that the level dips toward the center. This dip is called the *meniscus*. By convention, the level of the liquid in the buret is taken to be the level at the lowest point in the meniscus.

Open the stopcock to drain some liquid out through the tip into a container. Close the stopcock to stop the flow of liquid. Read and record the final liquid level in the buret. The difference between the initial and final volume readings is the amount of liquid delivered to the container. See Figure 3–4 for a summary of how to set up the buret and how to read buret liquid levels.

Finally, there is a correct way to position your hands on the buret. Most people have a coordinated hand and a not-so-coordinated hand, usually their right and left respectively. Use your coordinated hand to

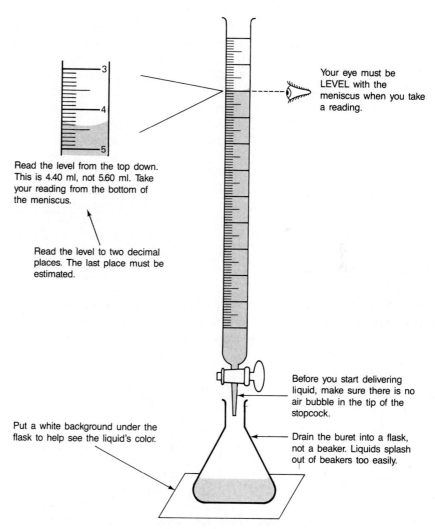

Your eye must be LEVEL with the meniscus when you take a reading.

Read the level from the top down. This is 4.40 ml, not 5.60 ml. Take your reading from the bottom of the meniscus.

Read the level to two decimal places. The last place must be estimated.

Before you start delivering liquid, make sure there is no air bubble in the tip of the stopcock.

Put a white background under the flask to help see the liquid's color.

Drain the buret into a flask, not a beaker. Liquids splash out of beakers too easily.

FIGURE 3–4 *Good technique for setting up and using a buret*

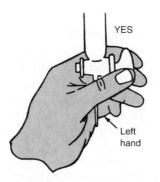 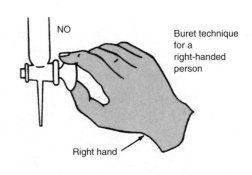

FIGURE 3–5 *Recommended buret operation for a right-handed person*

swirl the flask under the buret. Swirling to mix well is important, and only a coordinated hand can do this well. Use your less coordinated hand to work the stopcock. By wrapping this hand completely around the barrel of the stopcock (see Figure 3–5), you will find that your control over the flow of solution is excellent.

When you are finished using the buret, be sure to rinse it well. Ideally, a buret is stored vertically, filled with distilled water, and capped. However, it is not always practical to do this. Follow the cleanup and storage practices recommended by your instructor.

Will your experiment be a flop if you do not perform every step of its procedure in exactly the correct way? No. This is fortunate because it will take you time to develop your lab technique to the point where you are performing all operations correctly. We encourage you to persist in your efforts to improve your lab techniques throughout your lab experiences. As you acquire skill, it will pay off in both the quality of your results and the speed with which you obtain them.

Other Useful Laboratory Skills

Using a buret is one operation that you will need to master in order to get good results in your chemistry laboratory experiments. There are other skills as well, including:

Glassware skills
   Cleaning
      Choice of cleanser
      Rinsing
      Ways of drying
   Making equipment
      Breaking glass rods and tubing
      Bending glass tubing
      Firepolishing glass
   Inserting glass tubes into stoppers
   Heating glass

Bunsen burners
  Lighting
  Adjusting
  Using
Weighing skills
  Choosing the proper balance
  Using the balance correctly
  Weighing solids, liquids, gasses
Handling solids
  Transferring solids from reagent bottles
  Safely disposing of solids and solid wastes
Handling liquids
  Pouring liquids
    From regeant bottles
    From beakers and flasks
  Measuring volumes of liquids
    Using pipets and burets
    Using graduated cylinders and volumetric flasks
  Safely disposing of liquids and liquid wastes
Filtration
  Handling filter paper
  Doing gravity and suction filtrations
  Doing vacuum filtrations

Many laboratory manuals describe these operations. You may receive verbal instructions about them from your instructor as well. If you find verbal instructions hard to remember, you may want to jot down as many notes as possible so that you can refer to them later while performing the experiment. In any case, if you have doubts about your ability to perform an operation, ask your instructor for help. It is also appropriate to ask your instructor to observe your technique and offer you suggestions for improvement.

Learning to Record Laboratory Data

Another of your goals in working in the laboratory is to record your data in a professional manner. Many students find it difficult to record data during a lab. They focus so much on carrying out the experiment that they forget to make a written record of what they see. However, if you do not record your observations and numerical values safely in your lab notebook, you will not be able to write up your results.

We offer you two general suggestions as you record your data during lab. First, it is better to write down too much rather than too little. Second, try to make your writing legible. You, as well as your instructor, will need to be able to read what you wrote.

Let's look at some additional tips for recording data well.

Recording Observations

It takes practice to record accurately what happened in a chemical reaction. A good place to begin is to describe what you did. Did you heat a chemical? Add two chemicals together? How much time elapsed before you were able to see a change? Instantly? Five seconds? Never? Was there evidence for a chemical reaction: A gas evolved? A color change? A precipitate? A change in temperature?

When you see, hear, or feel things like these, be careful to record what you *actually* saw, heard, or felt, not what you *think* you saw, heard, or felt. For example:

NO   *I added pieces of magnesium to dilute HCl and immediately hydrogen gas was given off.*

(You cannot see that the gas is hydrogen.)

YES   *I added pieces of magnesium to dilute HCl and tiny bubbles of gas were evolved from the metal's surface.*

(Bubbles of gas are what you saw.)

Recording Numerical Data Precisely

When recording numerical data, you also need to state the units and give the correct number of significant figures. For example:

When recording the molarity of a solution

poor	.127
better	.127M
best	0.127M

When reading a buret

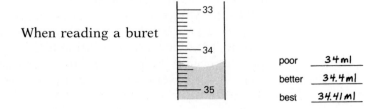

poor	34 ml
better	34.4 ml
best	34.41 ml

Learning to Interact with Your Lab Instructor

Like your interactions with all people, interactions with your lab instructor can be for better or for worse. Unlike most social interactions, however, interactions with your instructor can affect your grade. We suggest that you give some thought to the skills used in communicating with your laboratory instructor. For example, you are probably no more or less clumsy than anyone else in your lab. Some patterns of interaction, however, may give your instructor the impression you are less competent than you actually are.

In this section we will sketch some common situations and present some helpful and some not-so-helpful ways in which you may respond. Your instructor is likely to judge your competency as a lab worker by the responses you make to situations such as those shown in Figures 3–6 through 3–9.

DO   tell your instructor what happened

volunteer to clean it up

DON'T   shriek

use bad language

go overboard with your apologies

leave glass or chemicals on the floor

FIGURE 3–6   *Suppose you knock a beaker to the floor and it breaks . . .*

DO   consult with your instructor to see if you are wearing them properly

take a short breather outside the lab to ease your discomfort

DON'T   push the glasses to the top of your head

take them off

FIGURE 3–7   *Suppose your safety glasses hurt your head . . .*

DO   keep your mind on your experiment

ask your friend to wait until after laboratory is over

DON'T   use the lab as a place to socialize

give the impression that you are not serious about your work

FIGURE 3–8   *Suppose a friend comes over and starts a long, involved conversation . . .*

DO   take time to clean up your
      bench area

     put away all your equipment

     leave all instruments in an
     OFF or standby position

DON'T forget to wash your hands

     forget to lock your desk

FIGURE 3–9   *Suppose you want to leave lab in a hurry . . .*

Another important interaction occurs when you ask your instructor for help. There are helpful and not-so-helpful ways to ask questions. Here are some examples:

STUDENT 1:   What's the matter with my experiment?
INSTRUCTOR: Well, I don't know. What did you put in there? (How do you expect me to know what's wrong if you don't know what you did?)

STUDENT 2:   "I can't figure out what's wrong. I added silver nitrate to my solution of sodium chloride and didn't see a white precipitate."
INSTRUCTOR: You're right, you should have seen a precipitate. Try . . . (I can see this student is giving some thought to her results.)

STUDENT 1:   My Bunsen burner won't light . . . .
INSTRUCTOR: I'd better take a look. (Can't this kid do anything right?)

STUDENT 2:   I can't get my Bunsen burner to light. I've opened and closed the valve at the bottom and I've fiddled with the gas supply, but nothing seems to work.
INSTRUCTOR: I'd better take a look. (Sounds like he has done just what I would do.)

In each example, the second student appears more competent and conscientious. Yet, both students may have the same knowledge and skills. Only the second, however, has managed to communicate these adequately to the instructor.

Learning Safety in the Laboratory

Many students do not think of safety as a laboratory skill. Safety, however, can be demonstrated, learned, and practiced just like any other skill. If you are not safety-conscious in the laboratory, you may pay a high price: You may hurt yourself, you may hurt your neighbor, or your neighbor may hurt you. Do not work alone in the laboratory. Having another person nearby may make the difference between a major injury and a minor one.

Suppose you or your neighbor needs help in a hurry. Do you know where to find and how to use the following safety items? If you are currently working in a laboratory course, try to fill in the information in Table 3–1 from memory.

TABLE 3–1   LABORATORY SAFETY EQUIPMENT

Fire extinguisher

     Location _____
     Use:

Eyewash fountain

     Location _____
     Use:

Safety shower

     Location _____
     Use:

Fire blanket

     Location _____
     Use:

Emergency telephone

     Location _____

Emergency exit

     Location _____

If you know all of the information in Table 3–1, you have the tools to respond to a laboratory emergency. Most students, however, do not have this information instantly available. When you next go to the lab, take a moment to find this information. You could write the information on an index card and clip it inside your laboratory notebook. It could literally be a lifesaver.

Most laboratory manuals provide you with an impressive list of safety precautions. We urge you to take these seriously. The manuals usually speak to your personal safety, that is, protecting your eyes, keeping food out of the laboratory, and washing your hands after touching chemicals. Fewer manuals, however, tell you about social skills needed for safety. Laboratory is a social event, in the sense that you have to watch out for what other people are doing as you go about your own work. Give thought to these social skills:

Suppose you light a match:
   Are there any flammable substances around?
   Is your neighbor using anything flammable?
   Are you working with anything that could catch fire if your
      neighbor were to light a match?

Suppose you spill a corrosive chemical:
   Are your neighbors alerted to the spill?
   Do you need help with your experiment while you clean up the
      spill?
   Is the spill cleaned up well enough so that the next person who
      leans on the spot will not be harmed?
   If your neighbor cleans up a spill, is it likewise cleaned up
      satisfactorily?

Suppose you are heating a chemical in a test tube:
   Is the test tube pointed away from other people?
   Is your neighbor also heating a chemical? Is it pointed away from
      you?

For safety's sake, work to increase your sensitivity to the actions of others in the lab. In addition, becoming more aware of what others are doing will give you an informal check on your own results. If you notice that your results are different from those of your neighbors, check with your instructor to see if your work is proceeding properly. If you catch a mistake early, there may still be time to correct it. In any case, if things have gone wrong, try to avoid rushing about the lab. When you and your glassware start flying, accidents are more likely to happen.

WRITING UP YOUR WORK AFTER LAB

When you leave your lab bench, you should have a set of observations and measurements in hand. Most instructors will now require that you prepare a report to hand in. This is *your* chance to sit back and figure out either what happened—or what should have happened!

The sooner you start writing your report, the better your learning experience will be. Here are some reasons that may encourage you to start writing up your lab early:

- Details fade rapidly from your memory. If you wait too long, you may forget the information that you need to prepare the report.
- If you discover that you forgot to record some information from lab, you still may be able to obtain it.
- If you discover that you need help in interpreting your data, your instructor is more likely to help if you ask him or her early.
- Lab reports always take more time than you think. The sooner you start, the less chance that you will run out of time.

Graphs of Lab Measurements

Values of laboratory measurements that you carefully recorded may need to be graphed in order to draw conclusions from the lab. Figure 3–10 shows some do's and don'ts for drawing graphs.

Questions on Lab Reports

Certain questions pop up repeatedly as part of lab reports. Let's examine some of these in order to better understand what these questions ask of you.

What Are the Sources of Error in Your Measurements?

This question is *not* asking if you made a math error in your calculations. It is your job to correct any math errors before you turn in your report. Nor is this question usually asking you about personal errors, such as using the wrong chemical or tipping over your reaction vessel. Rather, the errors of interest to your instructor are those caused by limitations of the chemicals or limitations of the equipment. These are errors that always occur, no matter who does the experiment. For example, when you use a buret (see page 46), there may be an error because the solution you are using decomposes as you work with it.

Errors can also arise because you are not using equipment correctly. These are errors that you would hope to avoid by practicing good laboratory technique (see page 47). For example, Figure 3–11 shows some examples of avoidable errors in using a buret.

You may be asking yourself how you can be expected to identify sources of errors, particularly those arising from limitations of chemicals or of the experiment. Many sources of errors will be mentioned somewhere in the laboratory write-up. Otherwise, assume that all laboratory operations (weighing, transferring material, measuring volumes of liquids) are potential sources of error.

How Do the Errors Affect Your Results?

Once you identify a source of error, you are then likely to be asked what effect this error has on your results. The question might be phrased:

Suppose _____ happened in your experiment. Would the value of your results be too high, too low, or unchanged?

DON'T forget to title the
graph and label the axes.

DON'T start and stop the
graph at the first and
last points.

DON'T connect the dots.

DON'T draw a small graph on
a big piece of graph paper.

DO work to produce a
graph that looks
like this.

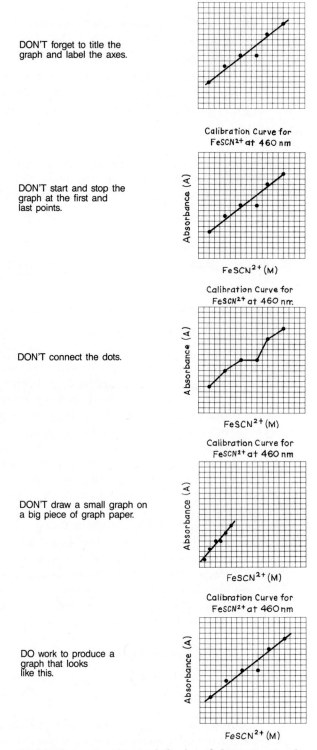

FIGURE 3–10 *Dos and don'ts of drawing graphs*

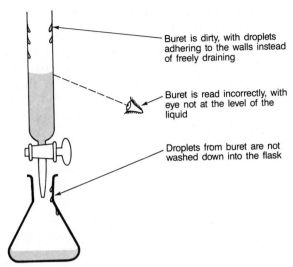

Buret is dirty, with droplets adhering to the walls instead of freely draining

Buret is read incorrectly, with eye not at the level of the liquid

Droplets from buret are not washed down into the flask

FIGURE 3–11 *Avoidable errors in using a buret*

This question is asking you to imagine a hypothetical situation and determine how it would affect experimental results. We label such questions **suppose questions** because they frequently begin with the words, "Suppose that . . . " This type of question appears easier than it actually is. Resist the temptation to guess or to answer it off the top of your head. For most students, responding quickly, without giving the question serious thought, results in an incorrect answer.

Let's look at an example of a suppose question about a lab experiment. Try to follow through the example, even if you have not yet begun work in the laboratory or if you have not yet studied the subject of molarity. However, if the example simply makes no sense, skip this section for now, but be sure to come back to it when you encounter a suppose question in your lab.

Assume, then, that in the lab you were instructed to make a 1.0 M (M = molarity) NaOH solution by weighing out 4.0 grams of solid NaOH and dissolving it in enough water to make 100 ml of solution. You have calculated the molarity as follows:

$$?M \text{ NaOH} = \frac{4.0 \text{ g NaOH} \times \dfrac{1 \text{ mole NaOH}}{40 \text{ g NaOH}}}{0.10 \text{ liter}}$$

$$= 1.0 \ M \text{ NaOH}$$

In the laboratory manual you encounter the following suppose question:

Suppose the NaOH you weighed out was contaminated with a small amount of an inert chemical. Would the molarity of your NaOH be greater, less, or the same as 1.0 M?

You can answer this question both by reasoning and by analyzing the mathematical calculation:

Reasoning: The 4.0 g of contaminated solid contains less than 4.0 grams of NaOH. So the solution I made up has less NaOH than it should. The molarity will therefore be less than 1.0 M.

Analyzing mathematically: The amount that I weighed out contained less than 4.0 grams of NaOH, so the numerator of the fraction decreases. This would make the molarity decrease.

$$M \text{ NaOH} = \frac{\overset{\text{decreases}}{\overset{\searrow}{4.0 \text{ g NaOH}}} \times \dfrac{1 \text{ mole NaOH}}{40 \text{ g NaOH}}}{0.10 \text{ liter}}$$

EXERCISE 1   Determining How Errors Affect Your Results

Here is a similar suppose question based on the above example. Answer it both by reasoning and by analyzing the mathematical calculation. Check the solution at the end of the chapter only after you have attempted an answer.

Suppose, in making up the NaOH solution above, you accidentally added too much water when dissolving the NaOH. How would this affect the molarity of the NaOH solution?

Can you see now why we encourage you to take these questions seriously? They're hard! But, like most lab skills, the ability to cope with this type of question improves with practice. Try writing out your reasoning on a piece of scrap paper before writing the answer in your lab report. Additionally, try arguing through the reasoning or math with some of your friends in the lab. Pool your collective wisdom.

There is one final question that you occasionally must face in lab.

What Went Wrong?

Sooner or later, one of your laboratory experiments will come out incorrectly. Although you may feel frustrated when this happens, it may not be a total disaster. You may receive part if not most of the credit for performing the experiment if you are able to account for your results.

Here are some actions you can take if your experimental results do not seem to be coming out right:

· Check your calculations. If you get stuck, do this with the help of a friend, if working together is permitted.

· If you discover what you did wrong, ask your instructor if you can go back into the lab to repeat that part of the experiment. This may be possible if your instructor teaches more than one lab section.

· If your instructor will not let you repeat the experiment, ask if you can have a set of data so that you can work through the appropriate calculations.

· Try to pinpoint your mistake. If you know what you did wrong, admit it.

· If you cannot figure out what went wrong, say so in your report. Include evidence for what you believe happened and why. Include in your report what you think should have happened.

If you are tempted to fudge your data to come out with the "right" answer, consider the consequences of this act. Falsified lab data is a great dishonesty in scientific work. The penalties for this action can be far greater than those for having a "wrong" answer. Even if you are not caught, you pay an emotional penalty for your act. We recommend honesty as the best policy.

The Finished Report

The quality of your report reflects on your work in lab. Accordingly, a messy report implies messy work in lab, even if this is not the case. Messy reports may also annoy your instructor, since many instructors find grading lab reports a long, tedious process. In order to earn the best score for your work in laboratory, make your report as concise and readable as possible.

To produce a readable report, you may find it helpful to do your calculations first on a piece of scrap paper. After completing and checking your work, transfer the figures neatly to the final report. Do the same with answers for essay questions. Avoid, however, writing down laboratory data in any place except your lab notebook. It is amazing how scratch paper with laboratory data tends to disappear!

Due dates for lab reports vary considerably. Some instructors want your write-up immediately; others allow a week or more. Usually you must work around whatever date your instructor has selected. If the only excuse for a late report is a death (preferably your own), take the hint. You might be better off to hand in an incomplete report rather than a late one. If your instructor is flexible about when you hand in your report, do not abuse this flexibility. Lab reports that straggle in late tend to be graded more harshly than those handed in on time.

One late report is probably not a disaster. It is a matter of concern, though, if you find that your reports are habitually late. Try to figure out why you are not getting your reports in on time. Do you misjudge the amount of time you need to prepare your lab report? How soon before the due date do you begin working on your report? If timing is a problem, start working on the next report a day or two earlier than usual. Mark the date on your calendar to help remind you to begin writing your report.

LEARNING THE BASIS FOR LABORATORY GRADES

Schools vary in how they grade your performance in laboratory. Some grade laboratory as a separate course. Others include it as a part of a general chemistry course. Schools also vary on the basis for assigning laboratory grades. You could be graded on your written report, on the accuracy of your results, on your skills while in laboratory, on what you know about the content of the experiments, or on any combination of these.

If you know what is expected of you, you will be better able to meet those expectations. Here is a checklist of possible areas on which you may be evaluated. Check those that are most important to the evaluation of your lab performance.

(   ) Written lab reports
(   ) Accuracy of lab results
(   ) Attendance in lab
(   ) Skill at laboratory procedures
(   ) Exam questions about the lab
(   ) Separate laboratory exams

If you are already taking a chemistry course with a lab and do not know how you are being graded, ask your instructor. If you have not yet begun your laboratory work, keep these possibilities in mind as you listen to your instructor explain the "rules of the course."

In our experience laboratory grading procedures are in part subjective. For this reason you need to make an effort to communicate clearly with your instructor (see page 51). If your instructor recognizes that you are well prepared and knowledgeable about the lab, your grade may reflect this.

Also, in our experience, few chemistry courses give **lab practicals,** or exams where you have to demonstrate your skills in front of an instructor. Pencil-and-paper tests are more often used to test your knowledge. Let's look at some types of lab questions that are apt to show up on exams.

Problems

Laboratory experiments often require you to perform calculations on your lab data in order to obtain a desired result. On an exam the laboratory situation may be described, and you may be asked to do a similar calculation. For example:

THE LABORATORY • 61

A 3.00 ml portion of acetic acid solution (vinegar) was placed in an Erlenmeyer flask. About 25 ml of water and 2 drops of phenolphthalein were added. The initial buret reading of a 0.107 M NaOH solution was 1.22 ml. The acetic acid was titrated until a pale pink color was seen in the flask. The final buret reading was 15.72 ml. What is the molarity of the acetic acid solution? Assume the density of vinegar to be 1.0 g/ml.

If you are familiar with the laboratory experiment where vinegar is titrated with sodium hydroxide, you may be able to make sense out of this question. Otherwise, the question may appear impossibly complicated. Test questions on laboratory usually are quite wordy because they are testing your ability to interpret a description of an experimental situation. Most can be rephrased in a more simple manner, one that asks the same question but removes it from the context of the laboratory. For example, the previous question could be reworded as:

What is the molarity of an acetic acid solution if a 3.00 ml sample requires 14.50 ml of 0.107 M NaOH for titration to an endpoint?

The first version of this problem requires that you translate the actions performed in the laboratory into the values needed for calculations. For example, to obtain the volume of NaOH (14.50 ml), you have to subtract the initial volume from the final volume. How do you prepare for laboratory questions like these on exams? Most students find it helpful to practice describing from memory how the experiment was done, what data were obtained, and how the data were used in the calculations.

Discussion/Essay Questions

Discussion/essay questions require you to generate from memory an entire procedure from laboratory. For example:

Describe how you could measure in a laboratory the molarity of vinegar.

Briefly explain how to prepare 500 ml of an approximately 0.1 M solution of NaOH.

You can prepare for such questions by writing out summaries of the many different procedures you have performed. This is not as easy as it sounds. You may be surprised at how difficult it is to write summaries for the first time. It takes practice to keep your writing brief, yet complete.

Questions from the Lab Manual

Questions on exams may be taken directly from your laboratory manual. You can prepare for these by reviewing all the questions you answered on your lab report, self-testing at intervals after the laboratory.

SUMMARY

In this chapter, we have described situations you may encounter in the laboratory and approaches to lab work that will help you achieve success in this important aspect of your chemistry course. Some of the difficulties you may experience in the laboratory include:

· Things can go wrong.
· Experiments may deal with material that hasn't been taught.
· Laboratory skills are difficult to teach.
· Some laboratory operations are boring.
· Laboratory write-ups may have "bugs" in them.

To conduct an experiment successfully, you must be emotionally and intellectually prepared. The laboratory worksheet gives you a systematic approach in five sections:

· Vocabulary to be learned
· Equations needed
· Summary of procedure
· Plan of action for lab
· Special things to remember

Allot yourself sufficient time to prepare for laboratory.

Acquiring correct laboratory skills is essential to success in lab. The proper use of a buret was used to illustrate the essentials of good laboratory technique:

· Knowing the purpose of equipment
· Cleaning the equipment
· Preparing the equipment for use
· Using the equipment

Other useful laboratory skills include:

· Learning to record laboratory data accurately
· Learning to interact with your lab instructor
· Learning safety in the laboratory

After lab you will be required to write up your work. If your write-up includes graphs:

· Title the graph
· Label the axes
· Don't "connect the dots"
· Use the whole sheet of paper

Questions that occur repeatedly on lab reports include:

· What are the sources of error in your measurements?
· How do the errors affect your results?
· What went wrong?

The finished report should be concise and readable.

Laboratory grades are determined in various ways. Learn what is expected in your course. Some typical test questions on labs include:

· Problems
· Discussion/essay questions
· Questions from the lab manual

SELF-ASSESSMENT

How well are you doing in laboratory? Here are some statements to complete to help you assess your current laboratory competency.

1. My background in laboratory is:

VERY _____ VERY
STRONG   WEAK

If your background is weak, you will need more time than average to prepare for lab and to write it up. Look for ways to use your time as efficiently as possible. The lab worksheet given on page 42 will be particularly helpful.

2. My ability to prepare for a laboratory experiment is:

VERY _____ VERY
SATISFACTORY   INADEQUATE

If you are feeling "lost" most of the time in the laboratory, your preparation is probably inadequate and needs strengthening. On pages 41 to 43, we discuss some of the questions you should ask yourself before going to laboratory. These questions may help you identify some of the information that you are missing. What information do you need before the lab? Write it below.

INFORMATION I NEED BEFORE DOING A LAB

WAYS I CAN OBTAIN THIS INFORMATION

3.   My laboratory skills and techniques are:

VERY _____ VERY
STRONG   WEAK

As we pointed out on page 48, laboratory skill is not acquired overnight. You must work to improve your skills in the lab, allowing yourself time to learn the correct procedures. What actions will you take to improve your lab skills and techniques? See pages 44 to 50.

WAYS IN WHICH I WILL WORK TO IMPROVE MY LAB SKILLS

4.   My lab reports are usually:

WELL _____ POORLY
DONE   DONE

What steps can you take to improve your lab reports? Should you start them sooner? Do you need to ask your instructor for help? Could you take better notes while you are in lab? See pages 54 to 60.

MY PLAN FOR IMPROVING MY LAB REPORTS

5.   Overall, my instructor is aware of my efforts to do good work in the laboratory.

YES _____ NO

Laboratory gives you the opportunity to interact with your lab instructor. Do you want to improve your ability to communicate with your instructor? See pages 51 to 52 for some helpful suggestions.

PATTERNS OF COMMUNICATION I WOULD LIKE TO IMPROVE

ANSWER TO EXERCISE

Exercise 1

Reasoning: If too much water is added, the solution will be weaker than it should be. Therefore, the molarity will be less than 1.0 *M*.

Analyzing mathematically: If the amount of water is increased, the denominator of the fraction will increase from 0.10 liter. If the denominator increases, the value of the fraction will decrease. Therefore, the molarity will decrease.

CHAPTER FOUR

Chemistry Tests

Taking tests is part of taking chemistry. That's not exactly a surprise, you may say. To do well on tests, you must learn the required material. In addition, you must be able to show your instructor the chemistry you have learned. In short, you need both chemical knowledge and good test-taking skills.

You will probably be frustrated if you know something and do not get credit for it on an exam. This happens to many chemistry students. We have seen students get low scores on exams when they knew a considerable amount of chemistry. We have also seen professors puzzled by the low scores of students who apparently knew more than their scores reflected.

What does a low score indicate? That is not an easy question to answer. Rather than laboring over it, we would like to point out two things: First, there are steps you can take to help ensure that your test score will show what you know. Second, you can strengthen your approach to preparing for exams so that you will learn more and do better.

In this chapter we make an important assumption: You *can* improve your ability to take tests. You may have taken chemistry exams in the past and felt that your grades did not reflect what you knew. Your unfortunate experiences with previous exams need not prevent your success on future exams. However, if you want to improve your performance, you will have to identify which skills are weak and take action to improve them.

You have been taking tests for many years. In the process you have formed test-taking habits—that is, typical patterns of actions that you use to prepare for and take exams. To improve your test-taking skills, you may need to form new habits. As you practice your improved skills, they will begin to become automatic.

66

There are specific test-taking skills that are used before, during, and after a test. As the first step in becoming aware of your current testing skills, complete Exercise 1 now. If you have already taken some chemistry exams, use your experiences with them to answer the questions in Exercise 1. If you have not yet taken a chemistry exam, recall the actions you took when faced with any other exam in a science course.

EXERCISE 1 My Current Test Strategies

Imagine that you have a chemistry exam five days from now.

BEFORE THE EXAM

In the space below, describe what you would do between now and the test to prepare for it. Specifically, what would you spend your time doing?

DURING THE EXAM

Imagine that you have just been handed your chemistry exam. How would you go about taking the exam? For example, which question would you do first? Are there any traps you would want to avoid?

AFTER THE EXAM

Imagine you have just been handed back your graded exam. What would you do with that exam now?

Keep your responses in mind as we discuss some helpful strategies to use before, during, and after taking an exam.

STRATEGIES TO FOLLOW
BEFORE THE TEST

Preparing for an exam does *not* begin the day before the test. Some tasks need to be started earlier to avoid a last-minute time crunch and to allow yourself adequate time for review. Let's look at some study methods to use in preparing for an exam:

**Prepare Topic
Summaries**

As your chemistry course unfolds, certain major topics will be taught. These are usually identified by your professor, probably in a syllabus. If all has been going well, you have been studying the parts of each topic as they were being taught. You have memorized the factual information, learned the meaning of new words, worked problems, and so on.

As the exam approaches, you must pull together all this required information about each topic. We call these **topic summaries.** Topic summaries can organize subject matter and thereby strengthen your knowledge of it.

In most courses the chief source of information for creating a topic summary is your lecture notes. Your professor has already selected the most important parts of topics to discuss in lecture. If you have worked through your notes and analyzed the contents (see page 26), you are prepared to collect this information to form an overview of the topic. An overview contains the following information:

· Major subtopics
· What you must know in each subtopic (words, terms, facts, rules)
· What you must be able to do with information in each subtopic (e.g., drawings to be reproduced from memory, types of problems to be worked)

For example, your professor may have spent three lectures discussing the topic of solutions: what solutions are, how to describe the dissolving process, ways of describing the composition of a solution, and so on. Your summary of this topic might be as follows:

BASIC INFORMATION ABOUT SOLUTIONS

To know (facts, concepts, rules)
    What solutions are
    Parts of solutions (solvent, solute)
    Classes of solutions (gas-gas, gas-liquid, etc.)
    Solubility of solutions
        What *solubility* means
        Units to describe solutions
    Types of solutions (unsaturated, saturated, supersaturated)
    Concentration
        What *concentration* means
        Names of concentrations
        Units of concentrations
    Classes of soluble/insoluble substances
To do
    Recognize soluble and insoluble compounds.
    Explain why substances do (or do not) dissolve in water.
    Explain how solubilities change with temperature.
    Draw molecular pictures of ionic substances dissolved in water.

Explain lecture demonstrations of solubilities:

Ethanol + I_2(aq)

Dichloromethane + I_2(aq)

MOLAR CONCENTRATIONS

To know

Definition of molarity

Abbreviation for molarity, M

Alternate ways of writing molarity (M = moles solute/liters solution)

To do

Given amount of solute and volume of solution, calculate molarity.

Given molarity and volume of solution, find amount of solute (conversion factor problem).

Given molarity and amount of solute, find volume of solution (conversion factor problem).

EXERCISE 2   Making a Topic Summary

Select an area of your course and produce a topic summary for it. Aim to provide in a concentrated form all the essential information about that topic.

If you had difficulty doing this exercise, you need to work on improving your summarizing skills. Two references that provide instruction in this skill are:

Walter Pauk, *How to Study in College*, 5th Ed. (Boston: Houghton Mifflin Company, 1993).

James F. Shepherd, *College Study Skills*, 3rd Ed. (Boston: Houghton Mifflin Company, 1986).

Topic summaries are powerful tools for reviewing your knowledge before an exam. Some students write their summaries on long strips of computer paper and hang them up in their rooms. Others devote specific sections of their chemistry notebooks to this purpose. Where might you put your summaries so that you could refer to them often? Ultimately, by reviewing the summaries, you will have in your memory all the information needed for each topic.

Test Yourself

How will you determine when you have studied a topic enough? Self-testing is the best way we know. Such testing may be informal or formal. For example, can you recite from memory the information on your topic summaries? Try to recall not only the major points but the specific detailed information in each part of your summary. What does each term mean? How are the words related? What rules do you need to know? What are the general steps for working each problem? You might try a variety of self-quizzing methods: Recite aloud the information or write it out.

We also recommend that you compose more formal tests for yourself to test your mastery of the material.. Sections in Chapters 3, 6, 7, 8, 9, and 10 give model questions for various types of chemical content; use them to make up these self-tests. Write out the answers to the self-test to check your total mastery of the information. In writing a test, give some thought to the level and format of the questions you have used. You want to make your questions similar to those on the coming exam. To do so, you should obtain the following information about your professor's tests:

Format: What will the test look like? How many questions will be included? How much time will be allotted? Which charts and graphs will be provided for you? Will you be given a periodic chart? Which factual information will be given on the test (e.g., Avogadro's number, metric-English equivalencies)?

Types of questions: Multiple choice? Matching? Problems? Fill in the blank? Will partial credit be given?

Level of problems: Will test questions be similar to homework problems? To problems done in lecture? Will some problems be different from anything you have ever seen before?

Coverage: What topics will be tested? Will certain topics be particularly emphasized? Will laboratory content be tested? Will information on handouts be covered?

Emphasis: Will you be asked to remember memorized facts? Give definitions? Give examples of concepts? Balance equations? Solve problems? What is the balance among these types of content?

Exams given in previous terms, especially those written by your instructor, are an important source of such information. Many instructors make these available to students. Students who have taken the course previously are also sources of old exams. If old exams are not available, you might ask your instructor to describe the test format and level. Explain that you are not trying to avoid work, but rather that you need the information to do a good job in preparing for the exam.

EXERCISE 3 Examine an Old Exam from Your Course

Obtain an old exam from your course. Use the questions above to obtain information about your coming exam:

- Format
- Types of questions
- Level of problems

- Coverage
- Emphasis

Use this information to determine how well you are preparing for the coming exam.

Good Advice

Self-testing should continue until you can remember the required information in an effortless, accurate way. Why effortless? Your chemistry exam will require you to think and reason. You want to be able to devote your energy to thinking and solving problems rather than to remembering information. Why accurate? Even small errors can cost you many points, as we will see in the next section.

Allocate Study Time Wisely

The ideas of chemistry build rapidly upon one another. Thus, the most useful study strategy is to work at the subject each day. What you study today becomes the foundation for what you will be taught tomorrow. This study plan is the first step in preparation for a chemistry exam.

As an exam draws near, you need a different strategy for your final study time. Now shift your emphasis to reviewing material and checking for forgotten or incompletely learned information. But don't forget the task of keeping up with the current material; otherwise, you will fall behind for the next exam.

Do you have time enough to learn all required chemical topics before an exam? Check either the right or the left column for each item in Table 4–1 to describe your actual (or anticipated) situation as your chemistry exam nears.

TABLE 4–1   DEMANDS ON MY TIME

( ) My other courses will not demand extra time, so I have sufficient time to study chemistry.	( ) Demands in my other courses are high, taking time from my study of chemistry.
( ) I am not behind in my chemistry work.	( ) I am behind in my chemistry work.
( ) I understood the chemistry topics as they were taught.	( ) I did not understand the topics as they were taught.
( ) I am in good health, and my mind is clear and ready to work.	( ) I am not feeling well, and I am preoccupied with other things.

If all your responses fall to the left, you will probably have sufficient time to master all required chemical topics before your exam. Continue to work at summarization and mastery of the exam material, as well as to work on the material currently being taught.

If you have any responses on the right, you may not have sufficient time to prepare yourself for the test. In this case, do not just study topics randomly. Instead, use this strategy: *Learn completely as many topics as you can.*

continue →

Avoid the pitfall of knowing a little about everything with mastery of nothing, even if this means that you cannot study some topics. Why is partial learning of several topics such a poor strategy? Simply put, chemical information is complex and detailed. Chemistry tests may give little or no credit for partial learning.

For example, you may be required to learn the name and structure of the sulfate ion:

$$\text{sulfate ion} = SO_4^{2-}$$

If you learn the charge incorrectly (e.g., SO_4^{1-}), you may lose full credit for any answer that requires you to use the sulfate ion in a chemical formula. You therefore receive no credit for what you know: that sulfate has one sulfur atom, four oxygen atoms, and a negative charge. Another place where you may receive no credit for less than 100 percent learning of a fact, concept, or principle is on multiple choice questions.

If you have already taken a chemistry exam, now work Exercise 4.

EXERCISE 4   Recognizing the Need for Complete Learning

Go back through a chemistry exam you have taken. Look for places where you received little or no credit, even though you knew most of the material. Note the amount of information that you were missing compared to the amount you knew. Note also how much you were penalized for missing that information.

Take Care of Yourself

Tests require you to think intensely and rapidly, and to sustain this thinking for an hour or two. If you are short on sleep, not feeling well, or emotionally drained, you may lack the stamina to maintain this high level of thinking over the time required. We encourage you, therefore, to take care of your physical and emotional health prior to an exam. If you eat sensibly and get sufficient rest, you increase your chances of performing well on an exam. You also decrease your chances of knowing something and not having the stamina to get credit for it.

Are you tempted to stay up studying the night before an exam? That is rarely wise. By staying up late you may learn some additional information. However, you will learn it at the cost of fatigue. Tiredness promotes careless errors and leaves you more vulnerable to anxiety. In short, you may be better off getting some rest, even if you must leave some topics unstudied.

Your body needs sufficient fuel as well as sufficient sleep. By eating sensibly before an exam, you will have enough energy to last through the exam. High-protein foods give more sustained energy than high-sugar foods. However, a sugar candy bar eaten just before the exam may be useful to revive your energy. If you are prone to jittery nerves, avoid coffee and high-caffeine colas. Some students have reported that drinking a glass of wine or beer before an exam calms them down. Since alcohol is a powerful depressant and may interfere with your ability to concentrate, we do not recommend this.

CHEMISTRY TESTS • 73

It is often helpful to do something fun or relaxing before an exam rather than studying right up to the last minute. For example, have you ever played a musical instrument or participated in a sports event? How did you release tension before a big meet or concert? Did jumping rope for five minutes ease your tension? Did running around the block ready your mind for intense concentration? Did eating a slice of pizza increase energy? Try to get in touch with the mechanisms that work in making you more comfortable and productive when you are under stress.

Manage Your Anxiety

If you have studied well for an exam, you may feel confident that you will perform well. Most people do not feel anxious about an exam if they are certain of their knowledge. Test anxiety, however, is not always a matter of logic. Some people feel anxious even if they are well prepared. In this section we confront the need to keep tension at a low enough level to permit you to work well on an exam.

Are you frightened about taking chemistry tests? What can you do if this tension prevents you from thinking clearly on the exam? Most people get somewhat nervous before tests. But nervousness does not affect everyone in the same way. Let's first look at how you react to the stress of taking tests. Check the boxes in Table 4–2 that describe your typical responses to taking exams.

TABLE 4–2   MY RESPONSES TO TEST ANXIETY

When I get nervous on an exam . . .

HELPFUL	*HARMFUL*
( ) I get extra energy.	( ) I make silly errors.
( ) I do better work.	( ) I cannot concentrate.
( ) My head is clear.	( ) My body is uncomfortable:
( ) My memory sharpens.	My muscles tense.
( ) I perform my best.	My heart pounds.
	I sweat a lot.
	My stomach hurts.
	I feel sick.
	( ) I forget what I have learned.
	( ) I cannot sleep the night before.

Have you checked any of the "harmful" responses? The difference between a helpful and harmful response is largely a matter of degree. Practically speaking, if any of the items you have checked interfere with your ability to perform well or affect your physical well-being, you are prone to being anxious about taking exams. We call this "test anxiety."

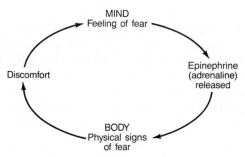

FIGURE 4–1 *Mind-body interactions*

If test anxiety hampers your performance, you can learn ways to lower your tension. One way to picture how your mind and body are connected is shown in Figure 4–1. When you feel stress, as with an exam, your body tenses. Muscles tighten, and epinephrine (adrenaline) is released in response to fear. Your mind then responds to these physiological signs by becoming more anxious. This, in turn, sends an even stronger fear signal to the body, which responds by becoming even more tense.

Learning to relax can help you to break this body-mind tension cycle. Many campuses have clinics that teach relaxation techniques for lowering stress. Using these techniques, many students have learned to control their reactions to stress. There are also self-help books that may accomplish the same purpose. Look for them in your local campus library or bookstore.

Attend to Last-Minute Details

If you are uncomfortable when faced with new situations, you may want to rehearse the process of taking your first chemistry exam. Try to scout out the room in which you will take the exam, particularly if it is different from your usual classroom. Where is the pencil sharpener? The nearest bathroom? The drinking fountain? What else do you think you might need?

If the room is new to you, sit in it for a few moments and become familiar with the space. Is the room hot, cold, drafty? What might make the seat more comfortable for you? Which seats have a clear view of the clock and chalkboard?

Decide in advance what you want to have with you at the exam. Here are some possibilities:

Calculator: Is yours in good working order? When was the last time you charged it? Do you have an extra battery?

Pencils/pens: Are your pencils sharp? Do you have a good eraser? Do you have a backup pen?

Books: Do you need to bring materials for an open-book test? Did your instructor tell you to leave your chemistry books at home?

Comfort: Might you get hungry during an exam? If permitted, might you bring a favorite snack, one that can be eaten quietly without disturbing others? A cold drink? A cup of coffee? Might you need a sweater to keep warm?

STRATEGIES TO FOLLOW DURING THE TEST

The big moment has arrived. You and your friends sit waiting for the test to be handed out. You now have it in your hands. You breathe deeply and begin.

Wait!

Before you actually begin answering questions, there are some actions you can take to improve your ability to perform well.

Read the Directions
Twice

Your instructor has not only decided what you are to know, but also how you are to show your knowledge. The test directions give you the ground rules for the exam. As you read through the directions for the exam, look for answers to questions such as these: Where do you put your answers? Is there a penalty for guessing? What is the time limit? In addition to the information on the exam itself, corrections or new directions may be written on the chalkboard. It is hard to resist the temptation to plunge into the exam at the earliest opportunity. If you do this, however, you may miss important corrections or directions that could cost you points.

Look Over the Whole Exam

What? Still not ready to start answering questions? That's right. We suggest you glance through the entire test before answering a single question. Look for information about the number of questions, the format, and the points allotted for each question or section. You can then make a rough estimate of how much time you should spend on each section of the test. Some of the questions may appear unfamiliar at first glance. Do not let this frighten you and do not get sidetracked trying to figure out the answers. Your sole purpose for the overview is to obtain enough information to guide your attack on the exam.

"Dump" Detailed Information You Will Need

As you look over the exam, you may see that you will need to use chemical or mathematical formulas and equations that you have memorized. As you identify these, immediately jot them down on the back of your exam. By "dumping" this information out of your head, you have cleared your mind for thinking. Once items are written down, you can then look them up instead of spending time and energy to recall them. See page 128 for more information on dumping.

Now start working on the test. But do not just start on any question. Rather, look for one that is familiar and answer it first. Success in completing a question can give you the lift needed to tackle the others. Work first on the problems that you think you can do.

Plan Your Answers

Before you start rapidly writing down the solution to a problem, take a moment to think about how you are going to answer it. In Chapters Ten and Eleven, we will teach you some powerful techniques for solving problems. As you plan your answers to problems, incorporate those suggestions into your solutions. Do not take shortcuts when problem solving, unless you want to risk receiving little or no credit for what you know.

Essay questions are occasionally included in chemistry exams. For these questions, as well as for problems, planning your answer is crucial. Outline the major points in your answer before you begin writing.

Work for Partial Credit

As noted earlier (page 72), you may receive no credit for partial answers on certain types of exam questions. However, you may have a chance for partial credit on complex problems with multiple steps. Put down on these as much information as you can. You want to receive credit for what you know, even if you are unable to work through the entire solution.

Use Appropriate Techniques for Multiple Choice Questions

Multiple choice questions are not all alike. Some multiple choice questions require you to solve a numerical problem. For these, write out your work right next to the question or put it on scrap paper, clearly labeled. You will then have your work to refer to when you check your answers. Why is careful checking so important here? Multiple choice questions usually have as wrong choices the answers resulting from simple errors, such as forgetting a minus sign. Therefore, obtaining one of the choices shown is no guarantee that you have solved the problem correctly. In order to have confidence in your answer, you must check it, looking for "classic" mistakes. Checking will go faster if you have your work organized so that you can refer to it.

Other multiple choice questions test principles or concepts. For these, do not stop reading the choices after you have located an apparently correct answer. Examine *all* choices that are listed before selecting an answer. If you are not sure of the correct answer, eliminate as many choices as possible. Then guess among the remaining ones. Answer all multiple choice questions unless you will be penalized for guessing. Even with a penalty, if you can eliminate one or two of the choices, you may be better off guessing than leaving the question blank.

Write Large and Legibly

If you want full credit, you will want your written exam work to be readable. As you check your work for accuracy, you are the first reader of your work. The next reader, the grader, must also be able to read it. If your handwriting is normally messy and practically illegible, you may want to copy parts of it over. As you write your answers, one simple way to improve readability is to write larger than usual.

Use Your Eraser Sparingly

There is always the risk that you will run out of time on your exam. Be on the lookout, then, for ways to save time. For example, erasing wrong answers takes time. Instead of erasing, draw a line through your error and begin again. Use the back of a page, if necessary, to complete the required answers.

Check Your Answers, If Time Permits

As you finish the last question on the exam, you may be tempted to get out of the exam room as fast as you can. But if you are working to get the best possible score, you have one task left: to check your paper. As you check, look for information included in other test questions that confirms answers you have written. For example, if for one question you needed the formula for ammonium nitrate, it may be given in another problem on the test. If time allows, you should also rewrite messy answers.

Resist Changing Uncertain Answers

During the checking process, you judge whether or not you have the correct answers down on the paper. As you check a problem or question, you may see another answer that also seems reasonable. Should you change your answer? By all means change the answer if you are *sure* the new one is correct. But, if you are not sure which is correct and would have to guess, stick with your first choice. It's more likely to be correct!

STRATEGIES TO FOLLOW AFTER THE TEST

Now the test is over. Are you sick of the subject? Do you never want to look at the exam again? Do you need to catch up in your other courses? Do you want to take some time for yourself?

This is a critical moment. If you want to stay in control of the material, you cannot afford to take a vacation from chemistry, no matter how much you may want to. You might temporarily decrease the amount of time spent on chemistry, but to avoid chemistry totally is taking a great risk. If you get even one lecture behind, you may not be able to catch up. You thereby set yourself up for trouble on the next exam.

What do you need to do after an exam?

Find Out the Correct Answers

What were the correct answers to the test questions? Most instructors will either discuss the correct answers in class or post a key. It is your responsibility to obtain the correct answers and to understand them. Make a record of the answers so that you will have them available when reviewing for the final exam.

Analyze Your Errors

Ask yourself the following questions about your mistakes:

What types of errors did I make?
  Errors in balancing equations?
  Errors in writing chemical formulas?
  Memorization errors? Concept errors? Rule errors?
  Errors in solving problems? Math errors?
Have I made any of these errors before?

Which errors showed up for the first time on this exam?

How can I plan to reduce these errors?

Use this information to help avoid repeating your mistakes.

Analyze the Test

Analyze the test by asking yourself the following questions:

What types of questions did the test contain?

Have I seen any of its questions before?

On old exams?

In the textbook?

In my lecture notes?

What topics were tested?

Lecture?

Laboratory?

Assignments?

Demonstrations?

Handouts?

Where was the information I missed available?

In lecture notes?

In the text?

In assignments?

In lab write-ups?

How should I have studied to master this material?

How hard were the questions?

Harder than assigned problems?

Easier?

This information tells you what kind of a test your professor has written. By implication, it also tells you what your professor wants you to know. You need this information so that you know how to focus your studying (see Chapter Two, page 18). You want to spend most of your study time learning the important material at the appropriate level of difficulty. You need to develop a clear picture of your instructor's expectations so that you can plan your future studying more effectively.

Notice how general the above questions are. We are not suggesting that you examine the test so that you can second-guess your instructor and take chances on what you can avoid studying. Our assumption is that nearly everything that your professor talks about in lecture is fair game for an exam and you should study it. However, how much emphasis to give each topic, what level of proficiency to reach, which topics to include that have not been emphasized in lecture—all of these are important study decisions. Analysis of your chemistry exams can help you make these decisions wisely.

Change Your Study Habits

If there is a difference between what you wanted to achieve on the exam and your actual performance, you will need to change your method of studying. Make some definite plans for strengthening your study process based on your analysis of the test and the errors you made. You may want to change your study approach totally (see Chapter Two for suggestions) or fine-tune your current study plan. You may want to increase the amount of time that you spend studying. Whatever the case, be aware that changing study habits can be a long and painful process. Expect to commit yourself daily to the new actions, just as you would if you were dieting or giving up smoking.

If you have difficulty changing long-standing study habits, find ways to make the change process easier. For example, write out for yourself the new activities that you plan to use. Post the new procedures where you can refer to them often. You could also enlist the aid of your roommate to remind you of the new actions that form your new study plan. In all of this, you are looking for mechanisms to remind yourself of the new actions that are needed and to encourage yourself to stick to them.

Do Not Forget the Final Exam

Most chemistry courses have cumulative final exams. It pays off if you review for the final each time you get an exam back. Six to eight hours of review distributed throughout a term will reinforce that knowledge more powerfully than an equal amount of time spent at one sitting at the end of the term. Therefore, when you get an exam back, consider reviewing it as well as reviewing any previous exams. You need not spend a lot of time on this.

SUMMARY

There is a skillful way to approach test taking in chemistry. This chapter discusses specific actions to use before, during, and after an exam.

To prepare for an exam:

- Write out *topic summaries*.
- Engage in *self-testing*.
- Allocate study time wisely.
- Take care of yourself.
- Manage your anxiety.
- Attend to last-minute details: Check out the exam room; find the nearest bathroom, pencil sharpener, etc.; and come prepared with calculator, pencils, books, comfort items.

Before beginning to work on the test:

- Read the directions.
- Look over the whole exam.
- Dump memorized information you will need.

While working on the exam:

- Pick a familiar question to start on.
- Plan out long answers.

- Work multiple choice appropriately.
- Work for partial credit on extensive problems.
- Write large and legibly.
- Do not waste time erasing.
- Check your answers.
- Be wary of changing answers.

After the test, don't take a vacation from chemistry. Work to:

- Find out the correct answers.
- Analyze your errors.
- Analyze the test.
- Change your habits as necessary.
- Review periodically for the final exam.

SELF-ASSESSMENT

Are you prepared for the test-taking demands of your course? Place an X on the line in the position that best describes your response to the following statements:

1. I do as well on chemistry tests as I would like.

YES ——————————————————————————— NO

You can learn strong test-taking skills. The skills we have discussed in this chapter are listed in the summary. Review pertinent sections in this chapter for suggestions on improving each skill.

SKILLS NEEDING IMPROVEMENT

MY PLAN FOR IMPROVING THESE SKILLS

2. When I take tests, I am rested enough to do my best.

YES ——————————————————————————— NO

Fatigue contributes to careless mistakes. If you begin your process of review early enough, you are less likely to stay up late cramming at the last minute. See page 72 for more about avoiding fatigue.

MY CURRENT LEVEL OF FATIGUE

MY PLAN FOR BEING MORE RESTED

3. When I take tests, nervousness interferes with my performance.

YES ———————————————————————————— NO

If excessive anxiety interferes with your exam performance, work to reduce it. See page 73.

MY CURRENT LEVEL OF ANXIETY ABOUT TESTS

MY PLAN FOR REDUCING MY ANXIETY

4. During an exam, I am never without a sharp pencil or a working calculator.

YES ———————————————————————————— NO

Before the exam is the time to attend to details such as pencils and calculators. See page 74 for other things to anticipate before an exam.

5. I take the time to relearn correctly the material I miss on an exam so that I do not make the same mistake twice.

YES ———————————————————————————— NO

If you find yourself making the same mistakes repeatedly, plan to take specific action to reduce those errors.

MY MOST COMMON ERRORS

MY PLAN TO REDUCE THOSE ERRORS

6. I have a reasonable idea of what to expect on a test before I take it.

YES ———————————————————————————— NO

Exam formats and questions should not be a total surprise. See pages 70 and 78 for techniques for anticipating what will be on your exam.

PART TWO

MASTERING THE CONTENT OF CHEMISTRY

Part One of this book focused on your course and how you could get the most from it. We hope you learned some constructive approaches to studying chemistry and are now able to work out a study plan that is effective for you. We also hope that you have the tools to carry out a laboratory experiment and to score your best on an exam.

Now, in Part Two, we shift the focus to the subject of chemistry itself and how you can master it. Imagine this scenario. You are sitting at your desk with your notebook open to today's lecture notes, textbook open to the appropriate section, and paper and pencils ready. What now? How do you proceed? How will you *learn* the required chemistry? Part Two will teach the actions needed for efficient mastery of chemical content.

We have organized Part Two around the different types of chemical content that form part of all chemistry courses: facts, concepts, rules, and problems. Since each type of content has its own characteristics, each will require different learning actions on your part.

The first chapter in Part Two will teach you to identify the four different types of chemical content. It also lists the major topics covered in most general chemistry courses and includes examples of the facts, concepts, rules, and problems that you may encounter under each topic. The remaining chapters will present in more detail the specific characteristics of each of these types of content: Chapter Six will concentrate on facts; Chapter Seven, on concepts; Chapters Eight and Nine, on rules; and Chapters Ten and Eleven, on problems.

Each of these chapters will give you practice in the activities required for mastery of the type of content.

CHAPTER FIVE

Identifying Types of Chemical Content

You learn different things in different ways. For example, when you meet a person, you may first learn his or her name by the process of memorization. You do not use this same process, however, to learn about the person. Instead, you bring together the content of many interactions with the individual, trying to see how they fit together in a meaningful way. Your thought processes are much more complex than the process of memorization.

Similarly, you learn the subject of chemistry using different thought processes. For example, you use different mental skills to memorize a fact than to develop a concept, use a rule, or solve a problem. The mental skills used for these differ in the complexity of the thought processes involved.

Your chemistry course is unlikely to proceed in a manner that starts with simple learning skills and builds to more complex ones. Instead, expect to find your chemistry course organized around a list of topics that the professor wishes you to learn. As each topic is presented, the pertinent facts, concepts, rules, and problems will be taught. For example, you might first be given a fact or two, then some concepts and a rule. These might be followed by a problem. In the course of doing this problem, some additional facts or concepts may become apparent. Thus, learning demands of differing complexity will be made on you all at once.

In making these learning demands, your chemistry course will not label chemical content for you as facts, concepts, rules, or problems. However, in order to be able to study appropriately, you may need to recognize whether a piece of information falls into one of these categories. This chapter will help you begin the process of recognizing different types of chemical content.

The latter part of this chapter contains summaries that list the facts, concepts, rules, and problems that you may encounter in a given topic of chemistry. We do not suggest that you try to memorize the summaries or even that you go through them at one sitting. Instead, use them as a reference as your course progresses. As each new topic of your course is introduced, look it up in this chapter. The summaries will alert you to the major learning demands for each topic.

TYPES OF CHEMICAL CONTENT

The four types of chemical content can be thought of as the tools with which to write the language of chemistry. This language, like the English language, is based on words that are constructed from an alphabet. These words can be used in sentences, which in turn can be used to construct paragraphs. In the language of chemistry, the letters of the chemical alphabet are the **facts** that you will learn. These are organized into chemical words, or **concepts. Rules** function as our chemical sentences. **Problems** are like the paragraph, built up from the facts, concepts, and rules. Thus, the four types of content differ in their complexity and are hierarchically related, as shown in Figure 5–1.

In the following sections, we will describe each type of content and explain what is involved in mastering it. First, let's look at the simplest type of chemical knowledge: chemical facts.

Facts

Chemical facts are statements about how the world is and how the world will be represented. Chemical facts usually can't be "figured out." They must simply be accepted and learned because they are currently believed to be true. Some examples of facts are:

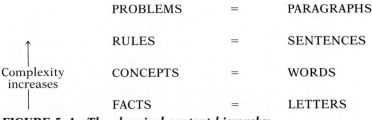

PROBLEMS	=	PARAGRAPHS
RULES	=	SENTENCES
CONCEPTS	=	WORDS
FACTS	=	LETTERS

Complexity increases

FIGURE 5–1 *The chemical content hierarchy*

Descriptions:

> The element chlorine is a pale green gas.

Names of chemicals:

> Acetic acid is the name of the chemical in vinegar.

Terms associated with specific ideas:

> Any substance that cannot be separated into simpler substances by a chemical reaction will be called an element.

Statements of relationships:

> To find the density of a sample, divide the mass by the volume.

The basic activity for learning facts is memorization. As you repeat the information to be learned and practice recalling it, you work toward mastery of the information. Chapter Six describes the process of memorizing chemical information. As you work through the topics in your course, you may be amazed at how little chemical information is mastered by memorization. Memorization is nonetheless important, though, for facts are basic to your building of concepts, rules, and problems. However, most of your learning time will be spent in doing more complex mental activities such as those we will describe next.

Concepts

A chemical concept is an idea about matter. This idea is represented by a single word or phrase. Examples of concepts are *element, compound, atom,* and *molecule.* Each of these words stands for a complex idea. When you learn a chemical concept, you engage in a struggle to learn fully what the concept word means and how it can be used.

There are five basic learning activities for mastering concepts. We will use the concept of *element* to illustrate these activities.

Finding definitions for the concept word:

> An element is a pure substance that cannot be separated into simpler substances by ordinary chemical processes.

Identifying the essential characteristics of a concept:

> An element can have only one type of atom present. The chemical formula of a substance that is classified as an element can have only one chemical symbol in it.

Identifying variable characteristics of a concept:

> The physical state of an element can vary; elements can be solid, liquid, or gas. Elements may exist as separate atoms, or atoms of the element may be combined into molecules.

Recognizing examples and nonexamples of a concept:

> Silicon (Si), sulfur (S_8), and hydrogen (H_2) are elements; water (H_2O) and table salt (NaCl) are not elements.

Determining relationship of the concept to other concepts:

> Element and compound are two mutually exclusive concepts; if a substance is an element, it cannot be a compound, and vice versa. Element is a part of the general concept, "pure substance." Elements can further be classified as metals, nonmetals, and metalloids.

Chapter Seven presents detailed information about how to master concepts. A glance at the topic summaries at the end of this chapter will convince you that *all* topics in general chemistry courses have large numbers of concepts to be learned. Your chemistry course is indeed a language course, with hundreds of new chemical words to be learned!

Rules

Chemical rules are generalizations about how the world usually works. Rules relate concepts to one another. Consider these examples of rules:

- Heat always flows spontaneously from regions of higher temperature to regions of lower temperature.
- Like electrical charges repel one another; unlike electrical charges attract.

There are five basic activities used to master rules. We will use the rule "Like electrical charges repel one another; unlike electrical charges attract" to illustrate these activities.

Identifying the precise relationship among the concepts:

> The statement of the rule identifies the relationship that like charges repel and unlike charges attract.

Identifying when the rule will apply:

> This rule applies to negatively charged particles (electrons) and positively charged particles (protons) in atoms. It also applies to compounds that contain ions (positively and negatively charged atoms) and to molecules of compounds that contain dipoles (parts of the molecule that have a slight negative and a slight positive charge).

Identifying when the rule will not apply:

> This rule does not apply to protons within the nucleus of an atom. There, special forces allow the protons to remain in the same region of space.

Identifying what the rule accomplishes:

> This rule allows one to predict when and how two atoms or two molecules will be attracted to one another.

Applying the rule to new situations:

> I can explain why electrons occupy regions of space as close as possible to the nucleus. I can also explain why it takes more energy to remove an electron that is close to the nucleus than to remove an electron that is far from the nucleus.

Rules are often given verbally, such as the two examples of rules given at the beginning of this section. Verbal rules can often be rephrased as "if–then" statements. For example, the rule above could be rephrased as: "If two electrical charges are of the same type (both positive or both negative), then they repel each other." Chapter Eight identifies techniques for mastering verbal rules.

However, rules also come in two formats other than words: mathematical formulas and graphs. For example, Boyle's law states: "The pressure and volume of an ideal gas are inversely proportional." This rule may be expressed mathematically as:

$$PV = k,$$

where k is the proportionality constant. It may also be shown graphically (see page 181). Chapter Nine presents strategies for mastering rules that are given in these formats.

Problems

A chemical problem describes a specific situation and then asks you to find some new information about that situation. Some examples of problems are:

· What is the weight percent of carbon in the compound carbon dioxide?

· How many grams of oxygen are contained in 100 grams of $CaCO_3$?

· What is the volume of an ideal gas, if 2 moles of that gas are collected at a pressure of 5 atmospheres and a temperature of 300 K?

· Write the net ionic equation for the reaction of hydrochloric acid and sodium hydroxide.

Many chemical problems will have a specified solution process that will be taught to you. An **algorithm** is a sequence of steps for solving a specific type of problem. As we will describe more fully in Chapter Ten, a problem that can be solved by use of an algorithm is called a **generic problem.** Mastery of generic problems comes from the following types of activities:

- Identifying the exact steps in the algorithm
- Identifying what the algorithm accomplishes (i.e., what information is given as the starting point, and what new information can be obtained by use of the algorithm)
- Practicing use of the algorithm until it can be employed with ease

Chapter Ten teaches a process for development of algorithms for chemistry problems that require you to manipulate chemical symbols. The fourth example of problems above is of this type. Chapter Ten also presents the algorithms for two common types of general chemistry problems: **mathematical problems** solved by use of a mathematical formula and **conversion-factor problems**—mathematical problems that are solved without a mathematical formula. The latter are also called **factor-label** or **dimensional-analysis problems.**

The essential characteristic of algorithmic problems is that they have a solution consisting of a series of steps that must be performed in a specified order to accomplish a specific goal. These steps may require recall of facts, classification of concepts, and/or application of rules.

Chapter Eleven considers **nonalgorithmic problems,** harder problems that do not have a totally specified solution. These problems are usually variations or combinations of the generic problems. In that chapter we present 12 common types of harder problems that you are likely to encounter, along with some strategies for solving each. To solve such problems, you must know the prerequisite facts, concepts, rules, and algorithms and be able to extend this information to new areas or conditions.

TOPIC SUMMARIES OF MAJOR LEARNING DEMANDS

In this final section, we summarize the more common areas of content taught in general chemistry courses. We have arranged these by title of sections, and list some common alternate titles. In each section we summarize the major learning demands by type of content. Refer to these listings as you progress through your chemistry course.

Note: Each chemistry course is different. We have included here *typical* demands of a *one-year* general chemistry course. Your course may include different subtopics within each topic or may include more or fewer mathematical problems than we indicate. These summaries are a guide to how topics are traditionally taught in such courses. If your course is only for one term or one semester, far fewer topics will be included than are listed here. Compare topics in your course to the descriptions here, then decide for yourself what the major learning demands are for each topic in your course.

**Forms and
Descriptions
of Matter**

ALTERNATE TITLES

Atoms, Molecules, and Ions

Atomic Structure

Pure Substances and Mixtures

The basic information of atomic symbols and identity of polyatomic ions and naming rules *must* be learned with 100 percent accuracy. This information is the foundation for chemical literacy, the ability to read and write the language of chemistry.

FACTS

· Names and corresponding symbols for elements
· Names, formulas, and charges for polyatomic ions
· History of development of atomic theory

CONCEPTS

pure substance	covalent compound
mixture	chemical formula
solution	empirical formula
atom	molecular formula
molecule	atomic weight
element	molecular weight
compound	molar mass
ionic compound	

RULES

· Rules for naming ionic compounds
· Rules for naming covalent compounds
· Law of multiple proportions (more than one compound may be made from the same two elements)
· Laws of conservation of mass and energy (energy and mass are conserved during a chemical reaction)

PROBLEMS

· Molecular weight problems: Given the formula and a table of atomic weights, calculate the molecular weight.

- Weight percent problems: Given the formula of a compound, find the percent by weight of one element in the compound.
- Empirical formula problems: Given the weight percents or actual weights of elements in a compound, find the simplest ratio of numbers of each element.
- Molecular formula problems: Given the molecular weight and the empirical formula, find the molecular formula.

Quantifying Matter and Energy

ALTERNATE TITLES

Metric System
Measurement
Dimensional Analysis
Problem Solving
Factor Label Problems

Problems in this topic are of the conversion-factor variety. Take the time to learn the process well because this algorithm will be used to solve problems throughout your course.

FACTS

- Names of metric units
- Values of metric prefixes
- Names of SI units

CONCEPTS

properties of matter	density
intensive properties	length
extensive properties	area
units of measurements	mole
heat	conversion factor
mass	concentration
volume	molarity

RULES

- Density = mass/volume
- Molecular weight = grams/mole
- Molarity = moles/liters

PROBLEMS

See conversion-factor problems, Chapter Ten, page 228.

Transforming and Quantifying Matter

ALTERNATE TITLES

Chemical Equations
Stoichiometry
Chemical Calculations
Mole Maps

Chemical equations are the symbolic descriptions of how chemicals react. You may need to seek your own understanding of this important topic, as it is a difficult topic to teach well.

FACTS

- Avogadro's number is 6.02×10^{23}.

CONCEPTS

mole	limiting reactant
chemical reaction	actual yield
chemical equation	theoretical yield
balancing an equation	solutions
reactant	titrations
product	neutralization
stoichiometry	

RULES

- Balancing equation rule: To balance an equation, you must have the same number of atoms of each type on each side of the reaction arrow.
- Typical reactions for classes of compounds
- Percent yield = (actual yield/theoretical yield) × 100

PROBLEMS

- Writing balanced chemical equations: Given reactants and products, obtain the same number of atoms of each type on each side of the reaction arrow.

- Predicting products of reactions: Given reactants and rules for typical reactions for those classes of reactants, predict products.
- Stoichiometry problems: Given a balanced chemical equation and an amount of one substance in the reaction, calculate an amount of another substance.
- Limiting reactant problems: Given a balanced chemical equation and amounts of more than one reactant, calculate which reactant will be entirely used up first; then calculate amounts of leftover reactants or amounts of products.
- Percent yield problems: Given two of the three quantities in the percent yield formula, calculate the missing quantity.

Gas Laws

ALTERNATE TITLES

Ideal Gases

States of Matter

For many students, the major difficulty in this section is the selection and transformation of the appropriate mathematical formula needed to solve a problem.

FACTS

- Values of STP (standard temperature and pressure)
- Postulates of kinetic molecular theory

CONCEPTS

gas	ideal gas constant
ideal gas	gas density
real gas	kinetic molecular theory
volume	diffusion
pressure	effusion
partial pressure	root-mean-square velocity
temperature	average molecular speed
Kelvin temperature scale	

RULES

- Kelvin temperature scale:

$$K = {}^{\circ}C + 273$$

- Ideal gas law (one sample of gas under one set of P, V, and T conditions):

$$PV = nRT$$

- Ideal gas law (gas under two sets of conditions):

$$\frac{P_1 V_1}{n_1 T_1} = \frac{P_2 V_2}{n_2 T_2}$$

- Ideal gas law variations (substitute in above):

$$n = \text{g/molar mass}$$
$$d = \text{g}/V$$

- Boyle's law:

$$PV = k$$

- Charles's law:

$$V = kT$$

- Avogadro's law:

1 mole of ideal gas occupies 22.4 l at STP

- Graham's laws of diffusion and effusion:

$$u = \sqrt{3RT/\text{molar mass}}$$

- Variations on Graham's law (comparison of speeds of two gases with different molar masses):

$$\frac{u_1}{u_2} = \sqrt{\frac{\text{molar mass}_2}{\text{molar mass}_1}}$$

- Variations of Graham's law (substitute in either equation above):

$$u = \text{rate/time}$$

- Van der Waals equation:

$$\left(P + \frac{an^2}{V^2}\right)(V - nb) = nRT$$

- Conditions for large deviation from ideality for real gases (low temperature and high pressure)
- Graphs:
  Maxwell's distribution of molecular speeds

PROBLEMS

Virtually all problems in this unit require appropriate use of one of the above mathematical formulas. In such problems you must select the correct formula, find values for all but one of the symbols in the formula, substitute the values into the formula, and calculate the one missing symbol value. See page 223, Chapter Ten, for a description of this type of problem.

Atomic Structure

ALTERNATE TITLES

Quantum Theory
The Bohr Atom
Electronic Structure of Atoms
Electron Configurations
Periodicity

This is a highly abstract topic. To make learning easier, imagine atoms and electrons as real objects. Quantum numbers are usefully viewed as descriptions of the location of an electron with respect to a nucleus (e.g., the principal quantum number, n, describes the distance of the electron from the nucleus).

This topic makes more sense if you have had a prior course in physics. If you have not, ask your instructor for some extra help in understanding physical concepts such as electromagnetic radiation.

The major learning demand is the learning and use of detailed rules.

FACTS

· Allowable values for quantum numbers
· History of atomic structure discoveries
· Order of orbital energy levels
· Names of families of elements on the periodic chart

CONCEPTS

atomic radius
Bohr atom
electromagnetic radiation
quantum
energy level
quantum numbers
principal quantum number, n
angular momentum quantum number, l
magnetic quantum number, m_l
electron spin quantum number, m_s
electron configuration

orbital
orbital diagram
ground state
excited state
emission spectra
paramagnetism
diamagnetism
periodic chart
periodic properties
ionization energy
atomic size

RULES

· Energy of electromagnetic radiation:

$$E = h\nu$$

· Relationship between frequency and wavelength:

$$\nu = \frac{c}{\lambda}$$

- Emission spectra of the hydrogen atom:

$$\Delta E = h\nu = R_H \left(\frac{1}{n_2^2} - \frac{1}{n_1^2} \right)$$

- Pauli exclusion principle: No two electrons in an atom may have the same four quantum numbers.
- Hund's rule: Electrons occupy orbitals singly, if possible, and with their spins parallel.
- Heisenberg uncertainty principle: It is impossible to know simultaneously the position and speed of a particle such as an electron.
- Rules for allowable values of quantum numbers.
- Rules for arrangement of elements on the periodic table.
- Trends in properties of elements, correlated with position of the element on the periodic table.

PROBLEMS

- Use any of the formulas above to solve for a missing value.
- Write the electron configuration for any element or ion.
- Write the orbital diagram for any element or ion.
- Give an acceptable set of quantum numbers for an electron in an atom.
- Rank a set of elements in increasing or decreasing order of values of their atomic properties (atomic or ionic size, ionization energy, electron affinity).

Chemical Bonding

ALTERNATE TITLES

Ionic and Covalent Bonding
Molecular Geometry
Chemical Bonding Theory

This topic contains a relatively large number of detailed rules. The problems based on these rules are difficult because it is easy to make careless errors in applying them. To minimize errors, write out problems in detail, skipping no steps. Keep careful track of your progress.

FACTS

- Lists of lone pair/bond pair electrons and resultant geometry of the molecules
- Bond angles in specific molecules

CONCEPTS

electron pair bonds   Lewis symbol (dot structure)
bonding pairs of electrons   electronegativity

lone pairs of electrons	dipoles
octet rule	VSEPR theory (valence-shell electron-pair repulsion)
ionic bonds	
covalent bonds	valence bond theory
coordinate covalent bonds	hybridization of atomic orbitals
multiple bonds	resonance
noble gases	geometric isomerism
bond angles	molecular orbital theory
bond lengths	bonding and antibonding molecular orbitals
valence electrons	

RULES

- Rules for representing electron pairs in molecules
- Octet rules (and exceptions to the rule)
- Rules for predicting charges of ions from position of the element on the periodic chart
- Multiple bonds and geometry of molecules: In determining molecular geometry, multiple electron-pair bonds count as single bonds
- Rules for predicting which pairs of elements will make ionic and covalent compounds
- Rules for predicting hybridization of orbitals within molecules
- Rules for constructing molecular orbital diagrams

PROBLEMS

- Given the formula of a covalently bonded molecule or polyatomic ion, draw the Lewis dot structure.
- Given the Lewis dot structure of a molecule or ion, predict its geometry.
- Given two nonmetallic elements, predict a formula from the octet and valence rules.
- Given the geometry of a molecule, predict the bond angles in the molecule.
- Predict the hybridization of orbitals within a molecule, given the geometry or Lewis dot structure.
- Draw a molecular orbital diagram for a simple molecule.

Thermochemistry

ALTERNATE TITLES

Energy Changes During Chemical Reactions
Thermodynamics

Concepts in this section are abstract and easily confused. Note below how many different concept terms contain the word *heat*. You must work to differentiate each concept from the others.

FACTS

- Names for units of energy
- Conventions
  Negative sign when heat is evolved
  Positive sign when heat is absorbed
- Values of T and P (for standard states)

CONCEPTS

heat	heat of reaction
work	heat of formation
exothermic reaction	heat of combustion
endothermic reaction	heat of vaporization
enthalpy	heat of fusion
enthalpy change	heat capacity
internal energy	specific heat
calorimeter	phase change
calorimetry	

RULES

- ΔH_{rxn} for a given chemical reaction will be obtained only when the molar quantities of the balanced chemical equation are reacted.
- Hess's law: The energy of a reaction does not depend on the path the reactants follow to form products.
- Calorimetry rules:
  Heat lost (or gained) during a process
    must be gained (or lost) by another part of the system.
  heat = $cm \Delta T$ (no phase change)
  heat = ΔHm (phase change)
- Heat of reaction is equivant to $-Q$ (calorimeter)/n.
- Sign conventions for energy changes during reactions: Exothermic reactions have negative heats; endothermic reactions have positive heats.
- Heats of formation for elements in their standard states are zero.
- Heat of reaction:

$$\Delta H_{rxn} = \Sigma \Delta H_{f_{products}} - \Sigma \Delta H_{f_{reactants}}$$

PROBLEMS

- Hess's law problem: Given a series of reactions and their enthalpy changes, sum them in appropriate ways to find the heat of reaction for a new reaction.
- Stoichiometry problem: Given a balanced chemical equation and a

heat of reaction for that equation, find the amount of heat evolved/ emitted when a given quantity of substance from the reaction is produced/reacted; can also be used to find an amount of substance produced/reacted for a given amount of heat.
• Use any of the above formulas to find a missing value.

Liquids and Solids

ALTERNATE TITLES

Phase Changes
Intermolecular Forces
States of Matter

Many students have difficulty in this section discriminating intermolecular forces (forces between one molecule and another) from intramolecular forces (forces that hold molecules together, i.e., ionic or covalent bonds). The concept words cause some of the confusion. For example, *hydrogen bonding* is not a chemical bond at all; it is an example of a type of intermolecular force.

CONCEPTS

liquid	freezing point
solid	melting point
ionic forces	phase diagram
dipole-dipole forces	vapor pressure
hydrogen bonding	evaporation
dispersion forces (London forces)	sublimation
crystal structure	critical temperature and
lattice energy	pressure
phase changes	triple point
boiling point	

RULES

• Relationship between intermolecular forces and vapor pressure, boiling points, and melting points
• Phase diagrams
• Rules for predicting intermolecular forces from molecular geometry or bonding within molecules
• Clausius-Clapeyron equation

PROBLEMS

• Given a set of substances (and their formulas), rank in order of increasing/decreasing boiling point, melting point, or vapor pressure.
• Problems using the Clausius-Clapeyron equation.

Solutions

ALTERNATE TITLES

Colligative Properties

Concentrations

When describing the composition of a solution—that is, its concentration—the emphasis is on how much *solute* is dissolved in a quantity of solvent. When the topic shifts to colligative properties, the emphasis changes. In colligative properties, you are concerned with how the *solvent* properties have changed by addition of a solute.

When describing a solution in various concentration units, keep in mind that you are merely changing the *description* of the particular solution. Thus, when you convert a molarity to a molality to a mole fraction, all three still refer to the same solution.

FACTS

· Boiling and freezing points of water
· Names of common nonelectrolytes
· Details of applications of colligative properties

CONCEPTS

solution	molality
solvent	solubility
solute	miscibility
electrolytes	colligative properties
nonelectrolytes	vapor pressure lowering
weak electrolytes	freezing point depression
concentration	boiling point elevation
molarity	osmosis
mole fraction	osmotic pressure
weight percent	

RULES

· Molarity = moles solute/volume of solution
· Molality = moles solute/kilograms of solvent
· Mole fraction = moles of one component/total moles
· Weight percent = (grams solute/total grams of solution) $\times$ 100
· Raoult's law:

$$P = P°X$$

· Freezing point depression:

$$\Delta T_f = K_f m i$$

- Boiling point elevation:

$$\Delta T_b = K_b m i$$

- Osmotic pressure:

$$\pi = MRTi$$

- Rules relating solubility of gases and solids in water with temperature

PROBLEMS

- Problems that require calculations using the above formulas.
- Given the formula for an electrolyte, predict the ions that form on dissolving the electrolyte in water.
- Given two or more solutions and their concentrations, rank these in order of increasing/decreasing solution properties.

Acids and Bases

If your course teaches both Arrhenius and Brønsted-Lowry acid and base concepts, you will have to distinguish when you are to use each concept. For example, only Arrhenius acids and bases may be identified from their chemical formulas. Brønsted-Lowry acids and bases can be identified only in terms of a chemical reaction in which they accept or give away hydrogen ions.

The pH scale is useful only for weakly acidic and basic solutions. Note that when you have one of the four fundamental quantities (pH, pOH, hydrogen, or hydroxide ion concentrations), you can obtain any of the others.

FACTS

- Identity of strong and weak acids and bases

CONCEPTS

Arrhenius acids and bases	pOH
Brønsted-Lowry acids and bases	strong and weak acids
Lewis acids and bases	and bases
conjugate acids and bases	neutralization reactions
pH	titration

RULES

- Class reaction: Arrhenius acids and bases react to form salts and water.
- Formula for pH:

$$pH = -\log [H^+]$$

- Formula for pOH:

$$pOH = -\log [OH^-]$$

- Relation between pH and pOH:

$$pH + pOH = 14$$

- pH curve for a titration of a
    Strong acid and strong base
    Weak acid and strong base
    Strong acid and weak base
- Formula for 1:1 acid/base reaction:

$$VM \text{ (acid)} = VM \text{ (base)}$$

PROBLEMS

- Given any Brønsted-Lowry acid and base, write the equation for the neutralization reaction and identify the acid, base, conjugate acid, and conjugate base.
- Given any molar concentration of strong acid or base, H^+ or OH^-, find any/all of the other quantities (pH, pOH, $[H^+]$, or $[OH^-]$).
- Use any of the above equations to find a missing quantity.

Reactions in Solution

ALTERNATE TITLES

Metathesis Reactions

Oxidation—Reduction Reactions

Ionic Equations

This topic is often not given as a separate area of study but is interspersed with others (e.g., electrochemistry or acid–base chemistry). Various types of reactions require different processes for predicting products and for balancing. To predict the process needed for balancing equations, you must be able to recognize when you have an example of each type. Work to answer such questions as how to tell a metathesis reaction from an oxidation-reduction reaction. Ask your instructor for help if you cannot find an efficient classification scheme.

FACTS

- Identity of strong and weak acids and bases
- Identity of soluble/insoluble substances in water
- Rules for assigning oxidation numbers

CONCEPTS

soluble	balancing equations
insoluble	molecular equations

precipitate
reaction going to completion
acids
bases
salts
weak and strong acids
weak and strong bases
oxidation number

ionic equations
net ionic equations
spectator ions
oxidation
reduction
redox reaction
half-reaction

RULES

- Reactions of acids and bases to produce salts and water
- Rules for predicting which reactions will go to completion
- Rules for assigning oxidation numbers
- Rules for distinguishing between metathesis and oxidation–reduction reactions

PROBLEMS

- Given the reactants, predict the products of a reaction.
- Given two or more reactants, write the ionic and net ionic equations.

Chemical Kinetics

ALTERNATE TITLE

Rates of Reactions

This is one of the most difficult topics in general chemistry because it is concerned with processes and how they proceed with time. Not only can the concentrations of reactants and products change with time, but the rate of change can change with time. Other difficulties arise because of the confusion of terms such as rate, rate of change, rate constant, and so on.

In identifying and learning generic problems, pay attention to the type of information that you are given and the type of information that each problem allows you to find. Problems in this topic are hard to distinguish from one another.

FACTS

- Factors affecting rates of reactions

CONCEPTS

rate of reaction
rate law
order of reaction

half-lives
radioactive decay rates
activation energies

zero-, first-, second-order reactions

integrated forms of rate laws

rate constants

transition states

catalysts

mechanisms

RULES

- Matching units of rate constants to order of reactions
- Graphs: forms of straight line graphs for zero-, first-, and second-order reactions
- Formulas relating rates of reactions and concentrations for zero-, first-, and second-order reactions
- Formulas relating concentration of a reactant (at time t), rate constant, time, and initial concentrations for zero-, first-, and second-order reactions
- Relation of half-lives to rate constants and concentrations for various orders of reactions
- Arrhenius equation (relating rate constant, temperature and E_a)

PROBLEMS

- Find the order of the reaction, given initial rate data.
- Use any of the appropriate equations above to calculate missing quantities.
- Use graphing or formula methods to determine rate constants, given concentration versus time data.
- Determine whether a proposed mechanism is consistent with the known rate law.

Chemical Equilibrium   ALTERNATE TITLES

Gaseous Equilibrium

Solution Equilibrium

Complex Ion Equilibrium

We have listed this as a single unit, although some courses break it up into separate units (e.g., gaseous equilibrium, solution equilibrium). The learning demands of each of those separate topics are relatively similar.

Each equilibrium constant, K, listed below has associated with it an equilibrium equation. Each equation has a required format. For example, the equation on which a K_a is based must have the weak acid written at the left of the reaction arrow and the anion and hydrogen ion species written on the right. This format is independent of the chemical system that leads to the equilibrium situation (e.g., add together hydrochloric acid and sodium acetate to form an acetic acid solution). This is another way of saying that the words *reactant* and *product* have changed their meaning. They no longer refer to the chemicals that react or those that are produced. Rather, reactants are species written to the left of a reaction arrow; products are written on the right.

The key to solving equilibrium problems is to be able to describe the major and minor species in a solution and species that react to a lesser or greater degree.

FACTS

· Solubility rules
· Identity of weak acids and bases
· Formulas for some complex ions

CONCEPTS

equilibrium	buffer
$K = K_c$	hydrolysis
K_p	acid salt
K_a	basic salt
K_b	neutral salt
K_d	complex ion
K_f	solubility product
K_{sp}	soluble
K_w	insoluble
position of equilibrium	slightly soluble
Le Chatelier's principle	solubility
stress on a system	dissociation
catalyst	formation

RULES

· Given the identity of two or more chemicals being mixed, predict the major and minor species after reaction.
· Rules for writing K_c expressions, given an equilibrium reaction.
· Rules for interpreting the numerical value of K (extent of reaction).
· Rules for writing chemical equations that correspond to various K expressions (e.g., K_a).
· Rules for writing species in different physical states in K_c expressions.
· Le Chatelier's principle: When a stress is placed on a system at equilibrium, the system will shift so as to relieve that stress.
· Rules for recognizing when you have a buffer system: After reaction, you have a weak acid/base and the salt of a weak acid/base.
· Rules for recognizing which types of chemicals will react with one another when mixed.
· Rules for recognizing which ionic or molecular species are related by stoichiometry in an equilibrium system.

CLASS 1 PROBLEMS: THOSE INVOLVING A SINGLE REACTION

- Given an equilibrium system and its K value, find concentrations of one or more species.
- Given one or more concentrations in an equilibrium system, find the K value.

CLASS 2 PROBLEMS: THOSE INVOLVING TWO SUBSTANCES (BUT ONLY ONE EQUILIBRIUM)

- Given a system with two substances mixed together, predict which species will react.
- Given a system with two substances, predict the major and minor species present after mixing.
- Given a system with two substances, write the appropriate K expression, and calculate concentrations of species at equilibrium.

CLASS 3 PROBLEMS: THOSE INVOLVING MORE THAN ONE EQUILIBRIUM (COMPETITION REACTIONS)

- Given more than one equilibrium system, predict which are the major and minor species present after reaction, calculate the K value for the overall reaction, and find the concentrations of species at equilibrium.
- Given a set of metal ions in solution, predict the order in which they will precipitate upon addition of an appropriate anion; given K_{sp}'s for the species, calculate concentrations of ions when precipitation just begins.

Electrochemistry

ALTERNATE TITLE

Electrochemical Cells

Many errors arise in this section from poor record keeping during problem solving. Be careful of sign errors, reading and writing redox reactions correctly, and so on.

Sign conventions for labeling electrodes differ from field to field. If you have studied physics or electrical circuitry, check that you understand the conventions that are used here.

FACTS

- Oxidation numbers for elements
- Specific electrochemical cells (e.g., lead storage battery)
- Value of 1 faraday (= 96,500 coulombs = 1 mole electrons)

CONCEPTS

$\mathscr{E}°$	redox reaction
emf	half-reaction
electrochemical cell	oxidation number
electrode potential	concentration cell
oxidation	voltaic cell
reduction	electrolytic cell
standard oxidation potential	coulomb
standard reduction potential	ampere
oxidizing agent	faraday
reducing agent	spontaneous reaction

RULES

- Rules for assigning oxidation numbers for elements in a substance
- Nernst equation:

$$\mathscr{E} = \mathscr{E}° - \frac{0.0591}{n} \log Q$$

- Predict the direction of the spontaneous reaction from the $\mathscr{E}°$ of the cell
- Rule for the $\mathscr{E}$ of a cell at equilibrium (must equal zero)
- Conventions for assigning cell potentials
- Rules for finding standard oxidation or reduction potentials from a chart

PROBLEMS

- Given a compound, find the oxidation numbers of all elements in the compound.
- Given an equation, identify the reactants that are oxidized and reduced and identify the oxidizing and reducing agents.
- Balance redox equations.
- Calculate the $\mathscr{E}°$ for a cell.
- Calculate the potential for a cell under nonstandard conditions.
- Predict the products of the electrolysis of an aqueous solution.
- Predict the products of the electrolysis of a molten salt.
- Stoichiometry-electrolysis problems: given some combination of the following quantities—coulombs, amperes, time of electrolysis, the electrolysis reaction—calculate the amount of substance plated out.
- Given the $\mathscr{E}$ of a cell, calculate the equilibrium constant.

Coordination Compounds

ALTERNATE TITLES

Complex Ions
Chemistry of Transition Elements
Coordination Chemistry

There are a number of difficult problems in this section caused by chains of rule application (e.g., "If this is larger, then that is smaller. If that is smaller, then the other value is greater."). Record keeping (writing down your reasoning) helps to reduce errors.

Use molecular models, if possible, to help you understand geometric and optical isomerism of complex ions. Three-dimensional thinking is required for these concepts. The models help by giving you a real object to manipulate before you try to draw two-dimensional representations.

FACTS

- Names of ligands
- Identity of monodentate, bidentate, tetradentate, and hexadentate ligands
- Formulas for specific complex ions
- Splitting patterns for *d* orbitals in octahedral, square planar, and tetrahedral geometry complexes
- Wavelengths of light and correspondence to colors of light absorbed or emitted

CONCEPTS

coordination compound	high-spin complex
complex ion	low-spin complex
coordination number	paramagnetic
ligand	diamagnetic
monodentate, bidentate, tetradentate, and hexadentate ligands	delta, splitting energy
	pairing energy
coordinate covalent bond	spectrochemical series
isomers	colors of complexes
geometric isomers	ligand field theory
optical isomers	valence bond theory

RULES

- Rules for finding number of *d* electrons of a metal ion in a coordination compound or complex ion
- Rules for writing formulas of complex ions or coordination compounds

- Relation of light absorbed by a complex ion to the color of the complex ion
- Relationship of the magnitude of the splitting of the *d* orbitals in a complex to the high-spin/low-spin *d* orbital pattern
- Naming rules for complex ions and coordination compounds
- Identification of complex ions that have no structural or geometric isomers

PROBLEMS

- Given the formula of a coordination compound, identify the coordination number and oxidation state of the metal ion.
- Given the geometry of a complex ion and the identity of the ligands, find all the geometric and structural isomers.
- Given two complex ions, assign the most likely color to each (based on the spectrochemical series of ligands).
- Predict which complex ions will be paramagnetic/diamagnetic.

Nuclear Chemistry

ALTERNATE TITLES

Radiochemistry

Radioactivity

The rules for writing nuclear equations are different from those for writing chemical equations. Note carefully the differences between "decay" reactions and "bombardment" reactions.

FACTS

- Names and symbols for various kinds of radiation
- Units for measuring radiation
- History of discovery of radioactivity

CONCEPTS

radioactivity	binding energies
radiation	chain reaction
alpha radiation and decay	fission
beta (+ and −) radiation and decay	fusion
	bombardment reactions
gamma radiation and decay	decay reactions
electron capture reaction	half-life
parents	radioactive dating
daughters	atomic bombs
decay series	hydrogen (thermonuclear) bombs

RULES

- In writing balanced nuclear equations, the sum of charges and weights of nuclei must be equal on each side of the reaction arrow.
- Rate of decay (first-order kinetics): rate of decay at time $t = kN$, with $kt_{1/2} = 0.693$
- Fraction of radioactive substance left after time t:

$$\log(N_o/N_t) = kt/2.303$$

- Graph of nuclear binding energy per nucleon vs mass number
- Graph of number of neutrons versus number of protons (identifying stable nuclei)

PROBLEMS

- Write and balance nuclear equations.
- Given three of the following—original amount of radioactive material, time, number of half-lives, value of the half-life—find the missing quantity.
- Use any formula above to calculate a missing value.

Organic Chemistry

Some courses introduce organic chemistry in a three-week unit. Others devote half the term to organic. Whether you learn a little or a lot, the basic learning demands of this content are similar. First, you learn some basic factual and conceptual information about organic compounds (e.g., geometry, hybridization, isomerism). Then, you consider various classes of organic compounds, learning to:

- Recognize compounds in the class
- Name compounds in the class
- React compounds in the class
- Make (synthesize) compounds in the class

Many students use flash cards for testing their recall of this information. As you do so, verbalize the information. For example, we encourage you to practice reactions by saying them in words, specifying what chemical bonds break and what new bonds form as the reaction proceeds. For example:

> When an alkene reacts with hydrogen gas, the carbon-carbon double bond breaks and the bond between the hydrogens breaks. Then, a new hydrogen-carbon bond forms to replace the missing bond for each of those carbon atoms.

Typical test questions for organic chemistry require you to classify the organic molecules involved in a reaction *before* you can predict what the products of the reaction will be.

FACTS

· Prefixes relating to number of carbon atoms ("meth-" = 1 carbon atom, etc.)
· Name endings for various functional groups
· Common names of chemicals (e.g., benzene)
· Uses of specific chemicals

CONCEPTS

hydrocarbons
hybridization
geometry of molecules
structural formulas
isomers
cis–trans isomers
optical isomers
classes of organic compounds
  alkanes
  alkenes
  alkynes
  cyclic hydrocarbons
  alkyl halides
  aromatics
  oxygen-containing compounds
    alcohols (primary, secondary, tertiary)
    ethers
    aldehydes
    ketones
    carboxylic acids
    esters
  nitrogen-containing compounds
    amines (primary, secondary, tertiary)
    amides
classes of reactions
  addition
  substitution
  oxidation
  nucleophilic substitution
  elimination
  saponification
  esterification
  hydrolysis
mechanism of reactions

RULES

- Naming rules for classes of compounds
- Rules for relating number of bonds to geometry to hybridization
- Rules for identifying *cis–trans* isomers
- Rules for typical reactions for classes of molecules
- General formulas for hydrocarbons
- Descriptions of mechanisms of reactions

PROBLEMS

- Given a structural formula, name the compound.
- Given a name, draw the structural formula.
- Given two reactants, draw the structure of the product.
- Given a product and the conditions of a reaction, draw the structure of the reactant(s).
- Given a name or structural formula, find all the structural or geometric isomers.
- Write the mechanism for a specific reaction.

Polymers

ALTERNATE TITLE

Plastics

If you have become practiced at recognizing functional groups in organic molecules, that skill will be needed here when difunctional organic molecules are combined to make polymers. We recommend the technique of verbalizing polymerization reactions to help you remember the process of reaction.

FACTS

- Names of specific polymers

CONCEPTS

monomer
polymer
addition polymer
condensation polymer
classes of condensation polymer
  polyesters
  polyamides
  nylons
initiator

free radical
catalyst
mechanism of polymerization
initiation step
propagation step
termination step

RULES

- Rules for recognizing monomers for addition and condensation polymers

PROBLEMS

- Given monomer(s), draw the structural formula of a segment of polymer.
- Given a segment of a polymer, identify the monomers from which it was made.
- Given a monomer and an initiator, write equations to illustrate the mechanism of polymerization.

Biochemistry

ALTERNATE TITLES

Chemistry of Life
Carbohydrate (Sugar) Chemistry
Protein Chemistry
Lipid Chemistry

The structures in this part of the course are extremely complex and detailed. You will need to build on the skill of recognizing the critical parts of complex molecules. You will need to practice writing from memory various complex structures with their precise details.

FACTS

- Names and formulas of amino acids
- Specific molecular structures (e.g., starch)
- Base pairs in nucleic acids

CONCEPTS

fats	enzymes
lipids	denatured proteins
fatty acids	hydrolysis
saponification	primary, secondary, tertiary structures
sugars	nucleic acids

carbohydrates	base pairs
saccharides	genetic code
alpha and beta links	DNA
proteins	RNA
amino acids	_t_RNA
peptides	_m_RNA

RULES

- Naming system for sugar rings
- Rules for drawing alpha and beta linkages in sugars
- Forces of attraction between base pairs (hydrogen bonds)
- Forces responsible for primary, secondary, and tertiary structure of proteins

PROBLEMS

- Given a sequence of DNA or RNA and the genetic code, derive the protein that could be made from the nucleic acid.
- Given a segment of DNA, make the corresponding segment of _m_RNA or _t_RNA.
- Link two sugar molecules with an alpha or a beta linkage.
- Hydrolyze a protein, breaking the primary structure.
- Construct a fat from three molecules of fatty acids and glycerol; given a fat, saponify it.

CHAPTER SIX

Memorizing Chemical Information

Without turning from this page, can you answer these two questions?

What element has the chemical symbol Na? _____

What is the chemical symbol for the element protactinium? _____

You may have known that Na is the chemical symbol for the element sodium. But we wager that few of you knew that the symbol for protactinium is Pa.

In asking these questions we are not concerned with whether you knew the answers. Rather, we want to raise a few additional questions. How are you to know that Pa is the chemical symbol for protactinium? Can you figure out that Na is the symbol for sodium?

The point here is that there is no way for you to know chemical names and symbols unless you have been given the information and you remember it. The process by which you deliberately learn something so that you can recall it at will is called **memorization.**

You may have heard your teachers say, "I don't want you to *memorize* chemistry; I want you to *understand* it." Is there something wrong with memorization?

116

In making a statement like this, your professor most likely is warning you not to stop your learning of chemistry at the memorization stage. You are not being encouraged, however, to neglect memorization. To attempt to do chemistry without having certain information memorized would be like trying to speak a foreign language without knowing any of the words!

Memorization is but the first step in learning chemistry. The factual material that you memorize gives you the information base on which to build understanding of chemical ideas and principles. Examples of chemical content that you may need to memorize are given in Table 6–1.

WHY MEMORIZE?

Memorization improves the efficiency of your work in chemistry. Let's look at some reasons why.

Memorization Saves You Time and Energy

Once you have memorized something, the information is instantly available. You do not have to waste time searching for it each time you need it. For example, it is more practical to memorize that Na is the symbol for sodium than to look it up each time you encounter it.

TABLE 6–1 TYPES OF INFORMATION TO BE MEMORIZED IN CHEMISTRY COURSES

Correct spelling and pronunciation of chemical words:
  phenolphthalein = fee-nol-THAY-leen
  neutron = NOO-tron
Names and symbols for chemical species:
  magnesium = Mg
  ammonia = NH_3
  methane = CH_4
  ammonium ion = NH_4^+
Lists of chemical species in a particular category:

strong acids = $\begin{cases} HClO_4 \\ HCl \\ HNO_3 \\ HBr \\ HI \\ H_2SO_4 \end{cases}$

insoluble chloride salts = $\begin{cases} AgCl \\ PbCl_2 \\ Hg_2Cl_2 \end{cases}$

Chemical facts:
  Chlorine is a pale green gas.
  Electrons have a negative charge and almost no mass.
  Atmosphere, kilopascal, and Torr are units of pressure.
  Oxidation is the loss of electrons.

On exams, of course, your only options are to recall memorized information or to derive it through a chain of associations. Having certain facts memorized usually costs you less time and energy.

Memorization Allows You to Communicate with Others

You learn chemistry by listening to and talking with others. In order to communicate, you need to know the basic chemical vocabulary. While conversing, you don't have time to look up the meanings of chemical words.

Memorization Frees Your Mind for Thinking

As you learn chemistry, much of your time will be spent reasoning and thinking. Thinking and reasoning require you to relate multiple ideas simultaneously. Unfortunately, the number of ideas you can hold in your mind at any one time is limited. Searching your memory for a needed fact will take up some of this capacity, leaving you with a diminished ability for higher-level thinking, such as problem solving. However, if you have memorized information well, you free your mind to work actively on the more difficult tasks.

We hope you are now convinced that memorization is a necessary first step for mastery of chemistry. On the following pages, we will discuss how memorization works, how to memorize efficiently, how memorized material will be tested, and techniques for minimizing errors when recalling memorized material.

HOW YOUR MEMORY WORKS

When you memorize information, you store it somewhere in your brain. Later, when you need the information, you bring the item back to your consciousness. This retrieval process depends on the formation of a mental link between two pieces of information. For example, the symbol Na triggers the associated name *sodium* and vice versa:

$$\text{sodium} = \text{Na}$$

If you memorize well, you put ideas into mental storage in such a way that you can retrieve them in a fraction of a second, without error and without effort.

Once you have memorized something, it usually does not stay memorized forever. As time passes, the links between pieces of knowledge fade until the association no longer exists. At this point you have forgotten. Forgetting is a natural process. Everybody forgets.

Fortunately, reforming a forgotten memory link is easier than making it for the first time. Learning for the second or third or fourth time takes less effort than the initial learning. Such **rememorization** is an essential part of the learning process when information must be retained over a long period of time.

There are actually two different kinds of memory—long-term and short-term. When we use the word *memory*, we are referring to long-term memory. It includes what you know and can freely remember over a long period of time. Long-term memory has unlimited capacity; you add to it continually throughout your lifetime.

Short-term memory is also called "working," or active, memory. It is the part of your mind that you use when you think and process information. Unlike long-term memory, short-term memory has a limited capacity. You can process only six to eight items at a time.

When you memorize, you transfer information from short-term to long-term memory. Such information is then available for use; its recall does not require extensive involvement of short-term memory.

In your chemistry course you will be required to memorize information such as that given in Table 6–1. This information is factual; it cannot be "figured out." You either know that magnesium has the symbol Mg or you do not. When you memorize information of this sort, you do it by **rote memorization.** This chapter is devoted to rote memorization, in which you deliberately build mental links between items.

MEMORIZATION TECHNIQUES

By now, we hope you are convinced that memorization is an important skill to master. In the following sections, we will introduce you to effective memorization techniques.

To illustrate these techniques we will use the following example, one that is frequently given as an assignment early in chemistry courses:

Memorize the names and symbols for the first 20 elements.

To allow us to work on this example together, write in the atomic symbols in the table on page 120, either with the help of a periodic table (see inside front cover) or from memory. Check your answers with a periodic chart if you are working from memory.

The ten techniques that follow will help you memorize such material efficiently.

Technique 1: Use as Many Senses as Possible

As you *wrote* answers in the chart above, you were more active than just reading or thinking. This is the first principle of memorization—*be active*, using as many of your senses as possible.

Always memorize with the aid of a pencil and paper. Write out a symbol, then see if you can write out the name. The action of writing helps keep your attention focused on what you are learning. It also allows you to check for errors visually. Be sure to learn information correctly. You will be frustrated if you learn something only to find later that you learned it incorrectly.

Go one step further than writing: *say* the names and symbols, spelling them out loud as you write them. *Listen* to yourself saying them. Check with your friends if you need help with pronunciation. Chemistry should have you talking to yourself from the first day on!

Atomic Number	Name	Symbol
1	hydrogen	_____
2	helium	_____
3	lithium	_____
4	beryllium	_____
5	boron	_____
6	carbon	_____
7	nitrogen	_____
8	oxygen	_____
9	fluorine	_____
10	neon	_____
11	sodium	_____
12	magnesium	_____
13	aluminum	_____
14	silicon	_____
15	phosphorus	_____
16	sulfur	_____
17	chlorine	_____
18	argon	_____
19	potassium	_____
20	calcium	_____

Technique 2: Look for Patterns

When memorizing, search for a general rule or pattern that all or parts of the material may follow. For example, in memorizing the names and symbols, you might notice that:

· All of the symbols consist of one or two letters, the first of which is capitalized.

· Most of the early elements (atomic number less than 10) have a single letter for a symbol.

- This letter is the first letter of the element name.

Generally, you will be expected to find rules and patterns for yourself.

Technique 3: Group Items into Manageable Chunks

As you begin the job of memorizing, group items in some sensible way. You will probably find it easier to learn five groups of four items than to learn one group of twenty items. This is true because of the limitations of your short-term memory—five chunks of material are easier to process than twenty individual items.

A good place to start is to separate the items you know from those you still must learn. You may also want to group confusing items or items that have something else in common. Here are some examples:

$$
\left.\begin{array}{l} Au \\ F \\ Bc \\ K \end{array}\right\} \text{a group of items that you do not know} \qquad \left.\begin{array}{l} Co \\ Cu \\ Cr \\ Cl \end{array}\right\} \text{a group of items that you confuse}
$$

Again, recognize that there are many useful and logical ways to group items. Select those that you find helpful.

Technique 4: Create Mnemonic Devices

Mnemonic devices are those that aid your memory. Almost anything can function as a mnemonic: a saying, a jingle, a picture. What you need to remember is linked to the mnemonic. When you recall the mnemonic, you recall that information as well.

For example, you may find it difficult to keep straight the processes of oxidation (loss of electrons) and reduction (gain of electrons). The phrase "LEO the GERman" may help you to remember which is which:

LEO = Loss of Electrons is Oxidation
GER = Gain of Electrons is Reduction

Here is a different sort of mnemonic. Suppose you are required to learn the order in which the elements scandium to zinc are listed on the periodic chart. The following sentence mnemonic might help you:

See Tina vault 'cross many fences counting nickels in cups of zinc
| | | | | | | | |
Sc Ti V Cr Mn Fe Co Ni Cu Zn

Vivid mental pictures can also be a powerful mnemonic. Can you imagine a picture that would help you remember the sentence above? Figure 6–1 gives you one.

Technique 5: Practice Associations in All Directions

Some memorization requires the association of only two items:

$$magnesium = Mg$$
OR
$$ammonium\ ion = NH_4^+$$

Learn associations like these in both directions. For example, learning that magnesium has the symbol Mg is only half the job. You must also be able to say or write the word *magnesium* when you see the symbol Mg.

FIGURE 6–1 *Creating vivid mental images can aid memorization*

You may find that the association is more difficult in one direction than in the other. For example, the formula for the ammonium ion, NH_4^+, contains many details: what atoms are present, how many of each, and the sign and magnitude of the charge. All these details must be learned.

Other information to be memorized comes as a list. For example:

$$\text{strong acids} = HCl, HBr, HI, HNO_3, H_2SO_4, HClO_4$$

Many students can successfully recite the strong acids. Fewer, however, automatically think "strong acid" when they see HNO_3 or HBr. Good students memorize in both directions.

Technique 6: Spread Memorization Over Time—Avoid Cramming

If you try to learn too much at once, you risk confusing the facts you are learning. For example, when you are working at memorizing Mn (manganese) and Mg (magnesium), it may help if you learn one first and then go back and learn the other. Similarly, with

$$C \quad Cl \quad Ca \quad Cr \quad Co \quad Cu$$

it may be a better strategy to master one or two of these at a time than to work on them all at once.

Memorization is also hard work. Many students find that a 30-minute session of memorizing is all that they can handle. You might set 30 minutes as a goal, but do not be afraid to stop sooner. Several short sessions are more effective than one long one.

Once you have completed your first memorization session, your job is not done. You begin forgetting as soon as you have finished memorizing. Allow yourself to forget by giving yourself some time (an hour or so) away from the material. Then go back and relearn what you have forgotten. On the following day check again to see what you have forgotten and relearn it. Each time you return to the material, you should find that you forget less.

What we have said here argues powerfully against cramming as a good learning technique. If you cram for an exam, recognize that you will probably need to rememorize the crammed material. Most crammed material disappears from memory in a day or so.

Technique 7: Practice Recalling Information in a Random Order, Using Flash Cards

When you review, practice recalling items in a *random* order. One technique for generating practice questions in random order is to use flash cards. A **flash card** is a small note card with part of the information to be memorized on one side and associated information on the other. Figure 6–2 shows a flash card for learning an element and its symbol. As you begin a memorization session, shuffle the pack well, mixing both the order and which side is up. To use the cards, do the following:

- Select a card.
- Read *out loud* the name or symbol.
- *Write* and *say* the answer.
- Flip the card to check your response.
- Put aside and review all cards on which you make even the smallest of errors.

After going through the entire pack, relearn the information that you missed.

When making flash cards for more complex information, you must decide how much information to put on a card. Should you make one card, with half the information on one side and half on the other, or make separate cards for each pair of items that must be associated? Either way of designing flash cards may be effective. Since it takes time to make each card, we suggest producing as few as possible. However, do not hesitate to make extra cards for those pairs of associations that are particularly difficult or important.

More and more schools are providing computer-assisted instruction. Some of the most popular programs are those that provide practice in the recall of factual information. The computer, like a set of flash cards, generates items in random order, requiring you to respond and telling you immediately whether your response is correct. See if this option is available for your use.

FIGURE 6–2 *Constructing a flash card*

Technique 8: Test Yourself in Different Ways

As you memorize, you have the opportunity to test yourself. Before sitting down to a practice session, do not review the memorized material. You want the opportunity to remember it "cold," without the help of your short-term memory.

The goal of your self-testing program is 100 percent accuracy. Nothing else is satisfactory. SO_4^{3-} is not an acceptable formula for the sulfate ion; only SO_4^{2-} will do. Yes, spelling counts.

Ask a friend to quiz you on the material. A good friend will not let you get away with any mistakes, even small ones. Working together will also lessen the boredom of reviewing material.

You may feel a sense of accomplishment as you recall material increasingly well. As you set goals for yourself, also provide rewards when you meet them. It is your success—enjoy it!

Technique 9: Keep Track of Your Mistakes

Self-testing allows you to pinpoint and correct your errors prior to an exam. Errors on self-tests are *good* errors. They tell you which items you have confused, incorrectly learned, or forgotten. In the process of spotting these errors, you strengthen what you have learned.

Errors may involve specific pieces of information. For example, do you consistently misspell the names of some elements (e.g., *florine* rather than *fluorine*)? Do you write P as the symbol for the element potassium? Items that you have learned incorrectly will require extra time and attention to correct—you must unlearn the error as well as learn the correct information.

Other errors are more general or repetitive. For example, a chemical ion has a positive or negative charge. You may generally forget to write the charges on ions, writing PO_4 rather than PO_4^{3-}, or NH_4 rather than NH_4^+. To eliminate this type of error, you must direct your attention to its cause, such as haste, carelessness, or the perception that charge is not important. Change your working patterns or beliefs in order to eradicate these mistakes.

Keep a list of your mistakes. This will help you to determine which errors you repeatedly make. Even after you think you have eliminated your errors, continue to practice the items that you missed. If you do not overcompensate for errors, they are likely to pop up again when you are under stress.

Technique 10: Keep Studying Until You Have Overlearned the Material

How many times should you review memorized material? Here is some information to help you decide for yourself when you have studied "enough."

You have studied a topic enough when you are able to recall the information without effort. Moreover, even if you do not review this information for a week or two, you can still readily recall it. This is called **overlearning.** Overlearning occurs only after you have had sufficient repetition of the material, either in practice sessions or by using it.

When you overlearn something, it becomes a part of you, just as your name is a part of you. You do not have to work to remember your middle name. Likewise, you do not want to work to remember that H_2SO_4 is sulfuric acid. Every time you must pause or strain to recall factual material, you disrupt your chain of thinking.

One way to check for overlearning is to monitor the time it takes for you to recall a fact. If you have used a set of flash cards to help you memorize, test yourself with them by writing down the response as rapidly as possible. Those cards on which you hesitate should be set aside for extra practice.

One final thought: Even overlearned material may be forgotten over time. When planning your study schedule for the final exam, build in some time for relearning material you memorized early in your course.

USING MEMORIZATION TECHNIQUES

The memorization techniques we have described are powerful. However, reading about these techniques is quite different from actually using them. If you want to improve your ability to memorize, your goal now is to use these techniques often enough so that they become a habit for you.

Try out these memorization techniques in the following exercise.

EXERCISE 1   Developing a Strategy for Memorization

Find something in your chemistry course that you are required to memorize. Below are some possibilities. Others can be found in Table 6–1.

- Names and formulas of acids and bases
- Names, formulas, and charges of polyatomic ions
- Types of radioactive decay processes
- Solubility rules
- Quantum numbers and their allowable values
- Names and formulas of organic functional groups

Plan a strategy for memorizing this information and then use that strategy to memorize it. The following summary can help you plan your activities:

- Work actively.
- Find patterns.
- Group items.
- Use mnemonics.
- Overlearn.
- Learn in both directions.
- Spread memorization over time.
- Practice items in random order.
- Test yourself repeatedly.
- Keep track of your mistakes.

TESTING MEMORIZED MATERIAL

On exams you will be asked to show what you have memorized. In part, your success will depend on how well you have learned the material. However, you may be tested in ways quite different from the way you learned. Thus, your success may also depend on your ability to anticipate how you will be tested.

To help you anticipate test questions, we will look at some common types.

Straight Recall of Memorized Material

What element has the symbol Mn? _____

NH_4^+ is called the _____ ion.

Write the formula for acetic acid. _____

These questions ask you to recall information. You will be prepared for these if you have accurately memorized information and have practiced recalling it in both directions.

Recall questions can be phrased in more complex ways:

An atom of beryllium would be represented by the symbol _____ .

Did you recognize this as the question: "What is the symbol for the element beryllium?"

Recognition of Memorized Material

Which of the following is the symbol for the element copper:

C   Ce   Cr   Cu   Co

Here, having the correct answer in the midst of reasonable alternatives may interfere with your ability to recall the correct association. If the alternatives confuse you, restructure the question to make it familiar. Ask yourself: "What is the symbol for the element copper?" Write down your answer before you search for it among the confusing alternatives. If, while you studied, you actively looked for confusing items (see page 121), you would be prepared for such a question.

Matching questions also can present confusing alternatives.

Match the following names and symbols:

_____ sulfate ion   a. SO_2^{2-}
_____ bisulfate ion   b. $S_2O_3^{2-}$
_____ sulfite ion   c. SO_4^{2-}
_____ thiosulfate ion   d. HSO_4^-
                            e. SO_3^{2-}
                            f. HSO_4^{2-}

As above, rephrase the question if you need to: "The sulfate ion is _____ ," and so forth.

Recognition of Errors

Which of the following is not a correct symbol for an element:

   Cl   Fl   Br   I

True or False? The chemical symbol for the element telenium is Te.

Recognizing "what isn't" is different from recognizing "what is." Your success with questions like these depends on how much attention you paid to details as you studied.

If the answer is not immediately obvious, try thinking like this:

Hmmm. Cl is the symbol for the element chlorine. That is OK. Fl could be the symbol for fluorine. But wait. Fluorine has the symbol F, not Fl. Could Fl be another element? No. At least none that I have learned. But I'd better check the other two to make sure. . . .

Hmmm. Te. Have I learned any symbols beginning with T? Yes, there was one; it was Te. Te stands for the element tellurium. So there's the mistake. The question gives the wrong name for the element.

Use of Memorized Information

The most common way that memorized material is tested is with questions that require its *use*. Let's look at a few examples to show how answering more complex questions may depend on using memorized information:

Write the formula for sodium carbonate.

If you cannot recall the correct formula for the carbonate ion, CO_3^{2-}, you cannot write the correct formula for sodium carbonate, Na_2CO_3.

How many grams of sodium carbonate are contained in 2.5 moles of sodium carbonate?

If you cannot recall the correct formula for sodium carbonate, you cannot calculate the formula weight needed to solve this problem.

The pH of a 0.01 *M* carbonic acid solution is:

   a. 2 or less
   b. 2–7
   c. 7
   d. 7–12
   e. 12 or more

To answer this question, you need to have memorized several facts:

· Carbonic acid is a weak acid.
· Acidic pH's are less than 7.
· A weak acid would not have a pH lower than 2.

Without these facts, you may have to guess to obtain an answer.

REDUCING ERRORS ON FACT QUESTIONS

The factual material you learn in chemistry is quite detailed. For example, in learning the formula for the carbonate ion, you must remember that:

· It contains 1 carbon atom and 3 oxygen atoms.
· The carbon atom is written first.
· The carbonate ion has a −2 charge.

Correct	Incorrect
CO_3^{2-}	CO_3, CO_2, CO_2^{-}, CO_3^{-}, CO_2^{2-}, etc.

"Silly" mistakes—ones that arise under stress during the exam—are most apt to occur in detailed material. For example, in spite of having learned the carbonate ion formula correctly, you might write some incorrect version on your test paper.

If test anxiety causes you to make errors, work directly on that anxiety. Help with test anxiety is available on most campuses, although the location of this service varies. Seek help from the appropriate agency on your campus—counseling center, health service, dean of students office, or wherever. In addition, make an extra effort to overlearn material. You must increase your sensitivity to the material so that an error "looks wrong" even when you are under stress.

Often, however, silly errors arise not because of stress, but because you are concentrating on a hard question. You focus so much attention on the problem that when you need a piece of memorized information, you give it too little attention and recall it incorrectly.

One technique to minimize such errors is called "dumping." For example, suppose you are being tested about solutions. As the test begins, quickly read through it to get some idea of the questions. If you see that you will need to use three types of concentrations—molarity, molality, and mole fraction—"dump" the following information on the back of your exam:

$$\text{molarity} = \frac{\text{moles of solute}}{\text{liters of solution}}$$

$$\text{molality} = \frac{\text{moles of solute}}{\text{kilograms of solvent}}$$

$$\text{mole fraction} = \frac{\text{moles of solute}}{\text{total moles (solute + solvent)}}$$

By writing out this information at the beginning of the test, you can refer to it when you need it rather than struggling to recall it. This leaves your short-term memory free to focus on solving a problem that requires use of this information.

Dumping has another use. Even the best of students may get behind in studying. If this happens to you, you may find yourself cramming factual information right up to the last minute. However, cramming usually does not put information into your long-term memory. Your only hope of having that information available during the exam is to keep it in your short-term memory until the test begins, and then dump it.

We do not recommend the "cram and dump" method. If you cram, you may neglect to go back after the exam and really learn the material. As you prepare for the final exam you may find yourself with an impossibly large amount of material to relearn. You also take the chance that you will dump information incorrectly on the exam paper.

In an emergency you may get away with cramming. However, if you find yourself repeatedly cramming, recognize this as a sign that you are not in control of your studies.

SUMMARY

In this chapter, we have discussed how memorization works and techniques for memorizing chemical material.

Why memorize?

· Memorization saves you time and energy.
· Memorization allows you to communicate with others.
· Memorization frees your mind for thinking.

Remember that your mind:

· When working ideally, stores information in a way that allows you to retrieve it quickly and effortlessly.
· Does not keep memorized material forever; forgetting is normal.
· Is able to rememorize information using less effort than learning it the first time.
· Can be thought of as containing long-term (unlimited capacity) and short-term (six to eight items) memory.

Effective techniques for memorizing include:

· Use as many senses as possible (look, write, speak, listen).
· Look for patterns.
· Group items into manageable chunks.
· Create mnemonic devices.

- Practice associations in all directions.
- Spread memorization out over time; avoid cramming.
- Practice recalling information in a random order, using flash cards.
- Test yourself in different ways.
- Keep track of your mistakes.
- Overlearn the material.

Test questions for memorized material typically ask for:

- Straight recall of memorized material.
- Recognition of memorized material.
- Recognition of errors.
- Use of memorized information.

Ways of reducing fact errors include:

- Reducing anxiety; seek help, if necessary.
- "Dumping" detailed factual information on the back of your test paper.

SELF-ASSESSMENT

Are you prepared for the memorization demands of your course? Mark an X on the line in the position that describes your response to the following statements:

1. The memorizing demands in my course are:

VERY HIGH ———————————————— VERY LOW
I am asked to   I am asked to
memorize lots in a   memorize little,
short period   *or* I already know
of time.   the material.

2. My memorizing skills are:

VERY STRONG ———————————————— VERY WEAK
I can memorize   Memorization is
rapidly and   difficult; I
efficiently.   seem to forget
                                                      everything.

You should experience little difficulty in your chemistry course if your responses look like this:

DEMANDS ————X————————————

SKILLS ————X————————————

OR

DEMANDS ——————————————————————— X ————

SKILLS ——————————————————————— X ————

However, you are in trouble if your course has high demands and your skills are weak:

DEMANDS ———— X ———————————————————————

SKILLS ——————————————————— X ————

This is a signal that you need to strengthen your skills. One way to do this is to select one or two of the techniques for memorizing and put them into practice. Work out a specific plan. We have written out one example for you:

SAMPLE PLAN

Technique: Keep track of my mistakes.

Plan: I will keep a section at the back of my lecture notes to record memorization errors. I will test myself on these errors at the beginning of each chemistry study session. After I remember an item correctly three times in a row, I will check it off and consider it learned. I will review the whole list before the exam.

YOUR PLANS

Technique:

Plan:

Technique:

Plan:

Technique:

Plan:

Most people find that they cannot improve their memorizing skills overnight, but improvement does come with practice. With this skill mastered, you will be ready to handle the more advanced thinking skills needed for success in your chemistry course.

CHAPTER SEVEN

Mastering Chemical Concepts

In the last chapter, we described how you could memorize chemical facts such as:

$$H_2SO_4 = \text{sulfuric acid}$$
$$HNO_3 = \text{nitric acid}$$
$$HCl = \text{hydrochloric acid}$$

Memorization is but the first step in mastering chemical content. A far more difficult task than memorizing the names of acids is learning what acids are. "Acid" is a chemical **concept**, that is, a chemical idea that can be represented by a specific word or term.

Chemical concepts are important. In our experience a frequent cause of failure in chemistry is the failure to learn chemical concepts well. In this chapter we will describe what chemical concepts are, how they are taught, how to master them, and how they will be tested.

WHAT CHEMICAL CONCEPTS ARE

Chemical concepts are ideas about matter. A one- or two-word concept will have the same meaning as the whole chemical idea. Chemists will then use the concept word interchangeably with the idea:

$$\text{concept word} = \text{idea about matter}$$

133

For example, the word *acid* may be linked with the idea:

acid = a chemical that, when dissolved in water,
gives a solution containing more H^+ than OH^-

As you study chemistry, you will need to learn the ideas associated with many chemical concept words. For example, each of the following terms represents an idea that you will have to master early in your chemistry course:

element	compound	mole
atom	molecule	ion
acid	salt	base
bond	covalent bond	ionic bond
density	volume	mass

Chapter Five provides a list of the topics covered in general chemistry and a summary of some typical concepts presented in each. If you have not already done so, go to page 91 now and quickly look through some of the topics. Note the large number of concepts that are required for mastery of those topics.

Thus, you should think of your chemistry course as a *language* course. Words like those above and in Chapter Five make up the chemical language. You will learn chemistry by learning the meaning of the new words, just as you would if you were studying a foreign language. For example, if you were studying Spanish, you would learn to associate the word *mesa* with the word "table" and associate both of these with the object table, as illustrated in Figure 7–1.

Similarly, in learning chemistry, you must form associations between chemical words and ideas. However, there is one important difference: in chemistry, both the concept word and its idea may be *new* to you. To understand this difference, imagine trying to learn the meaning of the word *mesa* if you had never seen a table. Before you could understand the meaning of *mesa*, you would have to learn what a table was. Likewise, as you are learning the chemical language, you may not be aware of any prior experiences with acids or bases. Before you can use the words *acid* and *base* in a meaningful way, you first have to formulate the ideas that are linked with these words.

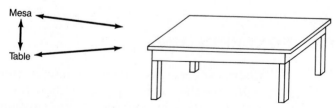

FIGURE 7–1 *Making associations to learn meanings*

It is often no easy task to formulate the ideas linked with concepts. Most chemical concepts are complex. They have many parts and are interrelated with other concepts. For example, earlier we gave one meaning for the word *acid*. There are other ways of conceptualizing an acid. These include:

· A chemical that gives a H^+ ion away during a reaction
· A chemical that has a sour taste
· A chemical whose formula usually begins with the symbol H
· A chemical that reacts with a base to form a salt and water
· A chemical that turns blue litmus paper to a red color

Each of these descriptions is important in a given context. For example, the sour taste of acids helps you learn which foods contain acids. The ability to turn blue litmus paper to a red color helps you to identify acids in the laboratory.

Your course may not require you to know all of this information about acids. When you learn about acids (and all the other chemical concepts as well), you must identify which aspects of the concept must be known. You will be better able to identify what is important if you understand the process by which you are taught concepts.

HOW CONCEPTS ARE TAUGHT

Figure 7–2 represents one way to visualize what might occur in a lecture or textbook presentation on acids and bases. Let's now relate this picture to how concepts are usually taught in general chemistry.

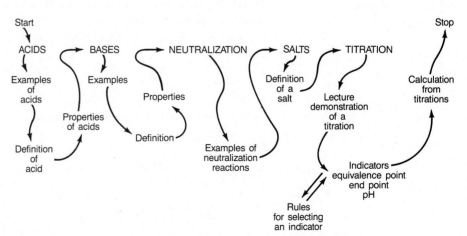

FIGURE 7–2 *Representation of a lecture on acids and bases*

Many Concepts Are Taught in a Class Period

It is not uncommon for 20 concepts to be introduced during a one-hour lecture. For example, there are nine concepts mapped in Figure 7–2. (Can you find them?) That content would take less than one hour to teach. Expect to be flooded with concepts!

Concepts Are Taught Without Their Relationships

Many instructors do not take the time to link one concept to another. For example, Figure 7–2 shows acids, bases, and salts each presented in turn, but not linked to each other. In this case, you have to discover for yourself how acids, bases, and salts are alike, how they are different, whether they are mutually exclusive categories, and so on. Expect often to be left with the job of interrelating the concepts.

Concepts Are Taught Simultaneously with Rules and Problems

Concepts are not taught in isolation. As you can see from Figure 7–2, once the concept of an indicator is introduced, you are then taught the rules for selecting an indicator. Similarly, as you learn the concept of a titration, you are shown how to work titration problems. Additional information about rules or problem solving may draw your attention away from the concept itself. As a result, you may find yourself trying to use a concept before you know exactly what it is.

Concepts Are Not Presented Completely

There is insufficient time in lecture for an instructor to tell you everything you need to know about a concept. Moreover, your instructor may not be aware of all of the subtle points that he or she expects you to know. Chemical concepts often have both microscopic and macroscopic properties (see page 8). A lecture may present only one aspect, requiring you to add the others.

Assume, then, that class presentations will be incomplete. Look for ways to complete your understanding of concepts on your own.

Concepts Are Extended in Later Class Periods

You do not usually get the whole picture of a concept at once. After a concept is mentioned, new pieces of information about it are frequently given in subsequent lectures. This new information may modify the meaning of the concept. For example, Figure 7–3 shows some ways in which the concepts from Figure 7–2 may be extended.

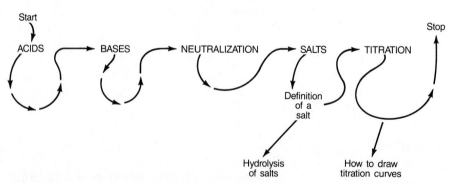

FIGURE 7–3 *Some extensions of concepts in a later lecture*

You cannot remain passive when it comes to learning concepts. You must process the information that you are given, finding out what words mean, filling in relationships, and developing each concept for yourself. In the next section, we will show you ways of doing this.

FORMING CONCEPTS

Once you have identified a particular concept that is to be learned, there are six questions you should ask yourself about it:

1. What does the concept word mean?
2. What are the essential characteristics of the concept?
3. What are some examples of the concept?
4. What are the parts of the concept?
5. What is the concept a part of?
6. With what other concepts is it mutually exclusive?

In many cases, you will be able to answer these questions by consulting your lecture notes and textbook. However, you may have to dig out the information from these sources, since your notes or text may not state it directly. In the following sections we provide some more detailed information about obtaining this critical information.

Meanings of Concept Words—Definitions

Suppose you were asked, "What is an atom?" Write down your response below:

If you wrote, "An atom is the smallest part of an element," or "Atoms are the basic building blocks of all matter," you gave a correct definition. Other definitions are possible as well.

These are examples of chemical definitions, as they state the essence of what a particular concept is. When you are introduced to a new chemical word, your first job is to find an adequate **definition.** To do this, check your lecture notes and your textbook or ask your instructor.

More than one definition of a concept term is possible, depending on the context in which the concept is introduced. For example, the concept *acid* may be defined in several ways, as illustrated on page 135.

Remember that definitions are *not* intended to be complete descriptions of the concept. Rather, they are the starting point from which you work.

Essential Characteristics of the Concept

Essential characteristics help you to pin down exactly what something is and is not. A definition usually identifies only some of the essential characteristics of the concept. For example, from the definitions given earlier, we can identify two essential characteristics for atoms: small size and building blocks of matter. But other properties are intrinsic to the nature of an atom (e.g., the existence of a nucleus with a positive charge).

Therefore, after obtaining a definition, your next task is to search out additional characteristics of the concept. Essential characteristics are the criteria you use to judge whether or not an item is an example of that concept. If an item is to be included as an example of a concept, it must possess *all* of the essential properties of that concept. To illustrate how the essential characteristics extend past a definition, we provide a definition and essential characteristics for three concepts: electron, solution, and salt.

ELECTRON

Definition

A subatomic particle that consists of a unit of negative electrical charge

Essential characteristics

Negative electrical charge
Relative mass $\frac{1}{1835}$ that of a proton
Absolute mass 9.11×10^{-28} grams

SOLUTION

Definition

A homogeneous mixture of two or more substances

Essential characteristics

Consists of more than one substance.
When the substances are mixed, each retains its identity.
The substances are mixed on the molecular level.
The mixture is uniform in appearance and properties.
The mixture does not separate upon standing.

SALT

Definition

An electrolyte formed by the reaction of an acid and a base

Essential characteristics

Composed of ions.
Must contain both positive and negative ions.
Contains equal amounts of positive and negative charges.
The positive ions cannot all be H^+.
The negative ions cannot all be OH^-.

Examples of the Concept

How do you recognize an instance that fits into a concept classification? The essential characteristics of a concept may be used to identify all the **examples** of the concept, that is, those items that belong to the concept class by virtue of possessing all the essential characteristics. **Nonexamples** of a concept are those items that do not contain all the essential characteristics. In order to be helpful to you, the set of essential characteristics must be sufficient to discriminate the nonexamples from the examples:

ELECTRON

Examples
   Electrons are represented by the following symbols: e, e⁻, and −.

Nonexamples
   Other atomic particles are identified by other symbols: p, +, n.

SOLUTION

Examples
   Name of solution is given (vinegar).
   Verbal description of a solution is given. (When copper sulfate was dissolved in water, a blue liquid, totally uniform in color, was formed.)
   Pictures (see Figure 7–4).

Nonexamples
   Names of suspensions, colloids, or emulsions are given (orange juice, smoky air, salad dressing)
   Verbal descriptions are given (a mixture of sulfur powder and iron filings)
   Pictures (any that show large clumps of one substance mixed with another)

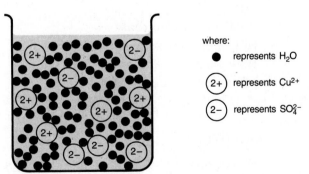

where:
   ● represents H_2O
   (2+) represents Cu^{2+}
   (2−) represents SO_4^{2-}

FIGURE 7–4 *Schematic picture to represent a solution of copper sulfate in water*

Note: Since many chemical concepts are abstract, we need to seek ways to represent them. In Figure 7–4 we represented a solution of copper sulfate on the microscopic level, that is, on the level of atoms and molecules. See page 9 for practice in visualizing chemicals and chemical processes at the microscopic level.

SALT

Examples
    Symbols (NaCl, $Ca(NO_3)_2$, KI)
    Names (sodium chloride, calcium nitrate, potassium iodide)
Nonexamples
    Symbols (H_2O, CO, HNO_3, NaOH)
    Names (water, carbon monoxide, nitric acid, sodium hydroxide)

Nonexamples of concepts are rarely taught in a chemistry class. Therefore, you must work to identify them for yourself. We will suggest a process for identifying some nonexamples in the section on mutually exclusive concepts.

Parts of the Concept

The next step in forming a concept is to identify the *parts* of the concept that must be understood. Many of these parts are concepts in their own right. In identifying them, you are still struggling to discover exactly what the concept is, rather than how the concept will be used.

Below, we have selected a few of the many parts of the concepts of electron, solution, and salt:

ELECTRON

Location of electrons within atoms
    Orbitals
    Energy levels
    Pairing of electrons
How electrons were discovered
How electrons are detected
The role of electrons in bonding

SOLUTION

Major types of solutions
    Solids
    Liquids
    Gases

Names of components of solutions
   Solute
   Solvent
Ways of preparing solutions
Ways of describing solution composition
   Dilute, concentrated
   Molarity, molality
   Weight percent, volume percent

SALT

Preparation of salts
   Neutralization of acid and base
   Direct combination of elements
Types of salts
   Acidic
   Basic
   Neutral
Hydrolysis of salts
Solubility of salts

The parts of concepts that are taught in any given chemistry course may vary. Even when two professors use an identical syllabus and textbook, they may teach the parts of concepts differently. Focus your energy first on the parts that are required by your course. If time permits, you can explore other concept parts that are of interest to you.

The Concept as Part of a Broader Topic

Most concepts are *part of* a larger topic. For example, electrons are part of the topic of atomic structure. When you learn about how atoms are constructed, you learn about the properties of subatomic particles such as electrons. Electrons are also part of the general topic of chemical bonding, because the sharing or transfer of electrons serves to hold atoms together. When you study chemical bonding, the characteristics of electrons as subatomic particles still exist—but are not of immediate interest to you. In worrying about how many electrons are shared between two nitrogen atoms, you don't care that each electron's weight is only $1/1835$ that of a proton. That aspect of an electron belongs to the subject of atomic structure.

Connecting a concept to its larger subject helps you to select the aspects of the concept that are currently important to study. Each concept "fits" somewhere. As you learn each concept, connect it to its appropriate place in the larger picture. Thus, you might learn about the intrinsic properties of electrons when studying atomic structure. You might learn about the octet rule and how electrons pair in bonds during the chemical bonding unit. At all costs, avoid learning isolated bits of information with no context, that is, with no sense of how they fit into a larger body of material.

Mutually Exclusive Concepts

Concepts are *mutually exclusive* when an example cannot belong to both at the same time. For example, the concepts solution and suspension are mutually exclusive. Since vinegar is an example of a solution, it cannot be an example of a suspension. Vinegar is automatically a nonexample of the concept suspension. When concepts are mutually exclusive, your task is to identify the shared essential characteristics and the differences.

Let's look again at the concepts of solution and suspension. These share the characteristic of being mixtures of two or more substances. In both, the type of fundamental particle remains unchanged upon mixing. However, solutions *must* be homogeneous whereas suspensions are not necessarily homogeneous. Moreover, suspensions do not mix on the molecular level and the large clumps of material will settle to the bottom of the container. This does not happen in solutions.

Not all concepts are mutually exclusive with other concepts. For example, the mole is an example of a concept that has no other concept with which it shares most, but not all, of its essential characteristics.

EXERCISE 1 Discovering Mutually Exclusive Concepts

From your course find some mutually exclusive concepts. Here are some possibilities:

- Element and compound
- Atom and molecule
- Ionic compound and covalent compound
- Oxidation and reduction

For the concepts that you have selected, determine the essential characteristics that the concepts share and those in which they differ. Remember, the characteristics that *differ* are what you use to assign examples to one or the other category. Work this exercise in your notebook.

MASTERING CONCEPTS

The process of forming concepts is an active one. You will have to search your notes or text for the critical information. You will have to think and reason and work at completing your understanding of chemical words as you use them in solving problems. The active process needed for formulating concepts helps you to learn them. By the time you have searched out definitions, essential characteristics, examples, and relationships, you will already have learned much of the required information. In this section we describe activities that can complete your learning.

Work Actively During the Study Process

Study with pencil and paper, writing out material from memory to see how much you remember. Say things out loud as well. Can you recite definitions without hesitation? Could you explain the meaning of a chemical concept to someone who has never taken chemistry?

Keep Lists of New Concepts

List in one place the concepts that are part of a general topic. As you study, be alert for additional concept words to add to your list. Use this list for review and self-testing.

Develop Flexibility with Chemical Language

Develop your ability to express chemical ideas in different ways. For example, when given a definition, practice expressing that definition in your own words.

Also be prepared to interchange the concept word and its meaning. For example, if a test question states, "A substance that contains only one kind of atom . . .", you need to recognize this as meaning, "An element . . ." See pages 148 to 153 for more information about the testing of concepts.

Increase Your Sensitivity to Chemical Words

Chemical words have peculiarities that can interfere with your ability to learn them. For example, a chemical word may have *more than one meaning*. Chemists use the word *oxygen* to mean either oxygen atoms (O) or oxygen molecules (O_2). You are expected to decide the meaning from the context. If, for example, the context is the air we breathe, the reference is to O_2.

It is also true that related words may be used *interchangeably*, even though they do *not* mean exactly the same thing. For example, an instructor may say, "The atomic weight of ^{14}C is 14," when he or she means that the atomic mass number is 14. Here are the correct definitions:

Atomic weight: Weighted average of all isotopes of a particular element

Atomic mass number: The sum of the numbers of protons and neutrons in a particular nucleus

In addition, many chemical terms look and sound alike. Here are some easily confused terms:

· Molarity and molality
· Heat, heat capacity, and specific heat
· Soluble, solubility, and solubility product
· Vapor pressure and pressure of a vapor
· Rate, rate of reaction, and relative rate of reaction
· Rate law and rate constant

Each of these represents a concept in its own right. You must work to distinguish terms like these.

Finally, chemical words are confused with "ordinary" language. Everyday speech and chemistry have many words in common. However, a familiar word may take on a different meaning in its chemical context. For example:

REDUCTION

Everyday meaning: The lessening of something

Chemical meaning: The gain of electrons

SPONTANEOUS

Everyday meaning: Happens without apparent external cause

Chemical meaning: May happen, but does not have to happen; has negative value of ΔG

INSOLUBLE

Everyday meaning: Does not dissolve

Chemical meaning: Dissolves to a small but measurable extent

As you become aware of the precise meaning of chemical words, you improve your knowledge of chemical concepts.

Seek Additional Examples for Concepts

In our experience, chemistry courses do not present students with an adequate set of examples of concepts. Therefore, you should seek examples on your own, refining your understanding of the concept as you do so. For example, you may have little difficulty identifying the following compounds as acids:

$$H_2SO_4 \quad HNO_3 \quad HCN \quad H_3PO_4$$

But what about these next ones? Are they acids?

$$CH_4 \quad H_2O_2 \quad HCO_3^- \quad CH_3COOH$$

As you come to recognize that CH_3COOH and HCO_3^- are acids, your understanding of the concept of acid will grow. Check your textbook or ask your instructor for help in identifying useful concept examples.

Expect Your Understanding of Concepts to Grow

Memorizing facts is a closed task: You know exactly what you are expected to learn. In contrast, learning concepts is open-ended: Your understanding of the concept changes as you study. These changes may be subtle. You may not even be aware that your understanding of concept words has changed over time. The first indication might be the need to replace your original definition with a refined one as you study for an upcoming exam.

For example, you may think you understand the concepts of heat and temperature. Only later, as you work problems involving heat and temperature, might the following questions occur to you:

· How is heat different from temperature?
· Do two substances at the same temperature contain the same amount of heat?

As you ask and answer questions like these, your knowledge of the concepts of heat and temperature will grow.

Decide on the Timing of Learning Related Concepts

Many students find it easier to learn confusing concepts one at a time rather than together. For example, if you must learn molarity and molality, select one of these to master before attempting to learn the other. This procedure minimizes the confusion between the two. Other students find it easier to learn related concepts simultaneously, working to identify similarities and differences.

Be aware that different strategies are possible. You might try one technique on one set of concepts; then try the other on a different set of concepts. See which works best for you. As you learn to control your study process and make decisions based on your responses, your studying becomes more efficient.

Relate Concepts to Previously Learned Concepts

Concepts give meaning to other concepts, as illustrated in this definition:

Ideal Solution: A solution in which the components have vapor pressures as given by Raoult's law

You cannot understand what an ideal solution is unless you know what *vapor pressure* and *Raoult's law* mean.

Moreover, concepts taught in introductory chemistry courses may also depend on concepts that you are expected to know from earlier schooling. In the Appendix we have provided a short test of basic concepts that are assumed to be known (and won't be taught) in most general chemistry courses.

Develop Relationships Among Concepts

Concepts relate to other concepts. Techniques for illustrating the relationships among concepts include circle diagrams (Venn diagrams), "tree diagrams," and outlines.

Circle diagrams can be used to demonstrate that categories include each other, partially overlap, or do not overlap at all. For example, Figure 7–5 shows some of the relationships among the words *man*, *woman*, *teacher*, and *occupation*. The categories man and woman are mutually exclusive since a person is either a man or a woman. The categories woman and teacher overlap, since it is possible to be both a

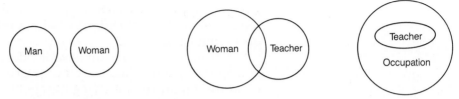

FIGURE 7–5 *Circle diagrams showing the relationships between categories*

woman and a teacher. Finally, being a teacher is one possible occupation, so the general category of occupations includes that of teacher.

We can draw similar pictures to demonstrate the relationship among chemical concepts such as *atom, molecule, element,* and *matter.* Figure 7–6 illustrates these relationships. When we consider the composition of the smallest unit of a substance, the concepts of atom and molecule are mutually exclusive. The smallest unit of a chemical species either will consist of an independent (unbonded) atom or will consist of two or more atoms bonded together to make a molecule. The smallest unit of a particular substance must fall exclusively into one, and only one, of these two categories.

The categories of molecule and element partially overlap. Elements are substances in which the atoms present are all of a single kind. Some elements occur as molecules, such as H_2 and S_8. But all molecules are not in the element class. Molecules like HCl are not elements (because more than one kind of atom is present in an HCl molecule). Moreover, some elements such as copper occur as individual atoms, rather than having those atoms bound into molecules.

Finally, elements are but one form of matter. Other forms of matter exist—for example, compounds, mixtures, and solutions. So the general category of matter includes elements as a subcategory.

Drawing such diagrams can help you refine your understanding of the precise relationships among concepts.

A second way of representing relationships is with tree diagrams. You may be familiar with tree diagrams that show the relationships among family members. For example, Figure 7–7 shows a short family tree. It is easier to grasp the relationships from the family tree than it is to

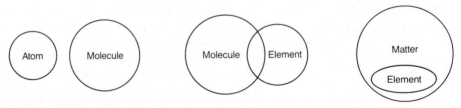

FIGURE 7–6 *Circle diagrams to illustrate chemical relationships*

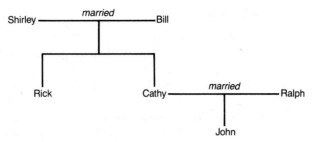

FIGURE 7–7 *Tree diagram showing relationships among family members*

understand them from a written description such as, "Shirley and Bill married. They had two children, Cathy and Rick. Cathy married Ralph. . . ."

Similarly, you may grasp relationships in chemistry more quickly if you use pictures. Figure 7–8 is a tree diagram showing the relationship among the concepts *matter, pure matter, mixture, solution, element,* and *compound.* Matter, the most general concept, is put at the top. It is then subdivided into two classes, pure and mixture. Pure matter is either an element or a compound, as indicated by a further subdivision. Likewise, mixtures (impure matter) are either homogeneous or heterogeneous.

As drawn, this diagram contains no details about the concepts, only their relationship to each other. Other information could be included if it did not obscure the relationships being illustrated.

Finally, you might choose to outline a topic in order to develop the relationships.[1] The concept of matter might be outlined in the following manner:

[1] See James F. Shepherd, *College Study Skills* (Boston: Houghton Mifflin Company, 1983), Chapters 8 and 9, for a thorough description of the skill of outlining.

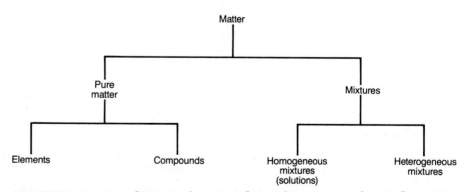

FIGURE 7–8 *Tree diagram showing relationships among chemical concepts*

MATTER:

A. Two general types
   1. Pure: One type of fundamental particle present
      a. Element
         (1) Cannot be separated by ordinary chemical means
         (2) Only one kind of atom present
      b. Compound
         (1) Can be separated into elements by ordinary chemical means
         (2) More than one type of atom present
   2. Mixture: More than one type of basic particle present
      a. Heterogeneous mixture
         (1) Not mixed on the molecular level
      b. Homogeneous mixture (solution)
         (1) Mixed on the molecular level

Some groups of complex concepts do not lend themselves easily to tree diagrams or to outlines. Therefore, stop diagraming relationships when the relationships become obscure. It is better to draw several simple diagrams than a single, unintelligible one.

Review and Self-Test, Using a Variety of Activities

Conceptual information, just like any other kind of learned material, will be forgotten over time. We suggest that you review and test your conceptual knowledge with the following activities:

- Skim through your lecture notes periodically, reviewing information.
- Cover up part of your notes and try to reconstruct from memory what you have covered.
- Reproduce from memory diagrams of related concepts.
- Using your diagrams as a guide, fill in the details about each concept: definitions, essential characteristics, and the parts of each. Produce examples of each when appropriate.
- Using your concept word lists, practice defining words. Use more than one set of words to say the same thing.
- With a classmate, rephrase assigned problems, substituting definitions for concept words and vice versa.

With these activities, you can test your knowledge of concepts before somebody else does. In the next section, we will look at the common ways of testing concepts on an exam.

TESTING CONCEPTS

Questions concerning concepts fall into four general categories:

1. Definition questions
2. Classification questions

3. Questions on concept parts and relationships
4. Questions using concepts

Let's now take a closer look at each of these.

Definition Questions

Given a Definition, Supply the Concept Word

> The temperature above which a gas may not be liquefied by an increase
>
> in pressure is called the _____ .

One way to make definition questions harder is to choose concepts that are readily confused:

> The number of moles of solute per liter of solution is called the
>
> _____ .
>
> The number of moles of solute per kilogram of solvent is called the
>
> _____ .

Another way to make definition questions harder is to use alternate wordings:

> A compound that produces more H^+ ions than OH^- ions when dis-
>
> solved in water is a(n) _____ .
>
> A compound that gives a solution with a pH less than 7 when dissolved
>
> in water is a(n) _____ .

Fill In the Missing Words in a Definition

> Sublimation is the process of a phase change from the _____
>
> state to the _____ state.
>
> The temperature above which a gas may not be liquefied by increasing
>
> the _____ is the critical temperature.

The missing words in such questions are often essential characteristics of the concepts involved.

Given a Concept Word, Supply a Definition

Define *chemical bond.*

Define *colligative property.*

It can be surprisingly difficult to generate definitions for concept words, especially under the pressure of an exam. Practice generating definitions beforehand, as described on page 137.

Recognize Whether a Definition Is Stated Correctly

True or false? An emulsion is a suspension of two liquids.

True or false? Molarity is defined as the number of moles of solvent divided by the number of liters of solution.

Expect definitions to look different on exams because of the substitution of synonymous terms for one another. For example, you may be taught the definition:

Isotopes are atoms with the same number of protons but different numbers of neutrons.

A true/false question written from this definition may look quite different:

True or false? Isotopes are atoms of the same element which differ in the number of neutrons in their nuclei.

True or false? Isotopes are atoms with the same atomic number but different mass numbers.

True/false questions may also be asked in the form of multiple choice. For example, this multiple choice question asks five separate definition questions for the price of one:

Which of the following is not true?

    a. The atom is the smallest particle of an element that still has all the properties of that element.
    b. The mass number of an isotope is equal to the weight of the protons plus neutrons in its nucleus.
    c. Isotopes are atoms of the same element with different numbers of neutrons.
    d. Cations are atoms that have a greater number of protons than electrons.
    e. Rutherford confirmed that the nucleus contains positive charges.

Earlier, in Chapter Four, we discussed some strategies for answering multiple choice questions (see page 76).

Classification Questions

Classification questions test your ability to identify all the examples of a concept and to reject from that classification all nonexamples.

Give an Example of a Concept

> Give three examples of diatomic gases.
>
> Write the formula for any weak acid.
>
> Give an example of a salt that dissolves in water to produce a slightly basic solution.

Given an Example, Name the Class to Which It Belongs

> In which of the following is the heat of formation equal to the heat of reaction?
>
> a. $HgO(s) \rightarrow Hg(s) + \frac{1}{2} O_2(g)$
> b. $H_2(g) + \frac{1}{2} I_2(g) \rightarrow 2\ HI(g)$
> c. $C(s) + \frac{1}{2} O_2(g) + 2\ H_2(g) \rightarrow CH_3OH(l)$
>
> Name the geometry of the following molecule:

> Circle and give the name for all functional groups in the following molecule:

This type of question can be made more difficult by asking you to classify more novel examples. For example:

> Which of the following are acids?
>
> CH_3COOH H_2 NaH $CO_2(aq)$

Two are acids. CH_3COOH is tricky because the H in acetic acid is not written first. For $CO_2(aq)$, you needed to know that CO_2 dissolved in water makes carbonic acid, H_2CO_3. The others contain hydrogen but do not give H^+ in solution, and they are therefore not acids.

The classification can also be made more difficult if an item contains an irrelevant characteristic. For example:

> Which of the following are isotopes of sodium-23?
>
> ^{22}Na $^{22}Na^+$ ^{23}Mg an atom with 11 protons and 13 neutrons

We call your attention to the second item, $^{22}Na^+$. This is a sodium *ion*, having one more proton than electron. But the question is about *isotopes*, which requires comparison of numbers of protons and neutrons, not protons and electrons. This answer is therefore correct, as is the first one, ^{22}Na. The others are not.

Classify, Based on a Verbal Description

> A chemist is given a block of metal to examine. The sample appears homogeneous both to the eye and under a microscope. The chemist melts the sample and then cools it, measuring the temperature as the metal solidifies. The temperature of the metal changes continuously as the metal solidifies. On the basis of these observations, *classify* the metal as a mixture, solution, compound, or element.

This question describes a hypothetical situation. The properties described are the essential characteristics of a solution (homogeneous, nonconstant temperature during a phase change).

In some classification questions, the properties are not described:

> Classify as solutions or suspensions:
>
> milk   6 M HCl   carbonated water   fog   brass
>
> Which of the following is *not* a solution?
>
> a. salt water
> b. a blue liquid formed by adding $CuSO_4$ to water
> c. orange juice
> d. bronze

In each of these questions, you must know how to discriminate solutions from other types of mixtures. You must also recall the properties of each of the na ned examples and provide your own description.

Questions on Concept Parts and Relationships

List or Describe Concept Parts

> List the five parts of Dalton's atomic theory.

> Draw a picture of NaCl dissolved in water, showing the solvation of the ions present.

> Describe two ways of preparing a buffer solution made up of acetic acid and sodium acetate.

These questions involve recall of concept parts. Often, professors illustrate characteristics of concepts by schematic drawings. As in the second question, be prepared to reproduce these drawings on exams.

Discriminate Between Related Concepts

Briefly explain the differences between suspensions and solutions.

What is the structural difference between a primary amine and a secondary amine?

How is molarity different from molality?

You will be prepared for these questions if you have compared and contrasted related concepts (see page 145) during study and review.

Questions Using Concepts

All of the previous questions directly test whether or not you know a chemical concept. However, many other questions test whether you can *use* a chemical concept. Your ability to apply chemical rules (see Chapters Eight and Nine) and to solve chemical problems (see Chapters Ten and Eleven) depends on your knowledge of chemical concepts. Here are some examples that illustrate the interdependency of concepts, rules, and problems:

The intermolecular attractive forces in liquid CO_2 are less than those in liquid water. Which of these two substances would have the lower critical temperature? Explain your answer.

The rule needed for this question is, "The less the intermolecular attractive forces in a liquid, the lower the critical temperature." It is impossible to understand this rule if you do not have an understanding of the concepts of intermolecular attractive forces and critical temperature.

What is the pH of a 0.1 M HCl solution?

To solve this problem you must be able to classify HCl as a strong acid, apply the rules for finding [H^+] of a strong acid, and know how to derive pH from [H^+].

SUMMARY

Chemical concepts are ideas about matter. Each concept is represented by a word or term. Concept words form the language of chemistry. Chemical concepts are usually taught in lecture in the following manner:

· Many concepts are taught in a class period.
· Concepts are taught without interrelating them.

- Concepts are taught simultaneously with facts, rules, and problems.
- Concepts are not presented completely.
- Concepts are extended in later class periods.

Such presentations force you to work *actively* to form complete chemical concepts. To master concepts, you must find answers to the following questions:

- What is a *definition* for the concept?
- What are the *essential characteristics* of the concept?
- What are the *examples* of the concept?
- What are the *parts* of the concept?
- What is the concept *a part of?*
- With which other concepts is it *mutually exclusive?*

Use the following techniques to master chemical concepts:

- Work actively during the study process.
- Keep lists of new concepts as you learn them.
- Develop flexibility with chemical language.
- Increase your sensitivity to chemical words.
- Seek additional examples for concepts.
- Expect your understanding of concepts to grow as the course progresses.
- Decide on the timing of learning related concepts.
- As you learn new concepts, relate them to previously learned concepts.
- Develop relationships among concepts.
- Review and self-test, using a variety of activities.

Several types of exam questions on concepts should be anticipated. Definition questions would include:

- Given a definition, supply the concept word.
- Fill in the missing words in a definition.
- Given a concept word, supply a definition.
- Recognize whether a definition is stated correctly.

Classification questions typically ask you to:

- Give an example of a concept.
- Given an example, name the class to which it belongs.
- Classify into a concept class on the basis of a verbal description.

Questions on concept parts and relationships ask you to:

- List or describe concept parts.
- Discriminate between related concepts.

Still other questions require you to use concepts.

SELF-ASSESSMENT

Here is your chance to evaluate how your chemistry course presents concepts and how well you are able to learn these concepts from the presentation. Mark an X along the line in the position that best describes your situation.

1. My chemical concept background is:

VERY _____ VERY
STRONG   WEAK

If your instructor assumes that you know concepts that you do not know, you may need to improve your science background. How will you do this? See the Appendix for some suggestions.

2. My understanding of the meaning of chemical words is:

VERY _____ VERY
HIGH   LOW

Successful chemistry students are aggressive about seeking the exact meaning of words. It is not enough that you know "something" about a chemical word. You must nail down its precise meaning. Are there any chemical words from your current work in chemistry that you are not sure of? Write them below.

WORDS I NEED TO LEARN

How can you improve your sensitivity to the meaning of chemical words?

MY PLAN

3. The number of chemical concepts introduced in my chemistry classes is:

VERY _____ VERY
HIGH   LOW

If you are not aware of how many new concepts are introduced in a class period, you will first need to find this out. Try counting the concepts mentioned in one of your classes. Try to write in your notes all concepts that your professor either mentions or writes on the board. You could even do this with a friend and compare lists.

The greater the number of new concepts, the more efficient your techniques for mastery need to be. Review pages 142 to 148 for activities that are effective for concept mastery.

4. My ability to form chemical concepts is:

VERY ————————————————————————— VERY
STRONG   WEAK

Suggestions for improving concept formation and mastery begin on pages 137 to 142 of this chapter. Determine in which of these skills you are weakest and plan some specific actions to improve your skills.

MY PLAN

5. My instructor provides useful definitions for new concept words:

ALWAYS ————————————————————————— NEVER

Useful definitions call attention to the essence of a concept and increase your sensitivity to the exact meaning of the word. If your instructor does not provide useful definitions, you must find them for yourself.

Plan specific steps for finding definitions. For example, you may decide for yourself, "I will check the text for the meaning of words right after lecture," or "I will pay more attention in lecture to writing down concept words that I am unsure of."

MY PLAN FOR FINDING DEFINITIONS

6. In my class, the amount of conceptual information that is stated indirectly is:

VERY ————————————————————————— VERY
HIGH   LOW

Here is an example of a direct statement of conceptual information:

This is concept A. This is concept B. A and B are alike in that . . . . A and B are different in that . . . .

When the last two points are omitted in your lecture, you must find them for yourself. Examine your lecture notes to determine how much information your instructor provides for you.

7. The set of examples/nonexamples I use to learn concepts is:

LARGE, ———————————————————————— SMALL,
VARIED   NARROW

You extend your knowledge of a concept by confronting examples and nonexamples of the concept. Nonexamples are particularly important in helping you to discriminate between related concepts.

If you are not exposed to a varied set of examples and nonexamples in your class, you must generate them for yourself. How will you do this?

MY PLAN FOR GENERATING EXAMPLES

It is impossible to learn chemistry if you do not understand the language of chemistry. In this chapter, we have indicated the importance of chemical words and their meanings. With a firm fact and concept base, you are now ready to advance to higher levels of work required by your chemistry course: rule using and problem solving.

CHAPTER EIGHT

Mastering Chemical Rules

The previous two chapters were concerned with chemical facts and concepts. We now take up the subject of chemical rules. It is no accident that facts and concepts were discussed first because, in order to understand and use chemical rules, you need to know some facts and concepts. The function of chemical rules is to organize this knowledge and to make it possible for you to predict new facts.

To understand what chemical rules are, let's first think about chemical facts and where they come from. Chemists obtain chemical facts by observing how matter behaves under a variety of conditions. For example, by observing what happens when sodium nitrate ($NaNO_3$), a white solid, is added to water, chemists discovered the fact that sodium nitrate dissolves readily in water.

The number of known chemical facts is incredibly large. We would all drown in a sea of chemical facts if it were not for the existence of chemical rules. A chemical rule is a generalization that *summarizes* the behavior of a number of different substances. For example, chemists discovered that not only sodium nitrate but also lithium nitrate, potassium nitrate, ammonium nitrate, calcium nitrate, titanium nitrate, and many other nitrates were soluble in water. After noting that all these nitrates dissolved, chemists stated the generalization: "All nitrate compounds are soluble." This rule efficiently summarizes the specific facts that were observed. The process of forming a rule from specific facts is summarized in Figure 8–1.

158

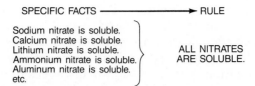

FIGURE 8–1 *The process of forming a rule*

The beauty of a chemical rule is that it frees you from having to learn many individual facts. Once you have learned the solubility rule for nitrate compounds, you do not need to remember the solubility of a large number of individual compounds containing the nitrate ion. Thus, rules play an important role in reducing the amount of factual information you must memorize.

What are you expected to do with the rules that are taught in your chemistry course? Rules are taught so that you can *apply* them to predict specific facts. When you apply a rule, you obtain new information. However, the rule often does not specify *how* you apply it to obtain this information.

For example, imagine that you are given the rule "All nitrates are soluble" in your class. This rule would be taught so that you could predict the solubility of any specific compound containing a nitrate ion. However, to apply the nitrate rule you must:

1. Be given a specific chemical (by name or by formula)
2. Know how to classify a chemical as a nitrate
3. Decide whether the compound fits the classification.

Finally, you use the rule to obtain the new information about whether or not the compound dissolves in water. Figure 8–2 summarizes the process of applying a rule. Most of the time the specific steps involved in applying a rule will not be spelled out for you. You will be expected to work out how to apply a rule on your own.

Rules are, by nature, generalizations that are restricted to specific circumstances. Some restrictions are obvious. For example, the nitrate solubility rule does not apply to compounds that are not nitrates. Other restrictions are less obvious. For example, although it is not stated as part of the nitrate solubility rule, the assumption is that we are discussing solubility in water (not any other substance), that the temperature at which we are measuring the solubility is approximately room temperature, and that we are restricting our rule to simple salts such as

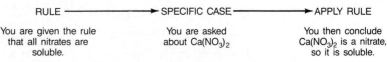

FIGURE 8–2 *The process of applying a rule*

those given in Figure 8–1. Compounds with more complex structures— for example, $[Ir(NH_3)_5(NO_3)](NO_3)_2$— are not very soluble in water, even though they are classified as nitrates.

Most rules that you will learn in your chemistry course will have exceptions—that is, specific instances in which the rule does not apply. Such exceptions do not invalidate a rule. Rules tell how the world *usually* is.

Rules relate not only to chemical facts but also to chemical concepts. The rule "All nitrates are soluble" cannot be understood if you do not know the concepts of nitrate and soluble. What is a *nitrate?* How do you recognize a nitrate when you meet one? What does the word *soluble* mean? You need to know the underlying concepts before you can expect to understand rules built on those concepts.

As another example, there is a chemical rule that states, "The volume and temperature of an ideal gas are directly proportional to each other." To understand this rule, you must know:

· What an ideal gas is
· What volume and temperature are
· How volumes and temperatures are identified and measured
· What "directly proportional" means (see page 187 for an explanation of direct and indirect proportions)

Again, you cannot expect to use a rule properly if you do not understand the concepts on which it is based.

One function of chemical rules is to relate concepts to one another. In the volume–temperature rule, the relationship between the two concepts is that of a direct proportion, a precise mathematical relationship. The nitrate solubility rule links two properties of a compound together: the identity of the compound and its solubility. In other words, if a compound is a member of the nitrate class, then it is also a member of the class of soluble compounds. Notice that the reverse relationship is *not* true: If a compound is soluble, it is not necessarily a nitrate.

Thus, in a real sense rules tie together the individual concepts that will be taught in your course. As you learn these relationships, topics take shape. The pattern of relationships that integrate different concepts makes the individual concepts easier to learn completely and to remember.

From what we have just described about rules, we hope you can see that your ability to use rules is critical to your success in chemistry. In this chapter we will examine rules closely. Our discussion will include the following topics:

· Recognizing a chemical rule
· Understanding the rule
· Learning the rule
· Applying the rule

- Developing your own chemical rules
- Modifying rules
- Testing rules

In the next chapter we focus on two special formats of rules: graphs and mathematical formulas.

RECOGNIZING A CHEMICAL RULE

Where will you encounter chemical rules? After reading our description of the origin of rules, you may be expecting to discover chemical rules by doing laboratory experiments or looking up a large number of facts. However, you will probably not get much chance to find rules in this manner. Instead, teachers and textbooks will present rules to you, often without mentioning how these rules were discovered.

Rules can be presented in many different situations throughout introductory chemistry courses. Most rules, however, are presented to help you answer one of the following four questions:

1. How does a class of chemicals behave?
2. How do the properties of substances change?
3. How are two or more properties of substances related?
4. How will chemicals be represented?

Here is an example of a rule for each of the questions:

1. How does a class of chemicals behave?

   Rule: An acid (containing H^+ ions) reacts with a base (containing OH^- ions) to form a salt and water.

2. How do the properties of substances change?

   Rule: The size of atoms increases as you descend a column on the periodic chart.

3. How are two or more properties of substances related?

   Rule: The density of an object is found by dividing the object's mass by its volume.

4. How will chemicals be represented?

   Rule: In writing chemical formulas for binary compounds (those containing only two elements), the more metallic element is written first.

As you read your text or study your lecture notes, you will encounter rules such as these. Sometimes they will be clearly labeled as rules, such as solubility *rules,* or *rules* for assigning oxidation numbers. However, at other times, rules will not be labeled and will occur in different forms and disguises. Let's look at the forms you can expect rules to take.

Statements

Rules are frequently presented as statements. For example, the rules just given as examples are rule statements. However, these statements will often be presented interspersed with facts, concepts, and problems. In this case the rule statements may be hard to spot. For example, as you read through the following wordy text passage, try to spot the rule that it contains:

Grams is a unit that describes the *mass* of a chemical sample. *Moles* is a unit that can be used to describe the *number of particles* (atoms, molecules, or ions) in the sample. There is a simple relationship between these two methods of describing the quantity of chemical, as illustrated for the element carbon: 1 mole C = 12 g C. This equation is a statement of the equivalence between the number of particles of carbon (one mole of carbon atoms) and how much that number of atoms would weigh (12 grams). In general, one mole of any element or compound and the molar mass of that element or compound both describe the same amount of the chemical.

This passage contains one rule: "One mole of any substance and the molar mass of that substance both describe the same amount of material." That is:

1 mole (substance) = molar mass (substance)

From this rule, it is possible to make many equivalencies, such as:

1 mole H_2O = 18 g H_2O
1 mole NH_3 = 17 g NH_3

In addition to this rule, the passage contains the following facts:

· Grams and moles are units.
· Grams measure mass.
· Moles can measure number of particles.
· 1 mole C = 12 g C

Laws and Principles

As you progress through your course, you will encounter statements labeled as "laws" or "principles." For example, you may be taught the law of conservation of mass, Le Chatelier's principle, or Boyle's law. These are all examples of chemical rules.

Chemical Equations for a Class of Chemical Reactions

Your lecture notes and textbooks will contain many chemical equations. These equations will fall into one of two categories. Some of them will describe specific reactions that you must memorize, such as the reaction that produces electrical energy in a car battery. Treat these as chemical facts. Other equations will be given as *examples* of how a class of chemicals react. Chemical equations that describe the reactions of *classes* of chemicals, rather than of unique chemicals, are chemical rules. The following is an example of a general equation:

$$HCl + NaOH \rightarrow H_2O + NaCl$$

The general equation could be written:

$$HA + MOH \rightarrow H_2O + MA$$
$$\text{acid} + \text{base} \rightarrow \text{water} + \text{salt}$$

Other acids (HBr, HNO_3, etc.) and bases (NaOH, $Mg(OH)_2$, etc.) react the same way as HCl and NaOH.

It may not be obvious whether an equation is a general equation (a rule) or a specific equation (a fact to be memorized). To a certain extent, the answer to this may depend on the context in which the equation is taught. Given a specific equation, you may need to ask your instructor whether you need be concerned with any other chemicals that will react in the same way.

Mathematical Formulas and Graphs

Mathematical formulas are also used to state rules. For example $V = kT$ is a mathematical statement of Charles's law. Likewise, Figure 8–3 is a graphical statement of this same law. Rules in the form of formulas and graphs require special techniques for complete learning and effective use. See Chapter Nine for the skills needed to master rules in these formats.

To sum up, the first step in mastering a rule is to recognize it. Because some rules are implied rather than explicitly stated, this is not always an easy task. Suspect that you are missing a rule when you cannot understand *how* some decisions are being made. For example, you may not understand how you were to know to write the chemical formula for calcium chloride as $CaCl_2$ and not CaCl. If you cannot find a missing rule on your own, ask your instructor for help in finding it.

EXERCISE 1   Locating Rules

Go to your notes from a recent chemistry lecture and identify the rules that they contain. Mark each rule in the margin. Note how the rules are interspersed with problems, facts, and concepts.

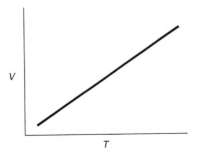

FIGURE 8–3   *Graphic representation of Charles's law*

UNDERSTANDING THE RULE

Let's look at some actions that can help lead you to a complete understanding of a rule.

Learn the Underlying Facts and Concepts

The first step in understanding a rule is to learn the facts and concepts on which the rule is based. As a start, you must know the meaning of every word used to state the rule. As you read through the rule statement, mark any unfamiliar words. Search out their meanings before struggling further with the rule.

Restate the Rule in Your Own Words

The next step in understanding the rule is attempting to restate the rule in words that have meaning for you. For example, the rule for writing symbols for isotopes may be given as follows:

> To write the symbol for a specific isotope, write the atomic mass number and the atomic number to the upper left and lower left respectively of the symbol for the element.

Restating this rule in your own terms, you might say, "If I want to write the symbol for an isotope, I first write the symbol for the element. Then to the upper left I write the mass number (the sum of protons and neutrons). At the bottom left I write the atomic number (the number of protons)."

Rules in textbooks may be written in complex, hard-to-understand language. This sometimes happens because the author is trying to be precise in stating the rule or wants to give some hint as to when the rule applies. While these are desirable goals, the result may be that the meaning of the rule is obscured. If you have difficulty understanding rules in your text, form the habit of rephrasing the rules, using short, simple sentences. Substitute the meaning of a concept word for the word itself (e.g., "the sum of the protons and neutrons" in place of "the atomic mass number"). It may help to pretend that you need to explain the rule to someone who knows little about chemistry.

Although rule statements in texts tend to be complex, the opposite is true for rule statements in lectures. These tend to be sparse. The context in which the rule has been developed often is omitted from the statement. To gain a better understanding of a rule given in lecture, you may want to try elaborating on it as you restate it, perhaps linking it to fundamental concepts.

For example, here is a typical rule that might be found in your lecture notes:

> Write the ion charge to upper right of element symbol. For example, Li^+.

As you restate this rule in your own words, you might include how you determine what the ion charge is (the difference in numbers of protons and electrons; an excess of protons gives a positive charge and an excess of electrons gives a negative charge).

EXERCISE 2   Restating Rules

> Go to the section of your lecture notes in which you identified and marked rules. Now restate those rules in your own words. Pretend that you are explaining the rules to a friend who has not taken a chemistry course.

Determine When the Rule Applies

When a rule is taught, more emphasis is usually placed on *what* the rule is than on *when* it should be used. If this is the case in your course, you may need to determine for yourself when a rule will be in effect. To do this, try taking your cue from the topic in which the rule is introduced.

For example, the ideal gas law ($PV = nRT$) is taught as part of the unit on gases. No one may explicitly state that you cannot use this law to determine the volume (or other properties) of liquids or solids. You may think it obvious that the ideal gas law applies only to gases. However, for years we have seen students incorrectly using this rule to calculate the volumes of liquids.

When you are presented with a rule, note whether there are other rules with which it may be confused. This is especially important when you have been taught rules that apply to separate classes of compounds. For example, two sets of rules for naming compounds are customarily taught in general chemistry courses. One set, for ionic compounds, is taught in the section of the course that deals with ionic compounds. At some later point, a second set of rules for naming covalent compounds is taught. It may never be pointed out to students that they now have a new decision to make whenever they name a compound: They must first determine whether the compound belongs to the ionic or covalent class before selecting the appropriate naming system.

Determine What the Rule Accomplishes

You learn rules so that you can apply them. The rule statement, however, does not tell you *how* to apply the rule. To determine this, you must translate the rule statement into a form that states directly what the rule will accomplish when it is used. For example:

Rule: The size of atoms increases as you descend a column on the periodic chart.

Use: If I am given two or more elements in the same column on the periodic chart, then the one farther toward the bottom is the larger.

We suggest that you reformulate all rules as "if–then" statements. Such statements identify specific cases for which the rule will be used and what decision you will make about that case as the rule is applied.

EXERCISE 3   Reformulating Rules

> Rewrite the following rules in an "if–then" format. Complete both questions before reading on in this section.

1. The size of atoms decreases as you go left to right across a row on the periodic chart.

    Rewrite

2. Positive ions are written first in the formulas of ionic compounds.

    Rewrite

In Exercise 3, correct answers would have looked something like this:

1. If I consider two elements in the same row of the periodic chart, then the one farther to the right will be the smaller.
2. If I am writing the formula of an ionic compound, then the positive ion will be written first.

Note that the "if–then" statements can lead you to question your ability to identify cases in which the rule will be used. For example, how will you identify when a compound is ionic? Unless you can answer that question, you will be unable to use the rule.

Identify Exceptions to the Rule

Most rules have exceptions, many of which find their way into exam questions. In the following example, the exceptions are stated as part of the rule:

All metal chlorides are soluble, except $AgCl$, $PbCl_2$, and Hg_2Cl_2.

Look at another example:

The ionization energy for atoms increases as you go from left to right along a row in the periodic chart.

This rule is generally true, as seen from data in Figure 8–4. Note, however, that there are some exceptions (B, O, Al, S). Occasional exceptions to a rule do not invalidate the rule.

H 1310							He 2372
Li 519	Be 900	B 799	C 1088	N 1406	O 1314	F 1682	Ne 2080
Na 498	Mg 736	Al 577	Si 787	P 1063	S 1000	Cl 1255	Ar 1519

FIGURE 8–4 *First ionization energies (kJ/mole)*

LEARNING THE RULE

Once you have recognized and understood a rule, you must then learn it; that is, you must place it in your long-term memory so that you can recall it at will. The nature of the rule determines how you will go about learning it.

Rules to Be Memorized

Some rules must be memorized because they cannot be figured out from other information. Such a rule may be arbitrary—for example, conventions about how to write the formulas of chemical compounds. Others may be descriptive, that is, a summary of factual information. As an example of the latter, see Table 8–1, which states a partial set of solubility rules that students are often required to memorize.

TABLE 8–1 PARTIAL SET OF SOLUBILITY RULES

NO_3^-	All nitrates are soluble.
SO_4^{2-}	All sulfates are soluble except $SrSO_4$, $BaSO_4$, Hg_2SO_4, $HgSO_4$, and $PbSO_4$. $CaSO_4$ and Ag_2SO_4 are slightly soluble.
OH^-	All hydroxides are insoluble except those of the alkali metals, and $Ba(OH)_2$. $Sr(OH)_2$ and $Ca(OH)_2$ are slightly soluble.
S^{2-}	All sulfides except those of the alkali metals and NH_4^+ are insoluble.

The amount of detail in these solubility rules makes them hard to memorize. Similarly, rules for naming chemical compounds are detailed, arbitrary, and difficult to learn. For learning detailed, arbitrary, or factual rules, we encourage you to use the memorization techniques outlined in Chapter Six.

Rules with Meaning

Other rules are linked closely to concepts. To learn these, rely more on increasing the number of associations with these concepts rather than simply memorizing. When a rule "fits into" other organized information, it is easier to remember. One way to build associations is to link the rule deliberately with its underlying concepts. When you study a concept, study the rules associated with it at the same time. In other words, as you attempt to learn what an acid is (a concept), also learn how acids act (rules about acids).

In addition, try to find out why a rule works. This will make the rule easier to remember. For example:

Rule: The more polar a substance, the higher its boiling point.

Rationale: The more polar the molecules of a substance, the stronger the dipole forces between molecules. The stronger the dipole forces between molecules, the stronger the intermolecular forces and the more energy needed to separate molecules from one another. Consequently, the more polar the substance, the higher its boiling point.

To find the reason for a rule, think about how the rule relates to other rules and concepts. If you have difficulty finding a rationale for the rule, you should feel free to ask your instructor. "Why does the rule work this way?" is a good question and is the mark of a strong student.

Reviewing Rules

Whether rules are arbitrary or linked to concepts, you need to test yourself to see if you have learned them. Use self-testing to practice recalling rules, to review when and why a rule is used, and to review exceptions to a rule. Your goal for recall is 100 percent accuracy.

When you must learn many rules, develop summarizing devices to provide rapid review. For example, here is a shorthand description of the solubility rules from Table 8–1:

Soluble
  Nitrates: All
  Sulfates: All except Sr^{2+}, Ba^{2+}, Hg^{2+}, Hg_2^{2+}, Pb^{2+}.
            Ca^{2+} and Ag^+ slightly.
Insoluble
  Hydroxides: All except alkali and Ba^{2+}.
              Sr^{2+} and Ca^{2+} slightly.
  Sulfides: All except alkali, NH_4^+.

To test your recall of the rules, write out this shorthand list from memory and then check how accurate you were.

The periodic chart (see Figure 8–5) is a useful summarizing device for atomic properties such as the sizes of atoms, ionization energies, electron affinities, metallic character, and electronegativities. When you use the chart as a summarizing device, you give yourself practice in associating variation in atomic properties with position on the chart, as in Figure 8–5. However, you could also review the rationale for some of these rules and any relationships among them.

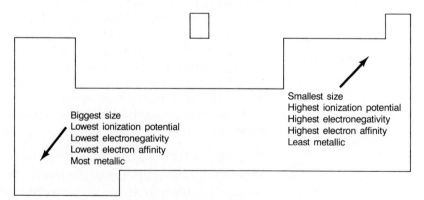

Smallest size
Highest ionization potential
Highest electronegativity
Highest electron affinity
Least metallic

Biggest size
Lowest ionization potential
Lowest electronegativity
Lowest electron affinity
Most metallic

FIGURE 8–5 *Using the periodic table to summarize rules*

Note: Summarizing rules for atomic properties is but one use of the periodic chart. The chart also provides factual information about elements (atomic numbers and weights), electron configurations, periodicity, and classification schemes (e.g., family names for elements). The periodic chart can help you in many ways—get to know it!

APPLYING THE RULE

Rules are taught so that you can use them—that is, so that you can predict the behavior, properties, and representations of specific chemical systems. Applying rules correctly takes practice. As you learn each rule, include with the rule statement some examples of the specific cases to which the rule can be applied. For example:

Rule: All nitrates are soluble.

Applications: $NaNO_3$ is soluble.
$Ca(NO_3)_2$ is soluble.

Rule: The size of atoms increases to the left and down on the periodic chart.

Applications: Co is bigger than Cu.
Ag is bigger than Cu.
Mo is bigger than Mn.
Is N bigger than S? Can't tell!

EXERCISE 4 Finding Applications

Go to the rules in your lecture notes that you have identified and analyzed (see Exercise 1). In your notes write several examples of varying appearance and difficulty of applications for each rule.

Anticipating some of the applications of a rule during study can help you recognize a test question that calls for the rule. In addition, look at some textbook questions to see how such questions might be phrased. It may not be easy to select the correct rule to use in a given problem. For example:

Problem: Which is bigger—an atom of cobalt or an atom of copper?

Rule to Apply: ?

The clues for determining which rule to apply are the names of two elements and the comparison word *bigger*. You are being asked to determine the relative sizes of two kinds of atoms. Atomic size was one of the properties linked to position of elements on the periodic chart. Recall of the appropriate rule comes about when you (consciously or unconsciously) ask the question, "What rule do I know for determining the sizes of atoms?" and find the answer in your memory.

Generate for yourself questions on which to practice using rules. The examples in your textbook or on old exams may help you get started. If you need more help, ask your instructor.

DEVELOPING YOUR OWN CHEMICAL RULES

Some rules will not be stated for you. Therefore, you will need the ability to generate rules for yourself.

Forming Rules from Data

Charts and tables contain many facts. What do you do with all the information? Learn it all? No. The individual facts are probably unimportant. However, the *patterns* or *trends* in the facts are important. Since these patterns or trends may not be stated, you will need to look for them yourself and summarize your findings as rules.

Table 8–2, for example, is a source of factual information used for various calculations. How is it organized? Take a minute to examine this table and look for patterns.

Note that electrons are gained in every reaction. The standard potential (V) is highest at the top and decreases irregularly as you go to the bottom. This much you can perceive, even if you do not know much chemistry. If you know some chemical concepts, you can find many more patterns. For example, at the top left of the table you find species that most want to gain electrons (e.g., F_2, metal ions and oxygen compounds in high oxidation states). At the bottom left you find species that least want to gain electrons (e.g., alkali metal ions, which prefer to form positive ions). Where do metal atoms appear? Metal ions? Hydrogen? Note these for yourself.

When organizing information from tables or charts, use the checklist in Figure 8–6.

A CHECKLIST FOR ORGANIZING DATA

Do the numbers increase or decrease as you go up, down, or across the chart or table, or do they appear to be randomly sized?

Are the increases or decreases between adjacent items approximately the same size throughout, or do the intervals get larger or smaller?

If the intervals change, can you link the change to any specific cause?

Do there appear to be any exceptions to the trend or pattern? If so, can you link these to any cause?

FIGURE 8–6 *A checklist for organizing data*

TABLE 8–2 STANDARD REDUCTION POTENTIALS

Reduction Half-Reaction	Standard Potential (V)
$F_2(g) + 2e^- \rightarrow 2F^-(aq)$	2.87
$Co^{3+}(aq) + e^- \rightarrow Co^{2+}(aq)$	1.82
$H_2O_2(aq) + 2H^+(aq) + 2e^- \rightarrow 2H_2O$	1.77
$PbO(s) + 4H^+(aq) + SO_4^{2-}(aq) + 2e^- \rightarrow PbSO_4(s) + 2H_2O$	1.70
$MnO_4^-(aq) + 8H^+(aq) + 5e^- \rightarrow Mn^{2+}(aq) + 4H_2O$	1.51
$Au^{3+}(aq) + 3e^- \rightarrow Au(s)$	1.50
$Cl_2(g) + 2e^- \rightarrow 2Cl^-(aq)$	1.36
$Cr_2O_7^{2-}(aq) + 14H^+(aq) + 6e^- \rightarrow 2Cr^{3+}(aq) + 7H_2O$	1.33
$MnO_2(s) + 4H^+(aq) + 2e^- \rightarrow Mn^{2+}(aq) + 2H_2O$	1.23
$O_2(g) + 4H^+(aq) + 4e^- \rightarrow 2H_2O$	1.23
$Br_2(l) + 2e^- \rightarrow 2Br^-(aq)$	1.07
$NO_3^-(aq) + 4H^+(aq) + 3e^- \rightarrow NO(g) + 2H_2O$	0.96
$Ag^+(aq) + e^- \rightarrow Ag(s)$	0.80
$Fe^{3+}(aq) + e^- \rightarrow Fe^{2+}(aq)$	0.77
$O_2(g) + 2H^+(aq) + 2e^- \rightarrow H_2O_2(aq)$	0.68
$MnO_4^-(aq) + 2H_2O + 3e^- \rightarrow MnO_2(s) + 4OH^-(aq)$	0.59
$I_2(s) + 2e^- \rightarrow 2I^-(aq)$	0.53
$O_2(g) + 2H_2O + 4e^- \rightarrow 4OH^-(aq)$	0.40
$Cu^{2+}(aq) + 2e^- \rightarrow Cu(s)$	0.34
$AgCl(s) + e^- \rightarrow Ag(s) + Cl^-(aq)$	0.22
$Cu^{2+}(aq) + e^- \rightarrow Cu^+(aq)$	0.15
$Sn^{4+}(aq) + 2e^- \rightarrow Sn^{2+}(aq)$	0.13
$2H^+ + 2e^- \rightarrow H_2$	0.00
$Pb^{2+}(aq) + 2e^- \rightarrow Pb(s)$	−0.13
$Sn^{2+}(aq) + 2e^- \rightarrow Sn(s)$	−0.14
$Ni^{2+}(aq) + 2e^- \rightarrow Ni(s)$	−0.25
$Co^{2+}(aq) + 2e^- \rightarrow Co(s)$	−0.28
$PbSO_4(s) + 2e^- \rightarrow Pb(s) + SO_4^{2-}(aq)$	−0.31
$Cd^{2+}(aq) + 2e^- \rightarrow Cd(s)$	−0.40
$Fe^{2+}(aq) + 2e^- \rightarrow Fe(s)$	−0.44
$Cr^{3+}(aq) + 3e^- \rightarrow Cr(s)$	−0.74
$Zn^{2+}(aq) + 2e^- \rightarrow Zn(s)$	−0.76
$2H_2O + 2e^- \rightarrow H_2(g) + 2OH^-(aq)$	−0.83
$Mn^{2+}(aq) + 2e^- \rightarrow Mn(s)$	−1.18
$Al^{3+}(aq) + 3e^- \rightarrow Al(s)$	−1.66
$H_2(g) + 2e^- \rightarrow 2H^-(aq)$	−2.25
$Mg^{2+}(aq) + 2e^- \rightarrow Mg(s)$	−2.37
$Na^+(aq) + e^- \rightarrow Na(s)$	−2.71
$Ca^{2+}(aq) + 2e^- \rightarrow Ca(s)$	−2.87
$Ba^{2+}(aq) + 2e^- \rightarrow Ba(s)$	−2.90
$K^+(aq) + e^- \rightarrow K(s)$	−2.93
$Li^+(aq) + e^- \rightarrow Li(s)$	−3.05

EXERCISE 5 Forming Your Own Rules

> In the space below, write two rules that summarize some facts in Table 8–2. Use the checklist in Figure 8–6 to help you find some rules. Some possible answers are given at the end of this chapter.

Forming New Rules from Old Rules

You may be expected to create new rules by drawing analogies from existing rules or by combining rules. For example, you can extend some of the rules based on the periodic chart. Knowing that AgCl is insoluble from the solubility rules, you might guess (correctly) that AgI is also insoluble since Cl and I are in the same group.

You may also need to extend a rule. For example, you may have been taught the following rules:

> The stronger the intermolecular forces, the higher the boiling point of a substance.
>
> The stronger the intermolecular forces, the lower the vapor pressure.

Are you justified in making the extension, "The higher the boiling point, the lower the vapor pressure"?

Yes, you can make this extension. Moreover, you may be required to do so on an exam.

Some Cautions on Forming Rules

Whenever you form a rule for yourself, you must consider it to be tentative until you confirm it by extensive use or until your instructor confirms it. For example, knowing the HCl, HBr, and HI are strong acids, you might guess that HF is also a strong acid since F is a halogen, just as Cl, Br, and I are. Your rule might be that all the binary acids formed from halogens are strong acids. Here, your guess would be wrong.

There is always the danger of forming a rule that is incorrect, either because you drew a wrong conclusion or because you were misled by a small data set. To avoid this, keep asking yourself if the rule you formed is giving you the correct answer *all* of the time. If your rule is not always working, this is your signal that it is incorrect or incomplete and must be revised.

Sometimes you will look for rules where none exist. For example, in using Table 8–2 you might try to form a rule that relates the magnitude of the standard potential to the position on the periodic chart of the element being reduced. There is no such rule. The trend in values is too irregular to be of much use in generating such a rule. The question of whether this rule exists, however, is still worth asking.

You can also form rules without being aware that you are doing so. For example, a common way to balance equations is to balance the left-most element first, followed by the element written immediately to its right, and so on until all elements are balanced. You may unconsciously form the rule that all elements must be balanced in turn, starting from the left to the right. This simply is not true. Your unconscious rule causes trouble in a case such as this:

$$O_2 + C_3H_8 \rightarrow CO_2 + H_2O$$

Here, you should balance the oxygen atoms last. A good rule to use when balancing equations is: "Leave until last any element that occurs in more than one substance on either side of the reaction arrow." The more aware you are of rules and how to form them, the less likely you are to form inaccurate or inappropriate ones.

MODIFYING RULES

In Chapter Seven we presented the idea that concepts evolve throughout a term. As concepts evolve, so may the rules based on these concepts. For example, you may initially learn that salts are ionic compounds that do not contain either the H^+ ion or the OH^- ion. So, when a salt dissolves in water, the solution that results is neutral—neither acidic nor basic. Later you may learn that some salts react with water (hydrolyze) to produce small amounts of H^+ and OH^-. These salts will produce either a weakly acidic or a weakly basic solution in water, depending on the particular salt that hydrolyzes.

Initial Rule: Salts dissolve in water to give neutral solutions.

Later Rule: Although many salts dissolve in water to give neutral solutions, some salts react with water (hydrolyze) to produce solutions that are weakly acidic or basic.

Since you will usually not be warned when a rule has evolved, you must learn to recognize this for yourself.

In addition, different rules may accomplish the same result. For example, the following two rules are used to determine relative melting points:

Rule: The more ionic the compound, the higher its melting point. (This rule allows comparison between ionic compounds or between ionic and covalent compounds.)

Rule: The larger the molecule of a nonpolar covalent substance, the higher the melting point. (This rule allows comparison between nonpolar covalent compounds.)

Both rules accomplish the same result, but each applies to a different class of substances. If you encounter such rules, it is up to you to determine which one applies in a specific case.

We caution you that some of the chemical rules you may be taught are likely to be simplifications. For example, it is a simplification to state that the larger the molecule of a nonpolar covalent substance, the higher the melting point, as stated in the preceding rule. This is not always true. For example, carbon tetrachloride, CCl_4, has a higher melting point than the larger molecule UF_6. Factors other than size are at work in determining melting points. Your instructor may or may not choose to teach you about them.

We have seen some students become truly upset when they learn that their rules have become obsolete or changed. They feel betrayed, as if they had been taught a lie. In one sense, they have been. They have been taught rules as if the world were simple. In actuality, the world is a complex system. For beginning students, some simplification of this complexity with "absolute" rules is helpful to get the process of learning started. Later, as students become more sophisticated, the messy nature of the real world can be admitted. Rules become less absolute, more in need of exceptions. In fact, in some areas there are no rules at all that can guarantee how the world works.

When you first begin your study of chemistry, you may find it useful to have rules on which you can rely. As you progress through the course, though, expect to give up some of the early rules. Instead of viewing these new rules as a source of frustration, look on them as a sure sign of your progress as a student of chemistry.

TESTING RULES

State the Rule

On the exam the simplest rule question asks you to recognize or state a rule. Such questions could have any of the following formats:

State Boyle's law.

What is the Pauli exclusion principle?

"Placing electrons into orbitals one by one from low energy to high energy" is one way of stating

   a. Aufbau principle
   b. Hund's rule
   c. Heisenberg principle
   d. Pauli exclusion principle
   e. Rydberg's principle

Deviation from the ideal gas law would be more pronounced at _____ (high, low) temperatures and at _____ (high, low) pressures.

Apply the Rule

The majority of rule questions you will encounter on tests ask you to apply a rule. For example:

> The formula of manganese(II) perchlorate is _____ .
>
> The molecules of which of the following gases have the same average velocity as nitrogen molecules at the same temperature?
>
> a. CO_2 d. C_2H_4
> b. He   e. If the temperature
> c. NH_3 is the same, all have
>   the same average
>   velocity.

Application questions can be made more difficult in several ways. Let's look at some examples.

Combining Rules

> How many protons, neutrons, and electrons are contained in an atom of tin-120?

Here we have three rules for the price of one.

Finding Disguised Clues for Rules

> Which of the following atoms would require the highest expenditure of energy in order to form a +1 ion?
>
> O   S   N   Na   He

"Expenditure of energy to form a +1 ion" is another way of describing ionization energy; the rule required is that of correlating ionization energy with position on the periodic chart.

Choosing Among Alternative Sets of Rules

> Name this compound: $Ca(C_2H_3O_2)_2$.

This question requires initial classification of the compound to determine whether naming rules for covalent or for ionic compounds apply.

Testing Exceptions to Rules

> Write the electron configuration for copper, Cu.

Copper has an irregular electron configuration.

Applying a Rule Repeatedly

> Rank the following atoms in order of decreasing electronegativity:
> P   Rb   Ca   H   Ni

This question requires the following actions: Locate elements rapidly on the periodic chart. Compare two elements and write them in decreasing order of electronegativity. Compare a third element to the first two and place it in its proper place in the order. Repeat for remaining elements. When finished, check to ensure you have decreasing and not increasing order.

Relating Rules to Other Information

Rb is a larger atom than Na; both are located in the same family on the periodic chart. Explain why you would expect Rb to have a lower first ionization energy than Na.

This question requires use of one rule to justify another. The reasoning is as follows: First ionization energy is a measure of energy needed to take the outermost electron away from an atom. The farther away that electron is from the nucleus and the more electrons between it and the nucleus, the less energy required to remove it. The outermost electron of Rb is farther from the nucleus and hence has a lower ionization energy.

Rules Used in Solving Problems

Rules are an essential part of problem solutions. Chapters Ten and Eleven will illustrate how rules are used in solving problems.

SUMMARY

Rules are generalizations that summarize chemical behavior. Most chemical rules describe:

• The behavior of a class of substances
• The systematic variation in properties of substances
• The relationship between two or more properties of substances
• Agreements about how to represent chemical systems

You must learn to *recognize* rules when they are presented in the following formats:

• Statements
• Laws and principles
• Chemical equations for classes of substances
• Mathematical formulas and graphs

Five activities can help you to *understand* a rule:

1. Learning underlying facts and concepts
2. Restating the rule in your own words

3. Determining when the rule applies
4. Determining what the rule accomplishes
5. Identifying exceptions

After understanding the rule, you must *learn* it by:

· Using memorization techniques (Chapter Six) for arbitrary or descriptive rules
· Building links to other chemical information (facts, concepts, and other rules) and finding a rationale for the rule, if possible
· Using summarizing devices for review of rules

Rules are taught so that you can *apply* them. To learn to apply rules:

· Develop practice sets of rule applications.
· Anticipate and prepare for test questions that will require rule applications.

Form your own chemical rules when necessary:

· Look for patterns and trends in factual data (use the checklist in Figure 8–6).
· Extend other rules that you have already learned.
· Observe some cautions to prevent yourself from forming inaccurate rules.

Since rules will evolve as your knowledge of chemistry grows, be prepared to *modify* rules to account for new information.

Anticipate how rules will be *tested*. Some questions will ask you to state the rule. Other test items will expect you to apply the rule to answer simple and more complex questions.

SELF-ASSESSMENT

1. I can recognize the rules that are presented in my course.

YES ——————————————————————————— NO

Rules can be presented to you in a variety of forms. See pages 161 to 163 for help in improving your ability to recognize rules.

2. In my course, rules are taught:

CLEARLY AND ——————————————————— NEITHER CLEARLY
COMPLETELY   NOR COMPLETELY

When rule presentations are unclear or incomplete, you must assume responsibility for teaching yourself about those rules and how to use them. The suggestions starting on page 164 can help you develop your understanding of rules. The suggestions starting on page 169 can then assist you in applying rules.

3. I can understand rules that are presented to me.

YES _____ NO

If you find yourself struggling with the rules that are presented to you, you may need to find some activities to strengthen your understanding of the rule. Review pages 164 to 166. Which of the activities from these pages seem particularly helpful to you? List these below to remind yourself of them:

4. I am able to learn rules efficiently.

YES _____ NO

Once you have recognized and understood a rule, you must then learn it. Pages 167 to 169 offer suggestions for learning rules. Are there any steps you want to take to help yourself learn rules? If so, write them below:

5. My course provides me with enough questions on which to practice applying rules.

YES _____ NO

As mentioned on page 169, you need a variety of problems on which to practice applying the rules you have learned. You may be able to make up some problems for yourself. Look for others in your textbook or on old exams.

6. I can form effective and appropriate rules for myself.

YES _____ NO

Do not expect that all rules will be spelled out for you. If you have trouble developing rules by yourself, look to pages 170 to 173 for help. Write below what you will do to improve your ability to form rules.

ANSWER TO EXERCISE

EXERCISE 5

Here are some possible rules from Table 8–2:

- Electrons appear only on the left side of the equations.
- When metal ions gain electrons to form (solid) metals, the standard reduction potential has a negative value (exceptions: Au, Ag, and Cu).
- Halogens (F_2, Cl_2, Br_2, I_2) appear only on the left side of the equation. They have positive standard reduction potentials when gaining electrons to form halides (F^-, Cl^-, Br^-, I^-).

CHAPTER NINE

Special Rules: Math Formulas and Graphs

Chemical rules can be expressed in the special formats of mathematical formulas and graphs. For example, here is a chemical *rule:*

> As the pressure of an ideal gas *(P)* is increased, the temperature *(T)* of the gas also increases in direct proportion, assuming constant volume for the gas.

This rule may also be expressed as a mathematical formula or graph, as shown in Figure 9–1.

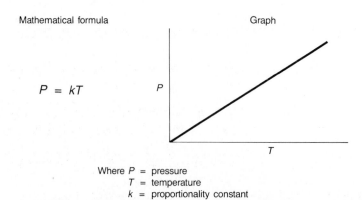

Mathematical formula

$$P = kT$$

Graph

Where P = pressure
T = temperature
k = proportionality constant

FIGURE 9–1 *Expressing a rule as a mathematical formula and as a graph*

Did you find the mathematical formula harder to understand than the verbal statement of the rule? Few people naturally think or reason in the abstract symbols that mathematical formulas contain. Most people tend to think in words or pictures. Yet, mentally operating with symbols is an essential skill for success in most chemistry courses. Mathematical formulas *are* rules; as such, they organize and relate chemical facts and concepts. Look for mathematical formulas to state exact numerical relationships among two or more properties of matter. Thus, formulas are "quantitative" rules.

Like any rules, mathematical formulas must have a class of situations in which they apply. Notice the difference between a mathematical *fact* and a mathematical *rule*, as illustrated in the following examples:

Fact: $\pi = 3.1416 \ldots$

Rule: $A = \pi r^2$

The fact states one, unchanging piece of information. The rule, on the other hand, gives the relationship between the area of a circle and its radius. You can apply this rule to different circles, each having a different radius and a corresponding area. To use the rule, you must be given values for one or more of the properties represented by symbols in the formula. You then perform the necessary mathematical operations to obtain a value for a property that has not been given.

Graphs represent even more of an abstraction than mathematical formulas. Graphs are "picture" displays of rules. In a graph, the value of one property is matched with a corresponding value of a related property. Each value is "plotted" on a grid as a single point that gives the simultaneous values for the two properties. When numerous points are plotted and a curve drawn to connect them smoothly, a graph results. To use graphs well, you need to be able to "read" the curve, extracting the rule—in words or in mathematical symbols—that is displayed in the graph.

You will need the ability to work with graphs and mathematical formulas in order to be successful in chemistry. This chapter will explain the unique characteristics of formulas and graphs and how to interpret and use them. It will conclude with some typical test questions for formulas and graphs.

UNDERSTANDING MATHEMATICAL FORMULAS

The mathematical formulas used in chemistry courses share many characteristics with the verbal rules discussed in the previous chapter. In particular, mathematical formulas, like verbal rules, specify the relationships among chemical concepts, typically among the properties of matter. However, math formulas represent these properties of matter in symbols rather than words. This use of symbols may initially make formulas difficult to understand and use.

Mathematical formulas have the following characteristics:

- Their symbols represent physical or chemical properties.
- Their constants are not always "constant."
- Their symbols have units associated with them.
- These units may have restrictions.
- These units must be consistent within the equation.
- The numerical values substituted for symbols may have restrictions.

We will use the formula $P = kT$ to illustrate these characteristics. This formula describes the relationship between the concepts of pressure and temperature of ideal gases, under the restriction that the volume of the gas remains constant.

Formula Symbols Represent Physical or Chemical Properties

The formulas taught in math class may be unrelated to any physical reality. In chemistry courses, however, the mathematical symbols usually represent specific chemical or physical properties. For example:

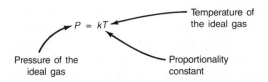

Only k, the proportionality constant, has no property associated with it.

When you first learn a formula, your most important task is to learn what each symbol represents. Be alert for symbols that can be easily confused. For example, T in the above formula is temperature, not time. Moreover, in determining what each symbol represents, recall how the present concepts relate to other concepts. For instance, you might link the properties in the formula with how you determine their values (e.g., pressures are measured with a barometer; temperatures are found with thermometers reading in Celsius or Fahrenheit degrees).

Translate formulas into words in order to check your understanding of the concepts represented by each symbol. By talking your way through the formula—that is, by replacing the symbols by the words that they represent—you strengthen your understanding of the formula.

Some Constants Are Not Always Constant

Some constants always have the same value, no matter what. For example, the value of pi is always 3.14159 or whatever decimal place you choose to stop the value of pi. In chemical systems, however, a constant may take on different values for different systems. For example, in the equation, $P = kT$, k is such a constant. As long as you are considering one particular gas sample with a specific volume, k keeps the same value, no matter how the values of P and T change. However, if you switch to a sample that contains a different number of gas molecules or that has a different volume, the value of k changes.

Symbols in Formulas Have Units Associated with Them

Values of physical or chemical properties are obtained by measurement. For all measurements you must specify the unit of measurement and how many of those units are present in the object being measured. For example, the measurement 4 inches represents a length in inches, equivalent to placing four one-inch lengths end-to-end.

Symbols in mathematical formulas that represent properties must have *appropriate* units associated with them. For example, appropriate units for measuring pressure include atmospheres, Torr, mmHg, and kilopascals. Liters or grams—units of volume and mass, respectively—would not be appropriate units for measuring pressure. See the Appendix for a brief review of properties and their units.

Units May Have Restrictions

Some property measurements may be restricted to certain units. For example, $P = kT$ holds *only* when the temperature of the gas is measured on the Kelvin scale, the absolute temperature scale. Other temperature scales (Celsius or Fahrenheit) cannot be used, because the pressure does not vary proportionally with these temperature values. Thus, $P = kT$ is not a true statement unless the temperature is a Kelvin temperature.

Remember from Chapter Eight that rules will be in effect only under certain conditions. Restrictions on units are a common way of restricting when mathematical formula rules will be in effect.

Units Must Be Consistent Within the Equation

Most mathematical formulas in chemistry are equalities. That is, one set of values is equal to some other set of values. The units on both sides of the equal sign must therefore be the same. For example, in the formula $P = kT$, suppose you want to obtain the value of P in the unit of atmospheres for a given value of T. T, as we have said, must be measured in Kelvins.[1] What, then, are the units of k (the proportionality constant)?

$$P = k \quad T$$
$$\text{(atm)} \quad ? \quad \text{(K)}$$
$$\text{units}$$

[1] By convention, the units of Kelvin are abbreviated as K, without a degree sign. This is in contrast to other temperature units, such as degrees Celsius (°C). Note that you must be careful to discriminate k, the proportionality constant, from K, the unit for the Kelvin temperature.

The units of the constant, k, must be such that when they are multiplied by K degrees, the units cancel to give pressure units of atmospheres. The units of k must therefore introduce atmospheres into the numerator and contain K in the denominator:

$$atm = \frac{atm}{K} \times K$$

EXERCISE 1   Using Consistent Units

Suppose the pressure in the above formula is measured in pascals (Pa). What would the units of k be? The answer is given at the end of this chapter.

Numerical Values May Have Restrictions

Quantities represented in a formula may have only certain allowable values. For example, T, the absolute temperature, cannot be zero or a negative number because of the way that the Kelvin temperature scale is constructed. Likewise, pressure must be a positive number. As long as some gas is present, it is impossible to have a gas pressure that is negative or zero. Since values of both T and P are positive, k, the constant relating them, must also be positive.

Note that you cannot discover the restrictions on the numerical values unless you understand the fundamental concepts that they represent. Work to understand concepts before you use rules involving these concepts.

Figure 9–2 is a checklist of questions worth asking about a mathematical formula. By answering these questions, you summarize the information needed about the formula.

A Checklist for Mastering Formulas

What is a verbal statement of the rule?

What concept or property does each symbol represent?

Is there another way to describe each concept or property?

Which symbols stand for constants? For variables?

For each symbol, what are the units used to measure the value?

For each symbol, what values are permitted? How can I obtain the value of this concept or property?

With what other concepts or properties may it be confused?

What common errors need I watch for?

FIGURE 9–2   *A checklist for mastering formulas*

FORMULA: $P = kT$

RESTRICTIONS ON USE: *Ideal gases only*
Volume (v) and number of gas
molecules (n) must be constant

VERBAL STATEMENT OF FORMULA: *The pressure and absolute temperature*
of an ideal gas are directly proportional
when v and n are constant.

FOR EACH SYMBOL:
   CONCEPT/PROPERTY REPRESENTED   *P = pressure*
   T = temperature (Kelvin)
   k = proportionality constant

   Alternative wording? *Barometric reading may be given for P.*

   Alternative calculation? *Pressure from barometer : P = g h d*
   Temperature: K = °C + 273
   °C = 5/9 (°F − 32)

CONSTANT OR VARIABLE? *P, T are variables.*
K is a constant for a specific gas sample.

UNITS: *P in Torr, mm Hg, atm, Pa, kPa*
T in K only

VALUES PERMITTED: *For P, T, k — all are positive and nonzero.*

CONFUSED WITH: *P may be confused with vapor pressure.*
T may be confused with time.

COMMON ERRORS IN FORMULA USE: *Forgetting to change T to Kelvin before*
using the formula.

FIGURE 9–3 *Formula summary sheet for P = kT*

A **formula summary sheet** can help you form the habit of asking these questions about a formula. We have filled out this sheet for the formula $P = kT$ (Figure 9–3) to illustrate how to use the sheet.

EXERCISE 2   Answering Questions About a Formula

Find a formula that has been taught in your course. Use the blank formula summary sheet in Figure 9–4 to fill in the essential information about this formula.

FORMULA:

RESTRICTIONS ON USE:

VERBAL STATEMENT OF FORMULA:

FOR EACH SYMBOL:
    CONCEPT/PROPERTY REPRESENTED

       Alternative wording?

       Alternative calculation?

     CONSTANT OR VARIABLE?

     UNITS:

     VALUES PERMITTED:

     CONFUSED WITH:

     COMMON ERRORS IN FORMULA USE:

FIGURE 9–4 *Formula summary sheet*

USING MATH FORMULAS TO MAKE PREDICTIONS

Rules are taught so that you can apply them to new situations. In this section we describe how you can use your mathematical formulas to answer nonmathematical, or qualitative, questions. We hold until Chapter Ten a discussion of how to use a formula quantitatively to solve a numerical problem (see pages 223 to 228).

Qualitative questions for formulas ask you to predict increases or decreases in one variable, given changes in the value of another variable. For example, given the formula, $P = kT$, you might be asked:

> Suppose the pressure is increased on a sample of an ideal gas (volume staying constant). Does the temperature increase, decrease, or remain the same?

Or, more simply put:

> Suppose P increases. What happens to T?

To answer this, you might reason as follows:

> If P increases, the value of the left-hand side of the equation increases. To keep the equality, the right-hand side of the equation must also increase. The constant k does not change its value. Therefore, if P increases, T must also increase.

EXERCISE 3   Answering Qualitative Questions

Fill in the blanks for the formula $P = kT$. Answers are given at the end of the chapter.

If P increases, T _____ .

If T increases, P _____ .

If T decreases, P _____ .

Direct Proportions

In the relationship $P = kT$, P and T are *directly proportional*. This means that as the variable on one side of the equal sign increases, the variable on the other side of the equal sign increases by the same ratio. For instance, if the value of T triples, P also triples; if P is halved, T is halved as well. There can be *no* added or subtracted terms in a directly proportional formula.

Two variables are directly proportional if the variables in a formula are located:

- On opposite sides of the equal sign *and* on the same side of the fraction line

OR

- On the same side of the equal sign *and* on opposite sides of the fraction line

All of the following are equivalent formulas in which P and T are directly proportional:

$$P = kT \qquad \frac{P}{T} = k \qquad \frac{1}{T} = k\frac{1}{P}$$

Inverse (or Indirect) Proportions

Two variables are *inversely proportional* if, as one increases, the other decreases by the same ratio. As with direct proportions, there can be no added or subtracted terms. For example, the pressure and volume of an ideal gas are inversely proportional. If P is doubled, V is halved. This inverse relationship may be stated mathematically in several equivalent ways. For example:

$$PV = k \qquad P = k/V \qquad V = k/P$$

Two inversely proportional variables in a formula can be recognized by analogy to the formulas for direct proportions. Try the exercise below.

EXERCISE 4 Determining Inverse Proportions

Fill in the blanks below. Answers are given at the end of the chapter.

Two properties are inversely proportional if they are located:

On opposite sides of the equal sign, *and* on _____ side(s) of the fraction line.

OR

On the same side of the equal sign, *and* on _____ side(s) of the fraction line.

Math formulas can relate more than two variables at a time. For example, $PV = nRT$ relates four quantities for ideal gases:

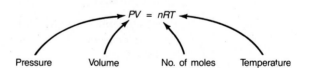

Note that R in this formula is the proportionality constant that relates the four quantities.

Direct or indirect proportions relate only *two* variables at a time. Thus, even if more than two variables are related in a formula, you are restricted to considering only pairs of variables at one time. The other variables would be considered constant (and therefore have no effect) on the relationship between the two variables you are considering.

EXERCISE 5 **Relationships Between Variables**

Fill in the following table for the formula $PV = nRT$. Answers are given at the end of the chapter.

Variables	Direct or Indirect Proportion	Variables Held Constant
P and T	_____	_____
P and V	_____	_____
V and n	_____	_____
n and T	_____	_____
n and P	_____	_____
T and V	_____	_____

Nonproportional Formulas

Some formulas taught in chemistry courses are not simple proportions, as in the following examples:

Converting between temperature scales:

$$5/9 \, (°F - 32) = °C \qquad \text{Fahrenheit to Celsius conversions}$$

$$K = °C + 273 \qquad \text{Celsius to Kelvin conversions}$$

Expressing acidity as pH:

$$pH = -\log[H^+]$$

Relating vapor pressure and absolute temperature:

$$(R)\ln P = -\Delta H_{vap}(1/T) + C$$

With formulas like these, it is more difficult to predict what happens to one variable as another increases or decreases. Therefore, if you are asked a qualitative question (i.e., does one variable increase or decrease when another increases or decreases), you may need to perform a sample calculation to answer it.

GRAPHS AS CHEMICAL RULES

Graphs are another format for presenting rules. Graphs are visual representations of how two properties are related. Individual "points" on the graph give the value of the property for a particular value of the other property. Let's look at an example:

For a sample of an ideal gas, measurements were made at three temperatures and the pressures that resulted at each temperature:

Pressure	*Temperature*
100 kPa	300 K
200 kPa	600 K
300 kPa	900 K

When these points are placed on the graph, the rule becomes visible: as the absolute temperature increases, the pressure of the gas increases proportionally, as shown in Figure 9–5.

You need to be able to construct graphs and to use them to obtain factual information and rules. In the following sections, we describe these skills.

Constructing a Graph from Data

Suppose you are conducting a laboratory experiment. You heat a solution and measure its temperature at 15-second intervals. From your data you can construct a graph of time versus temperature to illustrate how time and temperature are related. The data points may be the actual measurements of time and temperature, or some other value calculated from them. For instance, you might be asked to plot the reciprocal of time versus temperature (i.e., 1/time, temperature).

Graphs may be constructed from experimental or calculated data. For example, any time you have a mathematical formula, you can select two of the variables, assign a series of values to one of them, and perform a calculation to find the value of the other variable. This will give you the data with which to draw a graph. The shape of the graph might be related to a formula used to calculate the value (see page 192).

Although problem sets or exams occasionally require you to construct a graph, you will graph most often when writing up your laboratory results. Thus, we have included information on graph construction in Chapter Three, page 56. You might want to review that information now.

Stating the Rule from a Graph

Connect every graph you encounter with one or more verbal rules, as done with the example on page 180. The rule may be quantitative (an equation or exact mathematical relationship) or qualitative (general trends of increasing or decreasing values).

EXERCISE 6   Finding Qualitative Rules from a Graph

Figure 9–6 is a graph that shows the variation in vapor pressure with temperature for three different substances. Find several rules from this graph. Answers are given at the end of the chapter.

You may be asked to recognize graphs that correspond to mathematical expressions of direct and indirect proportions. When two variables

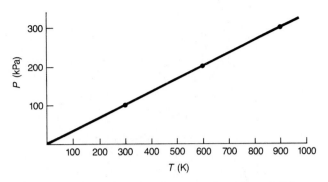

FIGURE 9–5 *Using graphs to make rules visible*

are directly proportional, a straight-line graph results (as in Figure 9–5). Note that the graph of two directly proportional variables passes through the origin, (0,0).

When two variables are inversely proportional (e.g., P and V of an ideal gas), the graph has the general shape shown in Figure 9–7. Notice, however, that the graph of two inversely proportional variables becomes a straight line if you plot one variable against the reciprocal of the other. Figure 9–8 illustrates this for a plot of P versus $1/V$.

Obtaining Factual Information from a Graph

When given a graph, you may be asked to find a specific point on it. For example:

> If the value of (one variable) is _____ , what is the value of (the second variable)?

Practice this skill in Exercise 7.

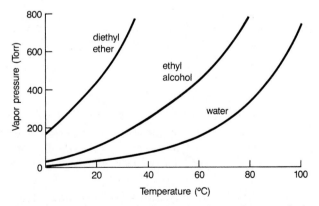

FIGURE 9–6 *Find several rules from this graph (see Exercise 6)*

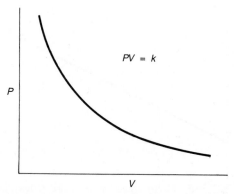

FIGURE 9–7 *A graph where P and V are inversely proportional*

EXERCISE 7   Obtaining Information from Graphs

Figure 9–6 is a graph of vapor pressure versus temperature for three substances. Obtain the following information from the graph:

1. The vapor pressure for diethyl ether at 20°C
2. The temperature at which water has a vapor pressure of 600 Torr

Answers are given at the end of the chapter.

Any linear graph can be represented by the general formula:

$$y = mx + b$$

Here, y is the vertical axis variable, x is the horizontal axis variable, m is the slope, and b is the intercept. Let's look at more information about each of these quantities.

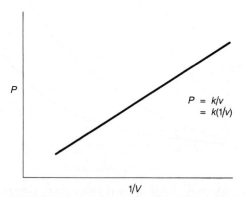

FIGURE 9–8 *A graph where P and 1/V are directly proportional*

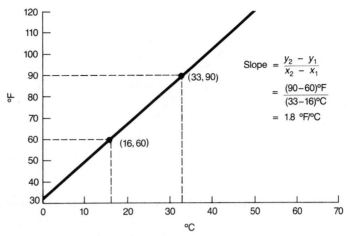

FIGURE 9–9 *Obtaining the slope of a line*

Slopes

The slope, m, gives the steepness of the line. It may be found by selecting any two points on the line, determining their x and y values, taking the differences between y values and between x values and then dividing those differences:

$$\text{Slope} = \frac{y_2 - y_1}{x_2 - x_1}$$

This is illustrated in Figure 9–9 for the graph of °F versus °C.

Since the x and y axes of graphs are usually assigned to properties of matter, the values of x and y will usually have units as well as magnitudes. Thus, the slope will also have units. For instance, in Figure 9–9, the slope has the units of °F/°C.

Slopes may be found without calculation in some special cases (see Figure 9–10). Line direction gives the sign of the slope (see Figure 9–11).

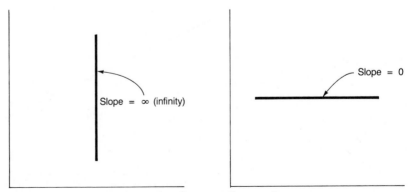

FIGURE 9–10 *Lines with infinite and zero slopes*

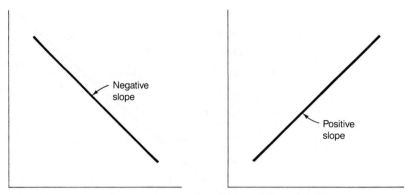

FIGURE 9–11 *Lines with negative and positive slopes*

EXERCISE 8 **Obtaining the Slope of a Line**

The natural logarithm of the rate constant, *k*, may be plotted against the reciprocal of the absolute temperature (i.e., ln *k* vs. 1/*T*) to give a straight line (see Figure 9–12). For this graph, determine the value, the sign, and the units of the slope. *Note:* ln *k* has no units; temperatures have units of K (i.e., Kelvin).

Intercepts

The *y* intercept, *b*, is the value of *y* when the line cuts the *y* axis. For example, in Figure 9–9 the value of the *y* intercept is 32. That is, when the Celsius temperature is zero degrees Celsius (0°C), the Fahrenheit temperature is 32 degrees Fahrenheit (32°F).

If you need more information on straight-line graphs, consult a basic math textbook.

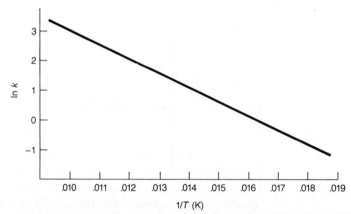

FIGURE 9–12 *What is the slope of this line? (see Exercise 8)*

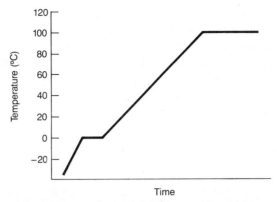

FIGURE 9–13 *A pure substance heated at a constant rate*

Linking Graph Data to Concepts

Conceptual information may also be obtained from graphs. Figure 9–13 describes the change in temperature when a pure substance is heated at a constant rate. Each part of the graph can be related to the concept or fact on which it is based. For example, the two horizontal portions describe the constant temperatures during phase changes and give the melting and boiling points of the substance (for water, 0° and 100°C, respectively).

Figure 9–12 illustrates the use of slopes to provide data linked to conceptual information. That graph is based on the equation:

$$\ln k \quad = \quad -(E_a/R)(1/T) \quad + \quad A$$
$$y \quad = \quad mx \quad + \quad b$$

The slope is equal to $-E_a/R$. R is a constant. Thus, when the slope value is found from the graph, it may be equated to $-E_a/R$ and used to calculate the value of E_a.

COMPLETING GRAPH MASTERY

Work for complete mastery of each graph. For example, are you able to draw a graph from memory? This is a high-level task because you have to supply all the information about the graph without any hints or prompts. The best way to ensure mastery at this level is by practice and subsequent self-testing to check that you still remember the information correctly. In the process of learning the information on the graph, you are able to check your understanding of the graph and what it represents.

Do not expect to be told to learn the graphs that are presented in lectures. We encourage you to do so, however, since test questions requiring graph reproduction occur surprisingly often. As you work to master a graph, use the checklist given in Figure 9–14 to ensure complete learning.

What does this graph describe? Does it have a title?

What rules are represented in this graph?

What can I use this graph to find?

What are the properties represented on each axis? Their units?

Are there restrictions on units for each axis?

What are typical values for each property?

What is the general shape of the graph?

Is there a general pattern or trend in the graph?

Does the graph represent an exact mathematical relationship which I am expected to know? If so, what is it?

Which parts of the graph are especially important (beginning and ends of lines, intercepts, horizontal or vertical portions, changes in directions of lines or curves, specific values, slopes, tops or bottoms of curves, etc.)?

To what concepts do these special points correspond? What are their units?

Can I draw this graph accurately from memory?

FIGURE 9–14 *A checklist for graphs*

TEST QUESTIONS FOR MATH FORMULAS AND GRAPHS

Test questions for mathematical formulas and graphs are similar to those for verbal rules (see Chapter Eight, page 174). Below, we list some examples of test questions for these two rule formats.

Give the Formula/ Graph

Write the formula for Raoult's law.

Draw the graph relating number of molecules to molecular speeds at two temperatures. Label the higher temperature.

Application Questions

The following three questions are listed in order of increasing difficulty.

According to "No Name's" law, as the pressure of a sample of helium gas doubles, the absolute temperature _____.

When the volume of a gas is doubled and its Kelvin temperature is also doubled, the pressure of the gas will

    a. increase four times
    b. increase two times
    c. stay the same
    d. decrease by half
    e. decrease by one quarter

Graham's law states that the molecular speed of a gas is inversely proportional to the square root of its molecular weight. If the molecular weight of one gas is four times that of another, how are their molecular speeds related?

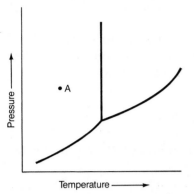

FIGURE 9–15 *Phase diagram for iodine*

Graph questions on tests will be similar to those described throughout pages 189 to 196 (e.g., constructing a graph from data). Here we give one final example of such a question.

In Figure 9–15, the point A represents a temperature and pressure in which

    a. $I_2(s)$ and $I_2(g)$ are at equilibrium
    b. only $I_2(s)$ exists
    c. $I_2(l)$ and $I_2(g)$ are at equilibrium
    d. only $I_2(g)$ exists
    e. only $I_2(l)$ exists

SUMMARY

Math formulas and graphs are two special formats for presenting chemical rules. Mathematical formulas have the following characteristics:

- Symbols in formulas represent properties.
- Formula symbols represent variables and constants.
- Quantities have magnitudes and units.
- Units may be restricted.
- Units must be consistent within formulas.
- Magnitudes of properties may be restricted.

Formula summary sheets provide the critical questions to be answered about a formula. Ask these questions about each symbol in the formula:

- What quantity does the symbol represent?
- What is its range of values?
- Is it a constant or a variable?
- What is its sign?
- What are its possible units?
- What alternative wording is used to describe this quantity?
- How can the value of this quantity be obtained?
- What is this symbol confused with?
- What common errors arise with this quantity?

Qualitative questions about a formula require no computations. Rather, they ask the effect on one variable when the value of another variable is increased or decreased. Such questions pertain primarily to formulas stating direct and indirect proportions.

We listed four common ways to use graphs in chemistry courses:

- Construct a graph from data.
- State the rule from a graph.
- Obtain factual information from a graph.
- Link graph data to concepts.

Mastery of a graph is complete when you can draw a graph 100 percent accurately from memory.

Test questions for math formulas may require you to state the formula or to use it. Test questions for graphs may ask you to draw the graph or answer questions from information on the graph.

SELF-ASSESSMENT

1. My understanding of the symbols used in mathematical formulas in chemistry is:

SOLID _____ WEAK

See pages 182 to 184 for a review of what symbols in formulas represent and how to develop an understanding of them.

2. I can reason qualitatively with the required math formulas:

YES, I CAN _____ NO, I CANNOT

If you need to improve this skill, review Exercise 5 and the sections preceding it.

3. Which of the following graph skills need improvement?

(   ) Constructing a graph from data
(   ) Stating the rule from a graph
(   ) Obtaining factual information from a graph
(   ) Linking graph data to concepts
(   ) Reproducing graphs from memory

If your math skills are not adequate for your chemistry course, you must improve them. Some possible actions include seeing your instructor for help, attending review math sessions or courses on your campus, or finding a friend who will tutor you. Whatever you choose, do not put it off. Do it now!

My Plans for Improving My Math Proficiency for Formulas and Graphs

ANSWERS TO EXERCISES

EXERCISE 1

Pa/K

EXERCISE 3

increases; increases; decreases

EXERCISE 4

opposite; same

EXERCISE 5

P and T direct; n and V constant
P and V inverse; n and T constant
V and n direct; P and T constant
n and T inverse; P and V constant
n and P direct; V and T constant
T and V direct; P and n constant

EXERCISE 6

Some possible rules from this graph:

· As the temperature increases, the vapor pressures increase.
· At higher temperatures, the vapor pressures rise faster.
· A given vapor pressure occurs at different temperatures for different compounds.
· The more polar the compound, the lower the vapor pressure at a given temperature.

Note: Do not despair if you did not find all these rules. The last rule particularly depends on concepts that you may not have learned yet. Rules depend on concepts, remember?

EXERCISE 7

1. approximately 450 Torr
2. approximately 94°C

EXERCISE 8

Slope (approximately) = −500 K

CHAPTER TEN

Solving Chemical Problems: Generic Problems

Chemistry students encounter lots of chemical problems. They read dozens of examples in their textbooks, see others worked out by their professor in lecture, and try many others by themselves. Few students, however, ask themselves how these chemical problems differ from one another and whether different strategies are needed for different kinds of problems. In this and the next chapter we examine these two questions. We believe that if you take the time to reflect on problems and how they can be solved, you can become a better problem solver.

What is a chemical problem? A chemical problem describes a situation and asks you to obtain new information about that situation. All chemistry problems are "word problems." They rest on the language of chemistry, requiring you to know chemical facts, concepts, and rules. Problem solving is impossible if you lack this prerequisite information.

How many different kinds of problems are there? Fewer, perhaps, than you think. Many students worry that they must learn how to solve hundreds, if not thousands, of different kinds of problems. Fortunately, this is not the case. In this and the next chapter, we explore ways of categorizing problems that will help you *limit* the numbers of *different* problems that you must learn.

For example, imagine you have been assigned 26 textbook problems on thermochemistry. You can learn to see these problems as belonging to only four or so different classes of problems. Rather than learning 26 unique solutions, you would learn four basic solution processes and some variations on each.

In this view of chemistry problems, we will therefore divide problems into two general categories—generic problems and harder problems:

Generic Problems: These are the "no frills," stripped-down problems, basic problems from which all other problems are built. Generic problems have a standard procedure by which they can be solved, which we call an **algorithm.** An algorithm is a series of steps that you perform, in sequence, to accomplish the goal of the problem. Each step in the algorithm produces a result that is used in later steps. The last step produces the desired result.

Harder Problems: More complex problems are formed by combining several generic problems, using more complex language, and/or extending the problem into an unfamiliar situation. You have *no algorithm* to solve such a problem.

In our estimation, there are but a *limited* number of generic problems—four to ten, perhaps—for each topic studied. We believe that if you approach problem solving by first looking to master these basic generic problems, you acquire for yourself the tools for solving more complex problems. You also reduce the problem-solving demands in your course to a manageable level.

In setting up these two general categories, we do not mean to imply that the line between them is sharp. As you will see in the next chapter, any problem for which the solution procedure is not clear can be treated as a harder problem. We also do not mean to imply that generic problems are easy problems. Rather, generic problems will require less creative thought than the "harder problems." In this chapter, we focus attention on generic problems, leaving harder problems for Chapter Eleven.

Our purpose in writing this chapter is to provide you with a powerful approach to solving any chemistry problem. Many students, when they first encounter a chemistry problem, ask themselves, "How can I solve this problem?" We encourage you to replace this question with the more powerful question, "What kind of problem is this?" Armed with this question, you begin the problem-solving process by seeking to relate the problem to others that you have already learned to solve. If the problem is similar to a generic problem you have already learned, then the solution process is already known. You then follow the appropriate algorithm to its conclusion.

Suppose you encounter a problem that does not resemble a generic problem you know. Now your job is quite different. First, you must engage in problem-solving activities that will lead you to understand and eventually solve the problem. Perhaps you can reason creatively, linking concepts and rules to accomplish the goal of the problem. Perhaps your professor will work the problem in class or you can find a worked-out text example to use as a model. However, your job does not end here. After obtaining the solution, you turn that problem into a generic problem by developing for yourself the solution algorithm. Thus, you add a new generic problem to your repertoire.

The process of becoming a strong problem solver in general chemistry will involve two tasks at first: (1) recognizing problems as belonging to classes of generic problems and (2) developing the ability to generate your own algorithms for generic problems. By building a complete repertoire of solution processes for each topic of your course, you provide yourself with the basic building blocks for solutions to many chemistry problems. When you encounter a harder problem, you can use these basic algorithms as tools, concentrating your energy and attention on the unique aspects of the problem.

In this chapter we will show you how to identify generic problems and how to develop algorithms for generic problems yourself. We will then describe a "package" of additional information that completes your understanding of the generic problem. Next, we will suggest activities that will improve your ability to solve generic chemical problems efficiently and effectively. We also will provide, as a addendum, a detailed look at the two most important algorithms for general chemistry courses: the mathematical formula algorithm and the conversion-factor problem algorithm. This is an opportunity to improve your mastery of these algorithms, both of which are useful throughout a general chemistry course.

IDENTIFYING GENERIC PROBLEMS

How do you recognize a generic problem when you meet one? As we pointed out earlier, generic problems are the basic, "no-frills" problems from which other harder problems are built. Therefore, you can expect generic problems to be clearly and simply worded, with little or no extraneous information in the problem statement. Here are some examples of generic problems:

How many grams of carbon dioxide are formed when 48.3 grams of carbon are burned in excess oxygen?

What is the density of a block of metal that has a mass of 71 g and a volume of 59 ml?

What is the pH of a 0.10 M solution of sodium hydroxide?

Not all generic problems involve mathematical calculations, as do those above. Some generic problems involve manipulation of chemical symbols and formulas:

> What is the electron configuration of Na^+?
>
> Draw the Lewis dot structure for PCl_5.
>
> Write the net ionic equation for the reaction of hydrochloric acid with sodium hydroxide.

Although such questions involve no computations, they are indeed problems because they require you to perform a series of steps in a specified order to solve them. Furthermore, they are generic problems because they have a standard solution process that you will be expected to learn.

Another characteristic of generic problems is that they constitute a *class* of problems. For each generic problem there are multiple problems that are essentially identical in structure and in solution. For example, suppose you have learned to solve the following generic problem:

> What is the weight percent of carbon in $CaCO_3$?

When you have learned the algorithm that solves this problem, you use that same algorithm to solve any of the following:

> What is the weight percent of oxygen in $CaCO_3$?
>
> Calculate the weight percent of carbon in CH_4.
>
> What percent is sodium by weight in $NaOH$?

Thus, these four problems should be perceived as being four examples of the *same* problem. They should not be viewed as four different problems.

You can look for generic problems in certain places. Recall from Chapter Two (page 19) that in most courses the lecture content most directly indicates what you are expected to know. Consequently, every problem worked by your instructor in lecture is probably one of the generic problems you are expected to master. By working these generic problems your lecturer is showing you how to solve a basic type of problem. Your job is to take that one worked-out example and generate from it a generalized solution process. Moreover, you will also be expected to recognize similar problems that will use the same algorithm for solution.

Textbook problems are also a source of generic problems. However, the text probably contains more generic problems than you are expected to learn. To identify those that are required, look to your assigned homework problems for guidance. Suppose you have learned the generic problems from lecture and still encounter assigned problems that seem to require a totally new solution process. This is an indication that you have encountered a new required generic problem. Look through the text chapter to identify a worked-out sample problem similar to the problem you need to solve. This sample problem is your source for identifying the algorithm for that type of generic problem.

Some lecturers and textbooks jump right to complex examples of problems, without working through the simpler, generic problems. In such a case, you might need to find generic problems for yourself. We can suggest two sources of generic problems. The first is a workbook:

Bassam Z. Shakhashiri, Rodney Schreiner, and Phyllis Anderson Meyer, *Workbook for General Chemistry Audio-tape Lessons*, 2nd Ed. (Philadelphia: Saunders College Publishing, 1981).

This book, with or without the audiotapes that accompany it, is an excellent source of worked-out generic problems.

Second is the list in Chapter Five of this book of topics taught in many general chemistry courses. In that chapter we identify commonly required generic problems within each topic. This listing indicates what kinds of generic problems you might need to learn. You would still have to seek out an example of each kind, on which you could begin the mastery process. With both sources, attempt to identify the required generic problems for your course, and concentrate your learning on them.

EXERCISE 1   Finding Examples of Generic Problems

> If you are enrolled in a chemistry course now, select a topic that has already been taught. Go to your lecture notes for that topic and identify all the generic problems therein. Be sure to include both mathematical and nonmathematical problems.

CHARACTERISTICS OF ALGORITHMS

An algorithm is a series of steps that you follow in order to solve a generic problem. Rarely will you be presented with the algorithm for a chemistry problem. Rather, you will need to devise the algorithm for yourself. To do this well, you will need some information about what makes an appropriate algorithm. In this section, we look at four characteristics of algorithms, illustrating each with some examples.

Algorithms Vary in Complexity; Choose the One That Is Right for You

Here is a generic problem which we shall call a "pH to $[H^+]$" problem.

Calculate the $[H^+]$ in a solution with a pH of 4.73.

One student's algorithm is as follows:

ALGORITHM	WRITTEN SOLUTION
1. Recall and write the mathematical formula pH = −log [H⁺].	$pH = -log\ [H^+]$
2. Solve for [H⁺].	$4.73 = -log\ [H^+]$ $1.9 \times 10^{-5}\ M = [H^+]$

A second student may write a different, more detailed version of this same algorithm:

ALGORITHM	WRITTEN SOLUTION
1. Recall and write the mathematical formula pH = −log [H⁺].	$pH = -log\ [H^+]$
2. Substitute pH into this formula.	$4.73 = -log\ [H^+]$
3. Enter the value for pH in my calculator.	$\boxed{4.73}$
4. Change the sign (hit +/− key).	$\boxed{-4.73}$ $\boxed{1.86208 - 05}$
5. Take the antilog by hitting the keys: inverse and log. This gives me the [H⁺]. (This last step may vary for you, depending on the calculator used.)	$1.9 \times 10^{-5} M = [H^+]$

Which of these is the "correct" algorithm? Both! Each is the proper algorithm for a particular student. For some students, using a calculator to determine the [H⁺] from pH is a source of confusion and hence of errors. These students, therefore, need to detail these steps carefully in their algorithm. Other students, however, may perform mathematical operations easily. They find it sufficient to write "calculate the pH," giving no instructions for doing this on their calculators.

Include in your algorithms what *you* need to remember to do. If you are in doubt as to what to include, it is usually better in include too much detail rather than too little. Months later, when you come back to an algorithm to review it for a final exam, you may appreciate the extra detail!

Different Algorithms May Exist for the Same Problem; Master One Algorithm Before Learning an Alternative

Here is a generic problem that we shall call an "[OH⁻] to pH" problem. It asks you to calculate the pH of a solution, given a concentration of hydroxide ion.

A solution of NaOH has a hydroxide ion concentration of $3 \times 10^{-4}\ M$. What is the pH of this solution?

This problem is similar to a number of other generic problems that ask you to calculate pH, pOH, H⁺, or OH⁻, given a value for one of these. Here is an algorithm that will enable you to solve this problem:

ALGORITHM

SOLUTION

1. Recall and write the mathematical formula pOH = −log [OH⁻].

$$pOH = -log\left[OH^-\right]$$

2. Use this formula to calculate the pOH.

$$= -log\,(3 \times 10^{-4})$$
$$= 3.5$$

3. Recall and write the mathematical formula pH + pOH = 14.

$$pH + pOH = 14$$

4. Use this formula to solve for pH.

$$pH = 14 - pOH$$
$$= 14 - 3.5$$
$$= 10.5$$

This algorithm, however, is not the only possible algorithm for this problem. Here is a second algorithm that works equally well:

ALGORITHM

SOLUTION

1. Recall and write the mathematical formula [H⁺] [OH⁻] = 1 × 10⁻¹⁴.

$$\left[H^+\right]\left[OH^-\right] = 1 \times 10^{-14}$$

2. Use this formula to solve for [H⁺], substituting information given in the problem.

$$\left[H^+\right] = \frac{1 \times 10^{-14}}{\left[OH^-\right]}$$
$$= \frac{1 \times 10^{-14}}{3 \times 10^{-4}} = 3 \times 10^{-11}$$

3. Recall and write the mathematical formula pH = −log [H⁺].

$$pH = -log\left[H^+\right]$$
$$= -log\,(3 \times 10^{-11})$$

4. Use this formula to solve for pH.

$$= 10.5$$

You may sometimes have the choice of several algorithms that solve a generic problem. Should you learn both? Not initially. If you are just starting to learn the algorithm, learn whichever seems appropriate, but learn *only* one. Stick with that one until you master it. After that algorithm becomes familiar, you can safely explore alternative algorithms. Ultimately, you want to have enough control of the process to choose the algorithm that works best for a given problem.

Algorithms May Involve Math Formulas and Unit Conversions; Learn Algorithms for Both of These Processes

The previous two problems have required the use of mathematical formulas for their solution (e.g., $[H^+][OH^-] = 1 \times 10^{-14}$). The process of using a mathematical formula to calculate some value is itself an algorithm. This mathematical-formula algorithm occurs as either the entire algorithm for some generic problems or as part of a more complex algorithm for other generic problems. One version of the mathematical-formula algorithm is as follows:

1. Write the mathematical formula.
2. Identify the value to be calculated and its symbol in the formula; assign values to all other formula symbols.

3. Transform the formula to isolate the symbol whose value is to be calculated.
4. Substitute values from step 2 into the formula.
5. Compute the numerical answer.

Can you use a mathematical formula smoothly and accurately? Alternatively, do you struggle when using a mathematical formula in solving a chemical problem? Beginning on page 223, we provide a detailed look at the steps needed for effective use of mathematical formulas. Work through that section if you need to improve your ability to perform calculations using a mathematical formula. Control of this algorithm is essential for success in solving general chemistry problems.

There is a second algorithm that commonly occurs within other algorithms. This algorithm also requires calculations but has no formula. The generic problem that this algorithm solves is called a conversion-factor problem. Here is an example:

A table is measured and found to be 48 inches long. How long is the table in feet?

A conversion-factor problem is one that involves changing a value in one set of units to an equivalent value in another set of units. Sometimes, as in the example above, the conversion-factor algorithm is all that is needed for solving the problem. In others, however, converting a value with one unit to another may be only one step in a larger problem.

Here is an algorithm for solving conversion-factor problems. This algorithm is referred to in some texts as the **factor-label** method, **unit-factor** method, or **dimensional analysis.**

1. Identify the situation and its stated description.
2. Identify the new description of the situation that is wanted.
3. Write an equation setting equal the stated and wanted descriptions.
4. Find the conversion factors that can transform the stated descriptions into the wanted descriptions.
5. Multiply the stated description by the appropriate form of the conversion factors from step 4 and cancel units.
6. Compute the numerical answer.

Just as with using mathematical formulas, some students can smoothly and accurately solve conversion-factor problems, while others need to attend carefully to the process. If you would like more information about working conversion-factor problems, study the section in the Addendum to this chapter beginning on page 228. In that section we describe more fully the algorithm's steps and how to use them.

Algorithms Include Two Kinds of Steps: Decision and Operation; Treat Each Kind Differently

Below we have stated the algorithm and solution for an example of a "Lewis dot" problem:

Write the Lewis dot structure for the F^- ion.

ALGORITHM	SOLUTION
1. Find the number of valence electrons in the atom (or ion) from its position on the periodic chart.	F $7e^-$
2. For an ion, add 1 electron for each negative charge; subtract one electron for each positive charge.	$\dfrac{+\ 1e^-}{8e^-}$
3. Write the symbol for the element.	F
4. Place dots around the symbol, one for each electron as determined in steps 1 and 2.	$\overset{\displaystyle\cdot\cdot}{\underset{\displaystyle\cdot\cdot}{:F:}}$
5. If the species is an ion, enclose the structure in a set of brackets and put the charge at the upper right outside the brackets.	$\left[\overset{\displaystyle\cdot\cdot}{\underset{\displaystyle\cdot\cdot}{:F:}}\right]^-$

Some of the steps in this algorithm are **decision steps**—that is, you must make the appropriate choice from a number of possibilities (e.g., step 1, deciding, from its position on the periodic chart, how many electrons to give to an atom). Other steps are **operation steps**; you need only follow the direction that is specified in the algorithm (e.g., step 5, placing brackets around the structure). Decision steps are often based on fundamental concepts and rules that you must have previously learned. For decision steps you must understand the basis for making the decision. For instance, to use step 1, you must know that the group number at the top of the column in which the element is located gives the number of valence electrons. Your algorithm will not be effective without this knowledge.

In this section you have seen some algorithms as well as explored some of their characteristics. You now know that the algorithm you make for a generic problem:

· Should be appropriate for you
· Should initially include no confusing alternatives
· May incorporate the mathematical formula or conversion-factor algorithms within it

· May contain both decision steps and operation steps

We are now ready to consider exactly how to determine the algorithm for a generic problem.

WRITING YOUR OWN ALGORITHM FOR A GENERIC PROBLEM

You will need an algorithm for each type of generic problem that you encounter. Few chemistry courses teach algorithms directly. Fewer still teach you how to form algorithms for yourself. Rather, most chemistry courses present you with models of worked-out problems, expecting you to find your own solution processes. In this section, we explore how to determine the algorithm of a generic problem, given an example of the problem. To illustrate the process, we will use the following problem:

Problem 1. Write the formula for calcium chloride.

If we were to describe verbally how to solve this problem, the description might be as follows:

Calcium chloride is an ionic compound, containing Ca^{2+} and Cl^- ions. Two negative charges are needed to balance the two positive charges from Ca^{2+}, so two Cl^- ions are needed. Thus the formula is $CaCl_2$.

This solution does not resemble the neat, step-wise algorithms that you have previously seen in this chapter. Let's work out the algorithm from the solution to problem 1 in order to show how you might create an algorithm for this or for any generic problem.

Identify All Steps in the Solution

Your first step in developing an algorithm is to identify all the steps used in solution of the generic problem example. Expect that this may require work on your part, as many examples will have essential steps implied rather than directly stated. For example, in working problem 1, your professor may have written only the following on the blackboard,

calcium chloride = $CaCl_2$

and said aloud, "You need two chloride minus one ions to balance the calcium plus two ion." This information is not an algorithm, but it does give you your starting point. Record it in your notes to use later when you develop the algorithm.

You begin the process of generating a complete set of solution steps by taking the initial information in the problem and reconstructing, in turn, all the actions leading to the final answer. One way to do this is to take the specific worked-out example and "talk" your way through that example, producing a verbal description such as we supplied earlier. It may help to pretend that you have to explain how to solve the problem to someone who does not know much chemistry. Your goal is to identify what you need to do at every stage of the solution process.

For example, the first step in writing a chemical formula for the compound calcium chloride is to identify the symbols for the elements (calcium and chlorine) and to identify their charges ($+2$ and -1, respectively). In Figure 10–1, we have written out a complete solution for problem 1. When you are talking your way through an example, do likewise and write down the steps you identify. You will find it easier to see what you are doing if you commit your steps to paper, rather than keeping them all in your head.

The series of steps you initially devise may be incomplete. It may take you several tries before you spot all the decisions and operations needed for complete solution of the problem.

Generalize Each Step in the Solution Process

Now comes the hard part. Each step must be generalized so that it describes not only how the information would be obtained for the specific example being solved, but also for any other example of that class of problem. Study Figure 10–1 now, noting how each step of the algorithm is written in general terms. Note that the generalized steps of the algorithm can be used as directions for writing the correct formula for many ionic compounds.

For another example of generalized steps, see the algorithm for problem 2, page 212. This and other examples of algorithms in this chapter may help you become more familiar with the generalized form of algorithm steps.

Generalizing steps in an algorithm can be extremely difficult, so don't be discouraged if your first attempts are less than perfect. Keep working toward your goal of being able to describe verbally how to solve a generic problem without referring to a specific problem. When stuck on a specific step, ask yourself questions such as, "Why am I doing this step?" or "What does this accomplish?"

SOLUTION   ALGORITHM

The compound contains Ca^{2+} and Cl^- ions.

1. *Identify the ions in the compound; find charges from periodic chart.*

Two negative charges are needed to balance two + charges from Ca.

2. *Rule: An ionic compound must have equal numbers of + and − charges.*

So two Cl^- ions are needed.

3. *Add more of the ion whose charges are in shorter supply until + and − charges balance.*

Thus, the formula is $CaCl_2$.

4. *Use subscripts to tell how many of each ion were needed to balance charges.*

FIGURE 10–1 *Developing an algorithm to write a chemical formula*

If you are really stuck on the process, ask for help from an instructor or friend in the course. Ask him or her to explain how such a problem should be solved, without specifying numbers or specific chemicals.

Modify the Algorithm for Different Examples

Once you have formed an algorithm, try it out on other problems of that same class. Different examples of a generic problem may require slightly different steps for solution. You may find that you must modify your algorithm somewhat in order to work easier or more complex examples. For instance, if you were to use the algorithm in Figure 10–1 to write the formula for aluminum carbonate, $Al_2(CO_3)_3$, you might want to add a step describing how to discover how many ions of each type are needed.

Algorithms should never be considered as absolute and unchangeable. Algorithms are guidelines for solving a class of generic problems. You may need to modify them continually as you encounter more sophisticated problems. This is the way algorithms are. Be flexible as you work with them.

EXERCISE 2 Expanding Algorithms

In Figure 10–1, write in additional steps that would allow you to write correct ionic formulas for calcium oxide (containing Ca^{2+} and O^{2-} ions) and aluminum carbonate ($Al_2(CO_3)_3$, made from the Al^{3+} and CO_3^{2-} ions). Answers are found at the end of this chapter.

Summarize the Steps in Simplified Wording

The elaborate algorithm that you initially develop exposes all the steps needed to solve a particular generic problem. However, it may be too cumbersome to use as you practice solving problems. You may want to produce a shorthand version of the algorithm that can be recited easily and quickly, resulting in a smooth, correctly ordered flow of steps. Such a summary can be rapidly reviewed, with each simplified step cuing recall of the more complete version.

The simplified algorithm for writing ionic formulas from names of compounds (Figure 10–1) might look like this:

1. Find charges on ions.
2. Write + ion first, then − ion.
3. Add + and − ions until the charges are equal.
4. Write subscripts.
5. Use parentheses for polyatomic ions.

EXERCISE 3 Simplifying Algorithms

Find a generic problem from your course. In your notebook, develop a written algorithm for that problem. Try using your algorithm to solve several examples of the generic problem, modifying your algorithm as necessary. Finally, write a shorthand version of your algorithm to enable you to recall easily the algorithm.

Suggestion: If you are expected to know how to balance net ionic equations in your course, try this exercise on that generic problem. Develop an algorithm powerful enough to balance the following equation:

$$SrCO_3(s) + HCl(aq) \rightarrow H_2O(l) + CO_2(g) + SrCl_2(aq)$$

Possible net ionic equation algorithms (full and simplified) will be found at the end of this chapter.

ESSENTIAL INFORMATION TO LEARN
ABOUT GENERIC PROBLEMS

To master a generic problem, you need a powerful algorithm—one that is complete and rests on an adequate knowledge base. This algorithm, however, is but one of several important pieces of information about generic problems. For any generic problem we suggest that you learn the following "package" of information:

· The "name" of the generic problem
· The formula, if any, that is used to solve the problem
· What the problem accomplishes
· The other problems with which it may be confused

This knowledge increases your ability to recognize an example of the generic problem and to use the algorithm successfully to solve it.

Let's now look at a generic problem to examine how acquiring this information completes your mastery of the problem.

Problem 2. Find the weight percent of carbon in CH_4.

ALGORITHM	SOLUTION

1. Determine the number of atoms of each element in the compound.

$$1C \qquad 4H$$

2. Multiply the number of atoms of each element by the atomic weight[1] of the element (to calculate the weight of that element).

$$\begin{array}{cc} 1 & 4 \\ \times 12 & \times 1.0 \\ \overline{12 \text{ wt } C} & \overline{4.0 \text{ wt } H} \end{array}$$

3. Add up the weights of all elements to obtain the total (molecular) weight.

$$12 + 4.0 = 16 \text{ Total wt}$$

[1]Obtained from the periodic chart.

ALGORITHM	SOLUTION
4. Recall and write the formula:	$wt \% C = \frac{wt\,C}{total\ wt} \times 100$
5. Substitute values (from steps 2 and 3) into the formula.	$= \frac{12}{16} \times 100$
6. Compute.	$= 75\% \ C$

What Is the "Name" of This Problem?

A descriptive title for a generic problem gives you a label under which you can collect all examples of the generic problem. The label can also help you identify the essence of the problem. For problem 2, the title could be "weight-percent" problem. Other generic problems that you may encounter will have titles such as "Hess's law," "limiting reagent," "mole map," or "gas law" problems. If a title is not given in class when the generic problem is introduced, make up one that has meaning for you.

What Formula, If Any, Is Used to Solve the Problem?

Generic problems such as "weight-percent" problems and "gas law" problems have formulas associated with them:

Problem	Formula
Weight-percent problem	$wt \% \ of \ element = \dfrac{wt \ of \ element}{total \ weight} \times 100$
Gas-law problem	$PV = nRT$

Other generic problems such as writing net ionic equations or drawing Lewis dot diagrams do not use mathematical formulas. Whenever a formula is needed to solve a generic problem, link the formula to the problem. In working with these formulas, give the same treatment to them as described on pages 181 to 186. For example, each symbol in the formula stands for a specific property, has certain legitimate units that may be used in representing the property, and so on. Check your understanding of the formula before attempting to use the formula in solving a generic problem.

What Does the Problem Accomplish?

This is one of the most important pieces of information needed about a generic problem. You know what a problem accomplishes if you can complete the statement:

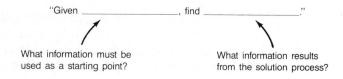

"Given _____, find _____."

What information must be used as a starting point?   What information results from the solution process?

You usually must restate the problem in your own words in order to put the problem into this form. For example, in problem 2 you could say, "Given the chemical formula, find the weight-percent of an element."

The "given–find" statement summarizes in an efficient way what the generic problem accomplishes. It may be easier to find this description after you have determined the algorithm for the problem, rather than when you first confront a new generic problem. Such a summary should be associated with every generic problem.

The summary statement helps you recognize examples of generic problems when you work homework assignments or test questions. Thus, when you meet a new problem, you restate what information is given in the problem and what information you are asked to find. This information may then be compared to the generic problems that you know how to solve to see if the new problem is a member of a known generic problem class.

With What Other Problems May It Be Confused?

As you learn to solve each generic problem, relate it to other generic problems in the same topic area. Compare and contrast these related problems to help you discriminate among them. Investigate how they are alike and how they are different. What kind of information is given in one type of problem compared to another? What kinds of results are possible with each? Especially confusing may be problems that accomplish the same result but are applied to different classes of substances. We will say more about easily confused problems in the next chapter.

These four questions help you summarize what is important about any particular generic problem. For example, with problem 2 you could now say:

- This is a "weight-percent" problem.
- Given the formula of a compound, I can find the percent by weight of a particular element in that compound.
- It uses a formula:

$$\text{wt \% of element} = \frac{\text{wt of element}}{\text{total wt}} \times 100$$

- This problem is the reverse of the one that finds empirical formulas when given weight-percents.

Note the similarity of the above package of information about generic problems with the information needed when learning chemical rules (see pages 164 to 166). This similarity is no accident. Chemical problems are often solved by applying several rules in a specific order. You need to treat the rules used in generic problems just as you would treat any rules.

PREPARING TO SOLVE GENERIC PROBLEMS

Your ability to solve generic problems will be tested on exams. In this section we will discuss how you can best prepare yourself to solve generic problems smoothly and without error.

Keep Lists of Required Generic Problems

As a topic is taught, one type of generic problem after another will be presented. In preparing for an exam you need to ensure that you have learned them all and that you can recognize an example of each type when you encounter it.

Many students find it helpful to keep a list of the generic problems that occur within each topic. Such a list would become part of your **topic summary,** the overview of each topic which you prepare before an exam (see Chapter Four, page 68, for a review of topic summaries). Include the entire "package" of information about each generic problem, not just its name and its algorithm. Also include a worked example of each of your generic problems to help you review the algorithm. Ultimately, you want to build in your memory a catalog of generic problems you have mastered. As you encounter a problem on an exam, you can search through that catalog to help you link the problem with the appropriate generic class.

Practice Using the Algorithm

Simply knowing an algorithm may not enable you to solve a problem on an exam. You must also be able to use the algorithm smoothly and effortlessly. You can develop your skill in using an algorithm by solving a set of practice problems. Look for practice problems in textbook problem assignments and on old exams.

As you practice solving problems, keep in mind the following suggestions.

Take No Shortcuts Initially

After you have used an algorithm several times, you may be tempted to take some shortcuts. Be cautious about this. If you find errors creeping in as you use those shortcuts, go back to your algorithm and work through it step by step, without shortcuts. Unless you work to eradicate errors during your practice sessions, these same errors are likely to show up on exams.

Focus on the Decision Steps in the Algorithm

Chemical algorithms have two kinds of steps: operations and decisions. Operation steps give directions for performing some action (e.g., "add up the weights of all elements") and often involve recall of facts or performance of a mathematical process. Decision steps require some form of judgment on your part, often based on chemical concepts or rules (e.g., "determine the number of atoms of each element in the compound," step 1 in the algorithm on page 212).

You usually need to pay more attention to decision steps than to operation steps in the algorithm. When planning the solution to a problem, concentrate on the decision steps before you actually begin writing anything down. In order to make the correct decisions, you must be sure of the basis for each decision and how to make it.

Identify Trouble Spots in the Algorithm

Trouble spots arise because a step is inherently difficult or because it is poorly defined in your algorithm. You also may have some weakness in chemical knowledge or in math that makes a particular step troublesome for you. Note where your errors occur as you solve generic problems. Plan specific actions to remind yourself of the places where you are most likely to make errors.

Do Not Change Your Process Too Soon During Practice

Chaos and confusion result if you change your notation, representation, or sequence of steps before you have mastered how to solve a problem. Stick with the method you are starting to learn until you master it. If a classmate or instructor tries to show you shortcuts or alternate processes, try (politely) to ignore him or her. If you alter steps before mastering the initial process, you are likely to mix up the new and the old steps and make errors. Later on, after mastery is achieved, you may allow yourself to look at alternatives that save time or energy.

Schedule Regular Reviews

After you have mastered an algorithm, plan short review sessions to maintain your control of it. How often you schedule these sessions depends on how well you understand the process and how involved it is. For material that is taught many weeks before an exam, weekly reviews are probably needed.

Work to Improve Your Accuracy

Some of the hardest errors to eradicate are the careless mistakes. Simply telling yourself to be careful does not work. If you have difficulty in doing accurate work, try the following:

Identify the Conditions Under Which You Make Errors

Are there particular times of day when you are most inaccurate? Do particular types of mathematical transformations cause difficulty? Become sensitive to your error-prone situations and avoid them if you can. For instance, you may schedule problem-solving activities in the morning, when your energy is highest, rather than late at night, when fatigue promotes errors.

Practice Working Problems Under Exam Conditions

Take practice sessions seriously. You may want to imagine that you are being graded on your practice problems. Work slowly and methodically, without skipping any steps in your algorithm. Write clearly so that you can see what you have written and check its accuracy.

As you work through an algorithm, check each step as you finish it. Put a check mark beside each step to indicate that you have gone back over it.

Keep Lists of Errors that Arise During Practice

In the process of practicing how to solve a particular class of generic problems, you will usually make some errors. These are "good" errors, since they alert you to areas in which your knowledge is incomplete or your problem-solving procedures need strengthening. Keep track of your errors. As you work additional examples, take note of similar errors. For example, when doing weight-percent problems, do you tend to add up the weights of the elements too quickly and come up with a wrong value? Do you forget to convert Celsius temperatures to Kelvin temperatures in gas-law problems? Whatever your errors, you need to become sensitive to them, so that you can work to eradicate them. Review your error lists on a regular basis to remind yourself of where you need to be especially careful.

Reward Yourself for Improvement

During each practice session, set an accuracy goal. Reward yourself for each session with fewer than _____ errors (you pick the number).

Accuracy is a *habit*. Work to build good habits during practice sessions so that you will not revert to sloppy behavior on exams.

Anticipate Variations of Generic Problems

Virtually all chemistry exams contain some generic problems. Let's look at some variations that you may encounter on exams.

Questions that Start in the Middle of the Algorithm

The first step in the algorithm for finding an empirical formula of a compound, for example, involves converting the weight percent of each element in the compound to grams of the element. A variation of the problem may begin by giving the weights directly.

Questions that Start at the End and Work Backward

Suppose you have learned a process for writing ionic compound formulas when given the name of the compound. A variation may give you the formula of the compound and ask you to write the name or tell how many ions of each kind are present in a formula unit.

Questions that Ask You to Write Out an Algorithm

You may be asked to explain how you would solve a problem—for example, how you would find the empirical formula of a compound, given the weight percent of each element in the compound.

SUMMARY

Generic chemistry problems are the basic problems from which all other chemistry problems are built. Generic problems:

- Are limited in number
- Have specified solutions, called algorithms
- Are clearly and simply worded
- May or may not involve mathematical computations
- Constitute a class of problems with multiple examples

The generic problems you need to learn to solve are usually worked out in lecture by your instructor or are found in homework assignments. Textbook examples can be used as models for solving generic problems.

Algorithms have the following characteristics:

- Algorithms vary in complexity. Choose the level of complexity right for you.
- Different algorithms may exist for the same problem. Master one version before learning an alternative.
- Algorithms may involve math formulas and unit conversions. Learn algorithms for both these processes.
- Algorithms include two kinds of steps: decision and operation. Each kind must be treated differently.

To write your own algorithms from worked-out examples of generic problems:

- Identify all steps in the solution process.
- Generalize each step.
- Modify the algorithm for different examples.
- Summarize the steps in simplified wording.

Complete your understanding of the generic problem by learning this essential information:

- What is the name of the problem?
- What formula, if any, is used to solve the problem?
- What does the problem accomplish?
- With what other problems is it confused?

To prepare yourself to solve new examples of generic problems, keep lists of required generic problems, and practice using the algorithms:

· Take no shortcuts at first.
· Focus on the decision steps.
· Identify trouble spots in the algorithm.
· Keep notation standard during learning.
· Schedule regular reviews.

Work to improve your accuracy:

· Identify conditions under which you make errors.
· Practice working problems under exam conditions.
· Keep lists of your errors.
· Reward yourself for improvement.

Anticipate the variations on generic problems that might be encountered on exams:

· Questions starting in the middle of the algorithm
· Questions in which you work backward
· Questions that ask you to write the algorithm

SELF-ASSESSMENT

1. My ability to spot a generic problem is:

VERY ———————————————————————————— QUITE
HIGH   LOW

It is important to identify generic problems because they are the basic problems that aid you in mastering chemical topics. Furthermore, they are the ones from which harder problems are built. Are you confident in your ability to recognize these basic problems when you meet them? If not, review the material on pages 202 to 204.

2. I must form algorithms for myself:

MOST OF ———————————————————————————— RARELY
THE TIME

Some chemistry courses do not provide direct instructions for solving particular kinds of problems. In these courses generic problems are taught primarily by example. How would you characterize your course? Are you the one responsible for forming the generalized solution process for required generic problems?

3. I am able to form algorithms:

EASILY ———————————————————————————— WITH
                                                              DIFFICULTY

Forming algorithms is a tough job. Suggestions for forming algorithms are found on pages 209 to 212. You may also want to try working together with other students to improve your ability to generalize problem solutions. You will find that the skill of forming algorithms is helpful for other courses as well.

MY PLAN FOR IMPROVING MY ABILITY TO FORM ALGORITHMS

4.   Usually, I can work generic problems:

EASILY AND _____ SLOWLY, WITH
SMOOTHLY   DIFFICULTY

Students have difficulty solving problems for different reasons. If you have trouble solving generic problems, try to identify the specific reasons for your difficulties. Check off on the following list the factors that might be important for you:

(   ) I do not always know what all the words in the problem mean. (Improve your concept and rule background before trying to solve generic problems.)

(   ) My algorithms give me the right answer only some of the time. (Perhaps you have missed some steps or are using an incorrect process.)

(   ) Mathematical problems are my downfall. (See the two algorithms at the end of this chapter.)

(   ) I cannot seem to recognize when to use each algorithm. (Pay attention to the "package" of information you need to learn about each problem. See page 212.)

(   ) I think I know my algorithms, yet I cannot solve problems on exams. (Review the information about preparing to use your algorithms in solving generic problems on exams. It begins on page 215.)

On which of these areas should you work to improve? Make some specific plans to strengthen your control of generic problems.

MY PLANS

5. My chemistry exams will probably contain:

MANY GENERIC ————————————————————————— FEW GENERIC
PROBLEMS   PROBLEMS

Look at old exams to estimate how many generic problems are on them. Compare the number of points for generic problems to the points given for memorized material, concept questions, rule questions, or harder problems. When you know the expectations of your course, you can effectively judge how much time and energy to put into mastering generic or harder problems.

ANSWERS TO EXERCISES

EXERCISE 2

Add the following steps:

Between 2 and 3:   If the ions have equal charges, use one of each.

Between 3 and 4:   It may be necessary to add some of one ion and also some of the other until charges balance. Or, use the charge of one ion as the subscript of the other and vice versa.

After 4:   Add parentheses around polyatomic ions before adding subscript.

EXERCISE 3

FULL ALGORITHM FOR NET IONIC EQUATIONS

1. Balance the molecular equation.
2. Identify each substance in the molecular equation which is solid (*s*), liquid (*l*), or gas (*g*).
3. Apply the rule: All solids, liquids, and gases are written as molecular compounds.
4. Classify all aqueous (*aq*) substances as acids, bases, or salts.

5. Further classify all acids as strong or weak; all bases as strong or weak.

6. Apply rules: All strong acids and bases are written as separated ions. All weak acids and bases are written as molecular compounds.

7. Apply rule: All salts (*aq*) are written as separated ions.

8. Cross out any species that occurs identically on both sides of the reaction arrow.

SHORTHAND ALGORITHM

Balance equation

Classify as *s, l, g* (keep together)

Classify (*aq*) as:

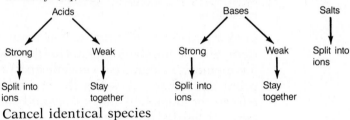

Cancel identical species

Addendum

In this Addendum we will examine the two most important algorithms for solving generic problems in chemistry: the mathematical-formula algorithm and the conversion-factor problem algorithm. We include these here not only because they occur as complete algorithms in their own right, but also because they form part of the algorithms for more complex generic problems. As important as these algorithms are, they are seldom explicitly taught in chemistry courses. Control of these algorithms will enhance your ability to succeed in your course.

ALGORITHM FOR USING MATHEMATICAL FORMULAS

Mathematical formulas are symbolic rules that state exact relationships among properties of substances. In Chapter Nine we presented the essential information needed for complete understanding of a mathematical formula. Review that chapter if you are unsure of what you need to know about the formula *before* you attempt to use it. In this section we will assume that you have already learned such information and are now prepared to use the formula to solve a chemical problem.

Figure 10–A1 presents a mathematical-formula algorithm. We will use the following problem as an illustration of how to use it:

> What is the volume of an ideal gas, if 3.0 moles of the gas have a pressure of 1.5 atmospheres at 27°C?

ALGORITHM FOR MATHEMATICAL FORMULAS

SOLUTION

1. Write the mathematical formula.

$$PV = nRT$$

2. Identify the value to be calculated and its symbol in the formula; assign values to all other formula symbols.

$V = ?$　　$T = 273 + 27$
$P = 1.5\,atm.$　　$= 300\,K$
$n = 3.0\,mol$　　$R = 0.082\,\frac{\ell - atm}{mol - K}$

3. Transform the formula to isolate the symbol whose value is to be calculated.

$$V = \frac{nRT}{P}$$

4. Substitute values from step 2 into the formula. Cancel units if possible.

$$= \frac{3.0\,mol \times 0.082\,\frac{\ell - atm}{mol - K} \times 300\,K}{1.5\,atm}$$

5. Compute the numerical answer.

$$= 49\,\ell$$

FIGURE 10–A1 *Algorithm for mathematical formulas*

223

This is a gas law problem that is solved by using the formula $PV = nRT$. It allows you to calculate one of the variables of P, V, n, or T, given the other three. To use this formula correctly, you must know that T represents the temperature in Kelvin. Thus, all data given in Celsius temperatures must first be converted to Kelvin before use in the formula.

We now elaborate on each step of the algorithm, describing the specific skills needed to perform each step correctly.

Write the Formula

CHIEF TASKS

· Choose the appropriate formula.
· Write it down without error.
· Know what each symbol in the formula represents.

When working a problem, always write down on your paper the formula to be used. This reminds you of the information you need to solve the problem and serves as a visual check that you have recalled the formula correctly.

Prepare for this step by developing an understanding of the formula and by identifying the generic problems that require its use. Note, however, that some formulas may be presented as definitions, requiring that you derive the mathematical formula for yourself. For example, given the definition, "Density is the mass per unit volume," you would derive the formula: $D = m/V$.

Identify the Unknown and Assign Values to Knowns

CHIEF TASK

· Associate the information in the problem with the symbols in the formula.

List all the symbols in the formula and after each, write an equal sign. Generic problems tell you clearly which quantity is to be calculated. Alongside the symbol corresponding to this quantity, write a question mark to remind you that it is unknown. Then assign the remaining values, being sure to record units. For example, from the gas law problem above:

$V = ?$

$P = 1.5$ atm

$n = 3.0$ mole

$T = 27°C + 273° = 300$ K (converts Celsius to Kelvin)

$R = \dfrac{0.082 \text{ L-atm}}{\text{mole-K}}$ (memorized value)

You may have to memorize the values of certain constants. Would you have been expected to know the value of R in this problem? Probably.

Some variables may be identified indirectly by their units. For example, the phrase in a problem, "at 27°C," identifies the Celsius temperature.

Transform the Equation

CHIEF TASK

- Use algebra to manipulate the mathematical formula.

You may need to manipulate the mathematical formula in order to isolate the symbol for the unknown on one side of the equation. The symbol for the unknown, when isolated, cannot be in the denominator. Such a process is called "solving the equation." The following algebraic rules can be used to solve equations for a symbol:

- You may multiply or divide by any quantity (except zero) provided you do so on both sides of the equation.
- You may add or subtract any quantity provided you do so on both sides of the equation.
- Usually, you should multiply and divide before you add and subtract.

These rules are sufficient for mathematical expressions that do not contain logarithms or exponents. Other rules are needed for these more complex cases.

Do you find yourself making "silly" mistakes in algebra, like "forgetting" to write a minus sign? These mistakes appear trivial, yet they can be costly in wasted time and in exam scores. To decrease careless errors, we encourage you to write down systematically all algebraic expressions and transformations. Do not take shortcuts, performing some steps mentally without writing them down. If you have all your work written out, you have a better chance of spotting and correcting errors.

We now offer you a chance to practice solving some equations for symbols, writing out each step completely. Read through the following example, and then work Exercise A1.

Given the formula, $D = m/V$, solve for m. Also solve for V.

Multiply both sides by V (puts V into the numerator) and solve for m.

$$D = \frac{m}{V}$$

$$V \times D = \frac{m}{\cancel{V}} \times \cancel{V} \quad \text{or} \quad m = V \times D$$

Divide both sides by D (removes D to isolate V).

$$D = \frac{m}{V}$$

$$D \times V = m$$

$$\frac{\cancel{D} \times V}{\cancel{D}} = \frac{m}{D} \quad \text{or} \quad V = \frac{m}{D}$$

EXERCISE A1 Solving Equations for Symbols

Solve, in turn, for each symbol in the following equations, just as was done in solving for V and m above. Answers may be found at the end of the chapter.

1. $PV = nRT$

2. $°C = (5/9)(°F - 32)$

3. Find a mathematical formula from your course. Solve, in turn, for each symbol in the formula.

If you had trouble with this exercise, you are likely to have trouble with any generic problems that require the use of a mathematical formula. You may need to improve your math skills. Ask your instructor to recommend an appropriate book for review or seek additional help from a friend or the instructor.

Substitute Values into the Transformed Equation

CHIEF TASKS

· Perform the substitution accurately.
· Check for consistency of units.

Now put into the transformed equations the values of each constant and variable. Cancel units, checking to see that they are consistent. For example, if the temperature had not been changed to Kelvin in the gas law problem above, units of temperature would not have cancelled.

Note also that the unit(s) remaining after cancellation must be appropriate to the property being calculated. In the gas law problem, the remaining unit is l (liter), an appropriate unit for volume.

Compute the Numerical Answer

CHIEF TASK

· Use your calculator rapidly and accurately.

Practice using your calculator until you can perform computations smoothly, even under the stress of exams. In practicing computation, work for the minimum number of operations that will give you the correct answer. For example, if your calculator has memory keys, you may be able to use them to simplify some operations.

Also, recognize the limitations of your calculator, notably:

· *Calculators do exactly what you tell them to do.* If you enter a wrong number into your calculator (e.g., punch in 3/2 instead of 2/3), it will give you the correctly computed wrong answer. After a computation, *always* ask yourself if the answer makes sense.

- *Calculators will not do algebra.* Work out algebraic manipulations on paper first so you know what sequence of numbers and operations to put into the calculator.
- *Calculators will not limit significant figures.* If you divide 3.58 by 1.32 on your calculator, the answer 2.712121 will be displayed. The answer, however, should be 2.71 according to the rules of significant figures.[1] If you write down 2.712121, you may be penalized.

Finally, chemistry problems may require you to do mathematical operations that you do not fully understand. For some students, this happens with formulas involving logarithms:

> What is the pH when $[H^+] = 0.023$ M?

To solve this problem, you need to use the formula: $pH = -\log[H^+]$. Even if you do not fully understand logarithms, you can still find the pH if you are able to carry out the following procedure on your calculator:

$pH = -\log[H^+]$	Memorized formula
$pH = -\log(0.023)$	Values substituted into formula

Use calculator: Calculator directions

1. Punch in .023.
2. Hit "log" key.
3. Change sign (usually +/− key).
4. Read out answer of pH = 1.64.

We are not suggesting that you forget about understanding the needed mathematics. However, you may not have sufficient time to understand fully both the chemistry and the math. On that rare occasion, solving problems without full mathematical understanding is preferable to not solving problems at all. When you have time, be sure to go back and learn the math.

EXERCISE A2   Solving Problems with Math Formulas

Practice the algorithm for math formulas on the following problems. Answers are given at the end of the chapter.

1. What is the density of a liquid, if 15 ml of the liquid weighs 22 g? $D = m/V$, where D = density, m = mass and V = volume.

---

[1] Significant figures, the selection of the correct number of digits to include with a computed answer, is a topic covered in many introductory chemistry courses and textbooks.

2. Calculate the Celsius temperature equivalent of 55°F. Formula: °F = (9/5)°C + 32.

ALGORITHM FOR CONVERSION-FACTOR PROBLEMS

Here is an example of a conversion-factor problem:

A table is measured and found to be 48 inches long. How long is the table in feet?

Like all conversion-factor problems, this one requires computation, but you will find no mathematical formula for its solution. Before we describe the algorithm for this problem, let's look at the problem's characteristics:

- The problem describes an object—a table.
- The problem describes one property of that object—its length, expressed in units of inches.
- The problem asks for an alternative description of that property—its length, expressed in units of feet.
- You must design a method by which the descriptions can be transformed. There is no convenient formula to use for this purpose.

One or more **conversion factors** are needed to change one description into another. A conversion factor is a fraction in which the numerator and denominator are equal in value, but different in numbers and units. For example,

$$\frac{1 \text{ foot}}{12 \text{ inches}}$$

is a conversion factor. Multiplying a measurement in inches by this conversion factor changes the description of the object from units of inches to units of feet. If you started with a measurement of 48 inches:

$$48 \text{ inches} \times \frac{1 \text{ foot}}{12 \text{ inches}} = 4.0 \text{ feet}$$

This conversion factor is derived from the fact that 12 inches = 1 foot. We call this fact an equivalency because it states that 12 inches and 1 foot represent the same length; that is, they are equivalent.

Two conversion factors may be made from any equivalency by the following method:

- Write the equivalency in equation form.
- Write one side of the equation in the numerator and the other in the denominator.

- Reverse numerator and denominator to make the second conversion factor.

Here is an example:

12 inches is the same length as one foot. In equation form:

12 inches = 1 foot

There are two conversion factors:

$$\frac{1 \text{ foot}}{12 \text{ inches}} \quad \text{AND} \quad \frac{12 \text{ inches}}{1 \text{ foot}}$$

These conversion factors transform inch measurements to feet and feet to inches, respectively.

Problems of this type are sometimes called **conversion-factor,** or **transformation,** problems. The algorithm to solve conversion-factor problems has been given several names: *factor-label method, unit-factor method,* or *dimensional analysis.* This is a powerful algorithm that may be used for both simple and complex problems.

We state the algorithm in Figure 10-A2 and illustrate its use with the following problem:

A pencil has a mass of 3.0 ounces. Express this mass in milligrams (454 g = 1 lb).

ALGORITHM   SOLUTION

1. Identify the situation and its stated description.

   3.0 oz.
   (English mass)

2. Identify the new description of the situation that is wanted.

   ? mg (metric mass)

3. Write an equation setting equal the stated and wanted descriptions.

   ? mg = 3.0 oz

4. Find the conversion factors that can transform the stated descriptions into the wanted descriptions.

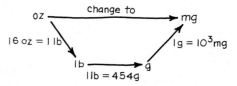

5. Multiply the stated description by the appropriate form of the conversion factors from step 4 and cancel units.

   $? mg = 3.0 \text{ oz} \times \frac{1 \text{ lb}}{16 \text{ oz}} \times \frac{454 \text{ g}}{1 \text{ lb}} \times \frac{10^3 \text{ mg}}{1 \text{ g}}$

6. Compute the numerical answer.

   $= 8.5 \times 10^4 \text{ mg}$

FIGURE 10–A2 *Algorithm for conversion-factor problems*

We will now describe each step of this algorithm in more detail.

Identify the Situation and Its Stated Description

CHIEF TASKS

- Picture the situation of the problem.
- Identify what property is known about that situation and the value (magnitude and units) of that property.

As you read the problem, picture the situation being discussed. Drawing a picture may help you visualize the situation.

Such visualization may be difficult when the situation is an *event in time*, not an object. Situations that take place over time are hard to visualize. Chemical reactions fall into this category:

> In the reaction
>
> $$N_2 + 3H_2 \rightarrow 2NH_3$$
>
> how many grams of NH_3 can be produced when 12 g H_2 are reacted?

This problem describes the chemical reaction between hydrogen and nitrogen gases. The property stated is the mass of hydrogen. Its value is 12 grams of hydrogen.

In some problems the property is difficult to recognize. Many students find it hard to think of the *number of objects* as a property of a situation. However, this property appears frequently as a stated or wanted property in problems involving grams and moles. Consider this problem, for example:

> What is the mass, in grams, of a lithium atom?

This problem is about an amount of the element lithium. The property stated is number of atoms. Its value is 1 lithium atom.

Here is another problem:

> How many atoms of hydrogen are present in 2.53 moles of H_2O?

The specific situation in this problem is a quantity of water. The property stated is the number of molecules, expressed in the counting unit of moles (one mole containing 6.0225×10^{23} molecules). The value of the counting unit is 2.53 moles of water.

Don't assume that every piece of information that is given in the problem may be needed to solve the problem. *Extra information* may be given as part of the problem. For example:

> The density of alcohol is 0.80 g/ml at 25°C. How many grams would 50 ml of alcohol weigh?

This problem is about a specific quantity of alcohol, 50 ml. The first sentence is an always-true statement about alcohol, not the stated description. You do not use the temperature in your calculation. Forming a mental image of the situation may help you discriminate the specific situation from other information given in the problem.

EXERCISE A3   Identifying the Situation

In the following problems, identify the specific situation (object or event), the property stated, and its value. Answers are given at the end of the chapter.

1. A pen weighs 3.2 ounces. How many grams is this?

   Specific situation:

   Property:

   Value:

2. What is the mass, in grams, of 0.76 moles of Ca?

   Specific situation:

   Property:

   Value:

3. $2Ca + O_2 \rightarrow 2CaO$
   How many grams of CaO can be formed from 22 g of Ca?

   Specific situation:

   Property:

   Value:

Identify the Wanted Description

CHIEF TASKS

· Identify the wanted description of the specific object or event.
· Note the property and the desired units.

In this step you determine what property you are looking for and the units in which it will be expressed. For example:

Calculate the mass, in grams, of one SO_2 molecule.

Wanted property: mass

Wanted unit: grams

EXERCISE A4 Identifying the Wanted Description

Identify the wanted unit and property in each of the following problems. Answers are given at the end of the chapter.

1. How many molecules of SO_2 are there in 0.20 moles of SO_2?

    Wanted property:

    Wanted unit:

2. Express 17 hours in seconds.

    Wanted property:

    Wanted unit:

3. How many milliliters of 0.26 *M* HCl are needed to provide 0.16 grams of HCl?

    Wanted property:

    Wanted unit:

Equate the Stated and Wanted Descriptions

CHIEF TASK

• Write an equation setting equal the stated and wanted descriptions.

This step may appear trivial, yet it is quite important. Here you actually state the purpose of this class of problem: to make the stated and wanted descriptions equivalent.

Write the wanted description to the left of the equal sign and the stated description to the right:

$$? \text{ wanted unit} = \text{stated magnitude and unit}$$

Write a multiplication sign after the stated value to remind yourself that you will multiply the stated value by some conversion factors. For example:

How many centimeters are equivalent to 5.3 feet?

$$? \text{ cm} = 5.3 \text{ ft} \times (\text{---})$$

Identify Needed Conversion Factors

CHIEF TASKS

- Find possible conversion factors.
- Select appropriate conversion factors.

This step of the algorithm is the most difficult because it demands the most decisions. Some problems will have an obvious path by which the stated description is converted to the wanted description. When this is not the case, you must look in the problem for some possible conversion factors to use in the transformation. Furthermore, you must analyze the units of stated and wanted descriptions for both the system of measurement (English or metric) and for the property being measured (length, heat, number of particles, etc.) as a basis for planning the conversion.

Some conversion factors will be given in equation form in the problem statement. But there are other sources of conversion factors.

Your memory is one source. For example:

> How many centimeters are in 5.72 kilometers?

To solve this problem, you will need to have memorized some common metric equivalencies (i.e., 1 kilometer = 1000 meters; 1 meter = 100 centimeters). Other information you may need to have memorized to solve chemistry problems includes:

Time units (e.g., 60 sec = 1 min)
English measurements (e.g., 3 feet = 1 yard)

Another source is previously learned chemical knowledge:

> How many moles are in 77 grams of CO_2?

Conversion Factor: 1 mole CO_2 = 44 g CO_2

You may be expected to know that the chemical formula of any substance is sufficient information to provide gram/mole conversion factors. You do this by adding up atomic weights (from the periodic chart) of all atoms in the formula and equating that weight in grams to 1 mole of the substance.

Verbal conversion factors are sometimes given in the problem statement:

> A rod is 5.5 yards. How many rods are in 15 feet?

Conversion Factor: 1 rod = 5.5 yards.

> You want to drive to Chicago, 250 miles away. Your beat-up old car takes 30 minutes to drive 15 miles. How many hours would it take you to get to Chicago?

Conversion Factor: 30 minutes = 15 miles

EXERCISE A5   Finding Conversion Factors

Write in equation form all conversion factors stated in the following problems. Answers are given at the end of the chapter.

1. A soft drink costs 40 cents per can. The neighborhood store will give you 5 cents for every returnable can you bring in. How many cans must you return in order to buy a six-pack of soft drink cans?

2. A dollar of American currency will buy 0.6 pounds sterling (English money) on the international money market. If you bought 6 shirts at 5 pounds sterling each, how much would they cost in dollars?

Compound units are still another source of conversion factors:

> The density of the liquid was 2.3 g/ml.

Conversion Factor: 2.3 grams = 1 ml

Note: 2.3 g/ml may also be written "2.3 grams per milliliter."

All percents can be expressed as conversion factors:

> Water is 11 percent hydrogen by weight.

This means that there are 11 grams of hydrogen contained in every 100 grams of water. Because this percent does not specify particular weight units, it is also true that there are 11 pounds of hydrogen for every 100 pounds of water.

Conversion Factors: 11 g hydrogen = 100 g water, or 11 lb hydrogen = 100 lb water, or other similar equivalencies

EXERCISE A6   Converting Compound Units

Write equation forms of conversion factors for the following. Answers are given at the end of the chapter.

1. The density of gold is 19.3 g/ml.

2. The molarity of the solution was 1.45 moles NaOH per liter of solution.

3. The compound was 17.5 percent carbon by weight.

4. The air was contaminated to the level of 15.6 parts per million SO_2, (i.e., there were 15.6 weight units of SO_2 for every 1 million weight units of air).

Identifying conversion factors in a problem gives you valuable hints as to how to plan a conversion path. In the following four problems, we illustrate how to map out a solution pathway for conversion-factor problems.

1. **How many milligrams are equivalent to 0.038 ounces? (454 grams = 1 pound)**

Transform: 0.038 ounces (English, mass) to milligrams (metric, mass).

Path:

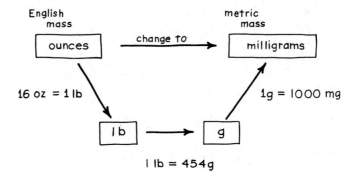

2. **How many milliliters of 0.534 M HCl solution would be needed to provide 25.8 grams of HCl?**

Transform: 25.8 g HCl (mass of HCl) to milliliters (volume of solution); all units in metric.

Path:

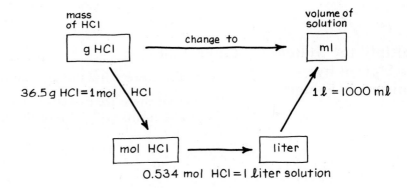

3. Express the speed limit of 55 miles per hour in terms of meters per second.

Two Transformations: Miles (English length) to meters (metric length). Also hours (time) to seconds (time).

Path:

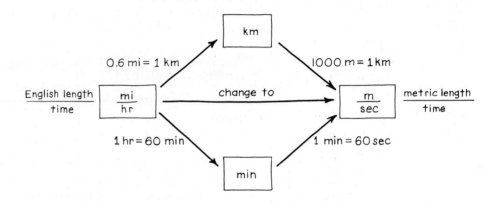

4. How many moles of Ca atoms are contained in 77 grams of $Ca(OH)_2$?

Transformation: Grams $Ca(OH)_2$ (metric mass) to moles Ca (counting numbers of atoms, metric). *Note:* This transformation involves a change of substance.

Path:

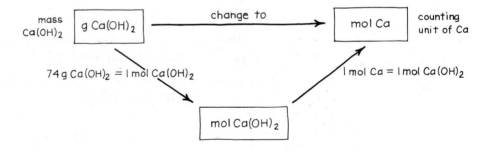

Multiply the Stated Description by Conversion Factors

CHIEF TASK

· Write the correct fractional form of conversion factors.

Recall that there are two fractional forms of a conversion factor. Only one of these forms will achieve the correct transformation:

$$48 \text{ inches} \times \frac{1 \text{ foot}}{12 \text{ inches}} = 4.0 \text{ feet}$$

If the wrong fractional form of the conversion factor is used, no units cancel and the stated description is not transformed:

$$48 \text{ inches} \times \frac{12 \text{ inches}}{1 \text{ foot}} = \text{ ?!}$$

Compute the Final Answer

CHIEF TASKS

· Use your calculator accurately.
· Check final units.

All points about computation (page 226) apply here. Note that the problem solution is not complete until you have checked the units to see if they are consistent with the wanted units.

EXERCISE A7 Solving Conversion Problems

In the space below, solve Problems 2 to 4 from above. Problem 1 is done to illustrate the entire process of using this algorithm.

1. How many milligrams are equivalent to 0.038 ounces? (454 grams = 1 pound)

$$? \text{ milligrams} = 0.038 \text{ oz} \times \frac{1 \text{ lb}}{16 \text{ oz}} \times \frac{454 \text{ g}}{1 \text{ lb}} \times \frac{1000 \text{ mg}}{1 \text{ g}}$$
$$= 1.1 \times 10^2 \text{ mg}$$

2. How many milliliters of 0.534 M HCl solution would be needed to provide 25.8 grams of HCl?

3. Express the speed limit 55 miles per hour in terms of meters per second.

4. How many moles of Ca atoms are contained in 77 grams of $Ca(OH)_2$?

ANSWERS TO EXERCISES

EXERCISE A1

1. $P = nRT/V$; $V = nRT/P$; $n = PV/RT$; $R = PV/nT$; $T = PV/nR$
2. $°F = (9/5)°C + 32$

EXERCISE A2

1. $D = ?$ $D = \dfrac{m}{V}$
   $m = 22$ g
   $V = 15$ ml
   $\qquad = \dfrac{22 \text{ g}}{15 \text{ ml}}$
   $\qquad = 1.5$ g/ml

2. $°C = ?$ $°F = \dfrac{9}{5} °C + 32$ $\dfrac{5}{9}(55 - 32) = °C$
   $°F = 55°$
   $\qquad °F - 32 = \dfrac{9}{5} °C$ $\dfrac{5}{9}(23) = °C$
   $\qquad \dfrac{5}{9}(°F - 32) = °C$ $13° = °C$

Exercise A3

1. a pen; mass, English; 3.2 ounces
2. an amount of calcium; number of Ca atoms; 0.76 mole Ca
3. an amount of calcium; mass, metric; 22 g Ca

EXERCISE A4

1. number of SO_2 particles; SO_2 molecules
2. time; seconds
3. volume of solution; milliliters

EXERCISE A5

1. 1 can = 40 cents
   5 cents = 1 bottle
2. $1 = 0.6 pound sterling
   1 shirt = 5 pounds sterling

EXERCISE A6

1. 19.3 g gold = 1.00 ml gold
2. 1.45 moles NaOH = 1.00 liter solution
3. 17.5 g C = 100 g compound
4. 15.6 g SO_2 = 1,000,000 g air

EXERCISE A7

2.

$$? \text{ ml} = 25.8 \text{ g } \cancel{\text{HCl}} \times \frac{1 \cancel{\text{ mole }} \text{HCl}}{36.5 \text{ g } \cancel{\text{HCl}}} \times \frac{1 \cancel{L}}{0.534 \cancel{\text{ mole }} \text{HCl}} \times \frac{1000 \text{ ml}}{1 \cancel{L}}$$

$$= 1.32 \times 10^3 \text{ ml}$$

3.

$$? \frac{\text{m}}{\text{sec}} = 55 \frac{\text{mi}}{\text{hr}} \times \frac{1 \text{ km}}{0.6 \text{ mi}} \times \frac{1000 \text{ m}}{1 \text{ km}} \times \frac{1 \text{ hr}}{60 \text{ min}} \times \frac{1 \text{ min}}{60 \text{ sec}}$$

$$= 25 \frac{\text{m}}{\text{sec}}$$

4.

$$? \text{ mole Ca} = 77 \text{ g Ca(OH)}_2 \times \frac{1 \text{ mole Ca(OH)}_2}{74 \text{ g Ca(OH)}_2} \times \frac{1 \text{ mole Ca}}{1 \text{ mole Ca(OH)}_2}$$

$$= 1.0 \text{ mole Ca}$$

CHAPTER ELEVEN

Solving Chemical Problems: Harder Problems

Imagine that you have just started a homework assignment. Upon reading the first question, you have a flash of recognition. "Aha, I know how to do this problem."

But as you continue to work problems in the assignment, you find that they become more difficult. While still somewhat familiar, less and less do they resemble the generic problems that you have carefully learned. Soon you are stuck and unable to use any algorithm to solve the problem.

Now, you are working *hard problems*. Hard problems are ones for which you will not have a solution algorithm. They can be made by:

- Combining two or more concepts, rules, or algorithms in one problem
- Extending an algorithm or rule into an unfamiliar context
- Making one or more steps in an algorithm more difficult than usual
- Wording the problem in complex language
- *All of the above*

Is there a sharp distinction between hard problems and generic problems? No. One student may see a particular chemistry problem as only a slight variation on a generic problem and solve it with ease, whereas another student may be totally baffled. Thus, we will not split hairs in attempting to distinguish between hard and generic problems. Any problem to which the solution is not immediately obvious is a hard problem for you. Treat it as such.

This chapter will strengthen your ability to solve hard problems. We will look at what hard problems are, how they are constructed out of simpler material, and how you can learn to solve them. We present the 12 most common types of hard problems and give suggestions for mastering each. We will next propose some problem-solving techniques for use with any chemistry problem requiring creative thought.

All chemistry problems, generic and otherwise, are word problems. They rest on the language of chemistry, requiring you to understand chemical facts, concepts, rules, and algorithms in order to solve them. If you do not know the prerequisite information needed for a problem, you will be unable to solve that problem. In such a case your problem-solving skills are not weak, but your knowledge base is. Thus, it is risky to attempt to work problems before you have studied the fundamental information related to those problems. None of the suggestions in this chapter for solving problems can overcome an inadequate knowledge base.

Prerequisite chemical knowledge is necessary but not sufficient for effective problem solving. Unfortunately, skills needed to cope with hard problems are rarely directly taught in chemistry courses. So how are you expected to learn to cope with hard problems?

The simplest answer is that you learn to solve hard problems by working at them. That is, you do all the problems that are assigned. By struggling to find solutions to them, you learn better how to cope with problems requiring creative thought. The information in the following sections can help you understand how each hard problem relates to the generic problems and other prerequisite information. You can learn to recognize and solve the common varieties of hard problems. The general problem-solving strategies we will discuss (beginning on page 252) can help to improve your approach to any chemistry problem.

Your chemistry course also offers help, even if it does not teach problem-solving skills directly. Ask your instructor to solve some problems out loud and let you observe how she or he goes about the process. Ask your instructor to watch you solve a problem and suggest improvements in your approach.

You can also work together with other students on ungraded problem assignments. Problem solving should often be a group activity. Learn from the approaches and mistakes of others in your group. Working together saves time in completing assignments and allows every participant to share in the group expertise.

Above all, when working problems, concentrate on *how* the problems are being solved. It is the *process* and not the answer that is important in learning to solve problems.

THE DIRTY DOZEN: TWELVE TYPES OF HARD CHEMISTRY PROBLEMS

Hard problems in chemistry are rarely totally new. They often involve familiar processes and knowledge put together in unfamiliar ways. In this section we present 12 ways in which generic problems are combined, extended, or otherwise disguised. When you work assigned or test problems, first try to identify which algorithms might be involved in the solution to the problem. Since these are hard problems, there will be some barrier to your use of a solution process in the usual manner.

We have organized the following 12 hard problems according to the barriers that prevent their solution. Each problem type will be introduced by a descriptive label, followed by a comment or question that you might mutter while struggling with such a problem. The characteristics of that problem type are then described, along with some possible ways of overcoming the barrier.

Magician Problems

STUDENT: I knew what to do and I did it. I just forgot to go back and answer the question that they really asked.

These problems ask you to solve a familiar problem, usually an involved one. However, at the end they do not ask you for the usual answer. Instead, they ask you to take the result of your work and apply it in some (usually) simple way to answer an additional question. Consider this example:

> Describe how you would prepare 100 ml of a 0.35 M NaOH solution.

This problem is based on the generic problem: Given the volume and concentration of a solution, find the amount of solute contained in it. The generic version might be worded: "How many grams of NaOH are needed to prepare 100 ml of 0.35 M NaOH solution?" Both the generic version and the "magician" version require the same calculation. But the magician version requires the additional step of describing how to convert that amount of NaOH into 100 ml of solution: Place some distilled water in the volumetric flask and add the solid NaOH to it; mix well to dissolve the NaOH; then add distilled water up to the 100 ml mark.

Students who miss a magician problem have done 90 percent of the work but have failed to complete the problem. The results of this error may be minor if partial credit is given or disastrous if it is not.

To minimize such errors, underline the specific question asked in the problem statement. When you have finished using the required algorithm, go back and check to see if the underlined question has been answered. Put check marks by your underlined question to note that it has been checked. When possible, verbalize your checking process out loud.

Many magician problems are not intended as such. Your instructor may simply be trying to show you that the processes you have learned have useful applications.

Red Herrings and Other Foul Fish

STUDENT: I thought I was supposed to use this algorithm, but it turned out to be the wrong one.

The problem statement for this type of question uses cue words or labels for one generic problem but the problem cannot be solved using that algorithm. For example:

> 81.65 grams of substance X reacts with 0.756 moles of substance Y according to the equation:
>
> $$X + 2Y \rightarrow Z$$
>
> What is the gram molecular weight of substance X?

You may have learned to find gram molecular weights when given the formula of the substance (by adding up the atomic weights of all atoms in the molecule). Since you are not given the formula of the substance, you cannot use this algorithm.

The correct solution to this problem depends on your knowledge of the concept of gram molecular weight, that is, the weight in grams of one mole of the substance, or grams per mole. You are given a gram weight of X (81.65 g) and can find how many moles of X this is:

$$0.756 \text{ mole } Y \times \frac{1 \text{ mole } X}{2 \text{ mole } Y} = 0.378 \text{ mole } X$$

$$\frac{81.56 \text{g } X}{0.378 \text{ mole } X} = 216 \text{ g/mole}$$

Divide grams X by moles X to obtain the molecular weight (grams per mole).

Problems that point you at the wrong algorithm can be some of the most difficult ones to solve. If you select an algorithm for a problem, but the starting information cannot be found, suspect that you are on the wrong track. Review the algorithms that might apply to similar situations. Which algorithms are related to the one you initially chose? If nothing clicks, perhaps there is no algorithm for this problem. If this is the case, go to the desired quantity (gram molecular weight in this example) and review what you know about that concept (e.g., what the term means). For these nonalgorithmic problems, use the checklist in Figure 11–1, page 253, for help in attacking the problem.

Hidden Questions

STUDENT: I couldn't figure out what they were asking me to do.

Hidden questions are those in which the final goal of the problem is unclear. For example:

> What part of the weight of calcium carbonate, $CaCO_3$, is due to oxygen?

This problem is related to the generic problem that asks: What is the weight percent of oxygen in calcium carbonate? (That is, given the chemical formula, find the weight percent of an element.)

If you do not know the meaning of chemical words, you will be unable to answer questions in which the meaning of a word is substituted for the word itself ("What part of the weight" is equivalent to "find the weight percent.") Such errors are concept errors. Strengthen your control of chemical language to overcome this barrier.

Hidden questions also occur when a new application of an algorithm is introduced.

> How many unpaired electrons are there in Mn^{2+}?

To solve this problem you must draw the orbital diagram and count the number of unpaired electrons shown by the diagram:

You may be prepared to work a problem that asks you to draw the orbital diagram of Mn^{2+}, but may never have noticed that whenever you draw the orbital diagram, you can count the number of unpaired electrons in the orbitals.

Your best hope for working such problems is to have been taught many of the applications for generic problems. If you are not taught applications yet are expected to answer application questions, form the habit of asking your instructor: "What can I use this process to find?" When confronted by a hidden question on an exam, cycle through your mental list of algorithms and try to link one with the hard problem.

Yellow-Brick-Road Problems

STUDENT: My answer came out exactly opposite to what it should have.

You may be confronted with a problem such as this:

> Compound A has a vapor pressure at 25°C of 15.8 Torr, whereas compound B has a vapor pressure of 28.9 Torr. Which is most likely a gas at 50°C?

The solution to this problem involves two rules: If a compound has the highest vapor pressure, then it has the lowest boiling point. If it has the lowest boiling point, it is most likely to be a gas at room temperature. So compound B is most likely the gas.

Notice that the two rules are applied in sequence. The conclusion to the first "if–then" statement is used as the starting "if" for the second rule. In essence, such questions ask you to make new rules by combining old ones. Errors arise not only when such rules (and their underlying concepts) are poorly understood, but also when you try to work such problems in your head. Write out all reasoning for such problems. Diagrams might also be useful, for example:

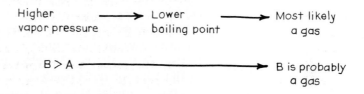

Eeny, Meeny, Miny, Mo Problems

STUDENT: Well, I knew it was a (generic) problem, but I couldn't decide what version of the formula to use.

In these problems, you must use the information given in the problem to choose among alternative versions of a math formula. For example, there are over a dozen versions of the ideal gas law ($PV = nRT$), each of which is used in different circumstances:

If a sample of an ideal gas has its pressure doubled and its absolute temperature tripled, what happens to its volume?

Here is the solution:

$$P_1 = P_1$$
$$V_1 = V_1$$
$$T_1 = T_1$$
$$P_2 = 2P_1$$
$$V_2 = ?$$
$$T_2 = 3T_1$$

$$\frac{P_1 V_1}{T_1} = \frac{P_2 V_2}{T_2}$$

$$V_2 = \frac{P_1 V_1}{T_1} \times \frac{T_2}{P_2} = \frac{P_1 V_1}{T_1} \times \frac{3T_1}{2P_1} = \frac{3}{2} V_1$$

Therefore, the final volume is 3/2 times the initial volume.

Consider another example:

If a sample of an ideal gas has its pressure doubled, what happens to its volume?

Note the differences in the solution:

$$T = \text{constant}$$
$$P_1 = P_1$$
$$V_1 = V_1 \qquad P_1 V_1 = P_2 V_2$$
$$P_2 = 2P_1 \qquad V_2 = \frac{P_1 V_1}{P_2} = \frac{P_1 V_1}{2P_1} = \tfrac{1}{2} V_1$$
$$V_2 = ?$$

Therefore, the final volume is half the initial volume.

The second example does not mention the temperature of the gas; you must assume that temperature is constant and will not affect the volume.

You prepare to solve such problems by learning exactly what each formula variation accomplishes and when each formula or process is to be used. Verbalizing the differences may help make you more sensitive to the type of data needed for use of each version. For example, the gas-law formulas above are used whenever the same gas sample is subjected to two sets of conditions. Practice making up problems for each version of the formula. When you work problems in areas that contain confusing formula alternatives, be especially careful in your use of the algorithm for mathematical formulas (see page 223).

"Play It Again, Sam" Problems

STUDENT: I knew what formula to use, but it seemed that the same information was given more than once.

Here is an example:

> A 25 gram block of metal requires 92 joules to raise its temperature by 1.5 Celsius degrees. How many joules would be required to raise the temperature of a 45 gram piece of that same metal by 15 Celsius degrees?

The formula needed is:

$$q = \text{specific heat} \times m \times \Delta T$$

Use the formula once with the first set of conditions ($q = 92$ J; $m = 25$ g; $\Delta T = 1.5°C$) to calculate the specific heat. Then use that value of specific heat in a second calculation with the same formula to calculate the missing quantity, q.

1st formula use: To calculate the specific heat for the metal from the first set of data:

$$q = 92 \text{ J} \qquad \text{specific heat} = \frac{q}{m \Delta T}$$
$$\text{specific heat} = ?$$
$$m = 25\text{g}$$
$$\Delta T = 15°C \qquad\qquad = \frac{92 \text{ J}}{(25\text{g})(1.5°C)} = 2.5 \text{ J/g}°C$$

2nd formula use: To use the value of specific heat calculated above with the second set of data to find q:

$$q = ?$$
specific heat = 2.5 J/g°C
$$m = 45\,g$$
$$\Delta T = 15°C$$

$$q = \text{specific heat} \times m \times \Delta T$$
$$= 2.5\,\frac{J}{g°C} \times 45g \times 15°C$$
$$= 1.7 \times 10^2\,J$$

When it seems that the same information is given more than once in a problem, suspect that you are dealing with two different situations involving the same substance. Use diagrams, pictures, lists of variables, and so on to distinguish one physical situation from another. Identify which aspects of the situation change and which remain constant. (Properties such as density, specific heat, and atomic weight are characteristic of a substance and do not change as the size of the sample changes.)

"What's in a Name" Problems

STUDENT: We were taught so many ways to do that. I just couldn't decide which process to use.

Each algorithm in a set may accomplish the same purpose but consist of totally different steps. Each algorithm may only be used with a specific class of chemical. If you use the wrong algorithm with a specific chemical, you calculate an erroneous answer. Consider these examples:

What is the pH of 0.1 M HCl?

What is the pH of 0.1 M HClO?

What is the pH of 0.1 M NaCl?

What is the pH of 0.1 M NaOH?

Each of the above problems has a different solution process. To select the correct algorithm, you must classify the chemical into its appropriate category (strong acid, weak acid, neutral salt, strong base, etc.) and use the algorithm that is appropriate for that type of substance.

Here is another example:

Complete the following equations:

Here again, the products of the reactions in organic chemistry depend on the classification of the reactants. Br_2 gives different products when reacted with an alkene (first equation) or an alkane (second equation).

Topics are taught in a linear fashion in chemistry lectures. For example, during one week, the reaction of bromine with alkanes is described, and you learn to write those equations. Later you learn to write equations for the reaction of bromine with alkenes. Now you have two processes that must be distinguished, each applying to a different class of compound. It is up to you to recognize that now you must classify the substance that is reacting with bromine to determine which algorithm to use.

Problems at the end of text chapters relate to material taught in that chapter. Only when you confront problems from multiple chapters in scrambled order do you see the necessity of classifying substances to identify the type of solution required. Working exams given in previous terms is one good way to practice this skill.

Hidden-Information Problems

STUDENT: I knew what type of problem this was. But there was a piece of information missing so I couldn't solve it.

In this common type of hard problem, a piece (or pieces) of information needed for the algorithm will not be directly stated but must be derived or inferred from other information in the problem. For example:

> The vapor pressure of water at 25°C is 23.8 Torr. What is its heat of vaporization?

This problem is solved by use of the equation:

$$P_1 = 23.8 \text{ Torr}$$
$$T_1 = 25°C$$
$$\Delta H = ?$$
$$R = 8.31 \text{ J/K-mol}$$
$$\left.\begin{array}{l} P_2 = ? \\ T_2 = ? \end{array}\right\} \text{MISSING}$$

$$\log\left(\frac{P_2}{P_1}\right) = \frac{\Delta H_{vap}}{2.30\,R}\left(\frac{T_2 - T_1}{T_2 T_1}\right)$$

Two sets of vapor pressure–temperature data are needed; only one is given in the problem (23.8 Torr at 25°C). The second set must be generated by the student from knowledge of the normal boiling point of water. Normal boiling points are temperatures at which the vapor pressure is equal to 760 Torr. For water, the substance in the problem, the normal boiling point is 100°C. The second set of values is then: 760 Torr at 100°C.

When confronting problems of this type, identify as clearly as you can what information is *missing* in the problem. Search your memory for alternative ways to obtain that information. Recall that in Chapter Nine we recommended the use of *formula summary sheets* (see page 185) to identify clearly the properties used in each mathematical formula. We then suggested that you determine the alternative ways of obtaining the value of each property. That suggestion was to aid you in solving hidden-information problems.

Deadly Duos

STUDENT: I couldn't match up the given information with what they wanted me to find.

These questions are combinations of generic problems in which the information given relates to one algorithm and the information desired relates to a different algorithm. For example:

> Is SO_3 a polar molecule? Show how you determined your answer.

You are asked to determine polarity of a specific substance. To determine polarity, you must know the geometry of the molecule. To know the geometry, you must first determine the Lewis dot structure of the molecule. The Lewis dot structure may be obtained from the formula. Thus:

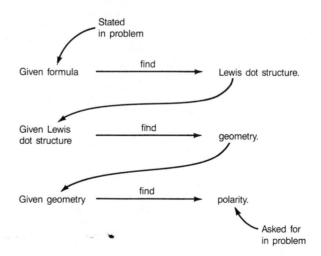

When you cannot match up the given and wanted information in a single algorithm, start by identifying what information you can obtain from the given information and what types of information can be used to obtain the quantity asked for in the problem. You are looking to find a common piece or pieces of information that will link the various algorithms together. This is why it is important that you identify the starting information and the goal of each generic problem that you are taught (see page 213).

Kitchen-Sink Problems

STUDENT: There was so much information that I couldn't even find the question, let alone the answer.

Here's an example of a kitchen-sink problem:

> When aspirin is produced commercially from salicylic acid, the raw product must undergo many purification steps before it is able to be used medicinally. This is because the product is contaminated with many by-products, and incomplete reactions often take place during manufacturing.
>
> The final step in the production of aspirin is the reaction:
>
> $$C_7H_6O_3 + C_4H_6O_3 \rightarrow C_9H_8O_4 + C_2H_4O_2$$
>
> salicylic acid   acetic anhydride   aspirin   acetic acid
>
> MW = 138   MW = 102   MW = 180   MW = 60.1
>
> A chemist reacted 25.0 grams of salicylic acid with 20.0 g of acetic anhydride and obtained 19.0 grams of aspirin. What was the percent yield from this reaction?

This is a limiting reagent and percent-yield problem. All the information that precedes the equation may be interesting, but it is not needed to solve the problem.

The extraneous information in this and similar problems is sometimes added to give a relevant context to the problem (as above) or to obscure the algorithm that is needed for solution of the problem. The extra information may be qualitative (i.e., words and ideas only) or quantitative (numerical information such as values of densities, melting points, temperatures). Kitchen-sink problems resemble problems in the real world. When you try to solve a real problem (as opposed to a classroom problem), you usually have more information available than will be needed for the solution. Thus, learning to reject irrelevant information is a useful skill.

Note in your own course how many problems contain extraneous information. Identify the information wanted and link it with the given information that can get you to the solution. If you find the extra information bothersome, lightly cross it out with your pencil. Don't black out the information so completely that you will not be able to read it if you should later find you need it.

Semantic Tangles

STUDENT: I kept getting lost in the question; it made no sense.

In these problems the language of the problem statement is unnecessarily convoluted (e.g., with multiple embedded subordinate clauses, multiple reversals, or negations). For example:

> Which of the following is incorrect?
>
> a. If dissolving a solid in water is exothermic, increasing the temperature reduces the solubility of the solid from that of its previous level.
> b. The solubility of a gas in the solvent depends on the partial pressure of that gas and not on the total pressure of all the gases above the solvent.
> c. The lowering of the vapor pressure of a solvent in a solution is given by the formula $VPL = X_2P_1°$, where VPL is the vapor pressure lowering, X_2 is the mole fraction of the solute, and $P_1°$ is the vapor pressure of the pure solvent.
> d. If a liquid is in equilibrium with its vapor at a certain temperature, the vapor pressure is independent of both the quantity of liquid in the container and the surface area of the liquid.

Some questions may introduce new concepts, vocabulary, or symbolism and expect you to operate immediately on them. Such questions are very difficult. Weaknesses in your understanding of chemical language will interfere with your ability to solve such problems successfully.

To untangle complex language, try to rephrase each part of the question. Make several short sentences out of a long one. Underline key verbs and important words like *not, incorrect, lesser than,* and so forth.

If "semantic tangles" seem to be harder for you than for most others in your class, your reading skills may need improvement. If there is a reading clinic on your campus, you might check to see what assistance is available.

Pie-in-the-Face Problems

STUDENT: Help!!!!!!

These are extremely complex problems, with multiple combinations of the previous difficulties. Essentially, you have to process so much information simultaneously that your short-term memory overloads and everything becomes hopelessly confused. For example:

> Given the following information about water:
>
> average specific heat of ice: 2.01 J/g-°C
>
> heat of fusion at 0°C: 6.02 kJ/mol
>
> average specific heat of liquid water: 4.18 J/g-°C
>
> average density of ice: 0.917 g/cm^3
>
> average density of liquid water: 0.998 g/cm^3

Suppose you have made some ice cubes in the freezer of your refrigerator. Each ice cube is 2 inches by 1 inch by 1 inch. Now suppose you take three of these ice cubes from the freezer (which is at a temperature of −4.0°C) and add them to 8 ounces of liquid water (which is at a temperature of 40.0°C). If the glass containing the water is insulated so that heat cannot be transferred into or out of the glass, what will be the final temperature of the contents of the glass?

Fortunately, these problems are more commonly found in problem assignments than on tests. No matter where they are found, however, they can be extremely frustrating and time consuming.

When confronting a pie-in-the-face problem, chip away at it. See if you can identify what the final calculation must be (i.e., what generic problem gives you the final answer). In the above example the ultimate calculation is the final temperature of a system in which one part of the system is losing heat and the other gaining heat. The liquid water will lose heat when the ice is put into it. The ice cubes will increase their temperature, then melt (completely or partially). If completely melted, the liquid water that results will then rise to the final temperature.

Identifying the final steps in the solution gives you clues as to what information you may need to calculate. Look back in the problem for some data that will give you the needed information. In this example, you will need to find the heat gained by melting the ice cubes. To find that, you will need to find the grams of ice. To find that, you will need to calculate the volume of the ice cubes and use the density to find the mass of ice.

In some problems you might start by looking at the data given and deciding what use you can make of it. For example, the volume and density of the ice cubes can be used to obtain the mass of ice. Then rephrase the question using the mass of ice in place of the density and volume.

GENERAL PROBLEM-SOLVING APPROACHES

In this section we outline general problem-solving strategies that are useful whenever you are solving chemistry problems. These have been suggested by our students, our chemistry colleagues, and those who study problem solving for a living.

Ask Constructive Questions About Hard Problems

In spite of the tips for solving hard problems that have been given in this chapter, you probably still will get stuck on some chemistry problems. When this happens, use the checklist in Figure 11–1 to gain a better understanding of the problem and find clues to its solution. Many of the questions in the checklist help you to redescribe the problem in a more meaningful way.

1. Are there words you don't know? Find out what they mean.

2. Would a drawing or diagram help? How about models?

3. Can you "tell someone" the problem in your own words?

4. Can you underline the key elements in the problem statement?

5. What questions do you ask yourself in this type of problem?

6. Can you make it look more like a generic problem you know how to do?

7. Try acting out the problem. (Sound bizarre? It can work!)

8. Describe a motion picture sequence for the problem. (This can be helpful for problems involving chemical reactions that occur over time.)

9. What will your answer look like? What will its units be?

10. Guess an answer and test your guess in the problem.

11. How large (or small) do you expect the answer to be?

12. Is there something you need to look up?

13. Should you organize a list? How about a table?

14. Can you use a set of "nicer" numbers (i.e., ones that enable you to work the problem in your head) as a clue to the solution process?

This list was adapted from one presented by Professor Billie Sparks at the First Governor's Conference on Basic Skills, Madison, Wisconsin, December 15, 1981.

FIGURE 11–1 *Checklist for understanding hard problems*

Relate Your Problem to Generic Problems and Their Common Variations

We recommended in Chapter Ten that you be aware of the generic problems for which you are responsible. Now you can add to your mental catalog common variations on generic problems such as the ones we have described in this chapter. As you solve harder problems on homework assignments, note how those problems differ from the generic versions. You may be surprised at how often similar variations show up on exams.

Solve Problems Qualitatively First

When you first read a problem, do not begin quickly writing down the first formula or process that comes into your head. Instead, reason through how you will go about solving the problem. Figure out your general approach, without using numbers or specific chemicals from the problem. Such a qualitative solution will resemble the generalized algorithms you have developed for generic problems (see page 210). If you cannot immediately plan the entire solution, make a guess as to where to start. Use the checklist in Figure 11–1 to select some activities that can start you on the solution path.

Follow Processes Systematically

In Chapter Ten we emphasized the need for a systematic approach to solving generic problems. That is, you minimize errors by following the algorithm faithfully and carefully. Since hard problems often require many of the same actions as generic problems, the same advice holds. For example, take the time to write out what you are looking for, what is given, the formula needed, and the values for each constant and variable. Do not skip algebraic steps. Do not do algebra and computations simultaneously. Write legibly. Restate problems when you have a partial solution. Work on paper, reasoning out loud (if possible) as you go. Putting work on paper, rather than carrying out operations or reasoning in your head, allows you to catch and correct errors.

Summarize the Solution After You Are Finished

When working problem assignments involving hard problems, it is important to go back and summarize each problem as you complete it. You should feel free to leave out the specific numbers and trivial details but include each major decision and operation step. Identify the clues that led you to the solution. Produce a smooth flow of generalized steps that led to the final correct answer. It is not the answer to the problem that is important. It is the *process* you went through to get the answer that will help you solve similar problems in the future.

Seek Help When You Are Stuck

You need not solve every problem by yourself (except on exams, of course). When working hard problem assignments, be realistic about how much time you can afford to spend on any one problem. As a rough guideline, if you cannot solve a problem in 30 minutes, you are probably missing some vital piece of information that prevents you from reaching the final solution. Spending additional time on the problem will probably not be worthwhile. Get help on that problem from an instructor, classmate, tutorial service—anywhere you can. When you find the answer, assess your error. Was it a missing fact, rule, or concept? Was an algorithm incomplete or in error? How were you supposed to have learned the missing material? Where was that information to be found? Work on improving your information-gathering or -processing skills. Then try some more problems.

Work Slowly

This may seem like strange advice, particularly if you have had the experience of running out of time on a chemistry exam. But you need to work slowly enough to work accurately. Read each problem carefully. Make sure you understand what you are expected to do and what information is given in the problem. You get no credit for answering a question that was not asked.

Question Assumptions

Here is a problem for you:

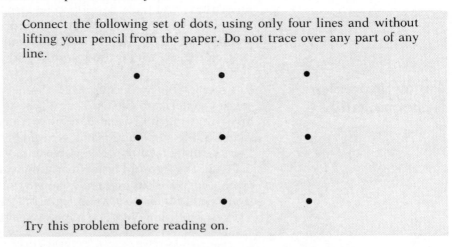

Connect the following set of dots, using only four lines and without lifting your pencil from the paper. Do not trace over any part of any line.

Try this problem before reading on.

The problem is impossible to solve if you assume that all lines must stay within the space outlined by the dots. It is solvable if you allow your lines to go outside of the dots. Try the problem again before checking the solution at the end of the chapter. The moral is: Question your assumptions when you encounter a seemingly unsolvable problem. Such advice is easy to give but, unfortunately, hard to follow.

We have encouraged you to draw analogies between hard problems and generic problems. All generic problems contain some assumptions, some of which you may hardly be aware of. But some hard problems will require you to modify or even discard these old, familiar solutions and to produce unique ones. Some feature of a new problem may be so different that one or more of the usual approaches must also change. Some hidden assumption in your original problem may prevent you from seeing what changes must be made. We hope you will meet such problems in classroom discussions or homework assignments before meeting them on exams.

Relate Ideas from Different Topics

Recall that you should work problem assignments only after having mastered the facts, concepts, rules, and generic problems for that topic. You may need to combine this information with information from other topics that were taught earlier in order to solve a particular problem. For example, hard problems that require two or more algorithms for their solutions often take those algorithms from different topic areas. Thus, you might have to combine a stoichiometry algorithm and a gas law algorithm in order to solve a specific gas law problem. Your instructors will rarely tell you when or how to do this. However, textbook problems at the back of chapters often include a reasonable number of these. Note how topics are integrated as you work assigned problems from your text.

Write Some Problems

Nothing demonstrates your mastery of a topic like the ability to write a solvable problem in that area. When you study with other students, see if you can solve their made-up problems and vice versa. Write both generic and hard problems, following the models shown in this chapter.

Cultivate Positive Problem-Solving Attitudes

More than skills are needed for successful problem solving. If you cultivate the following constructive attitudes, your chances of success will improve.

Believe You Can Learn to Solve Problems

The information load in chemistry courses is high; some of the problems will be very difficult. Still, with a good knowledge base, an understanding of how problems can be made more difficult, and some good problem-attack skills, you can eventually learn to solve many of them. But you must be convinced that this is possible so that you are willing to make the effort to learn. If you don't try, you won't learn.

Take the Risk of Being Wrong

Suppose you are taking an exam and encounter a problem that you aren't sure how to solve. Should you leave it blank? No way! Suppose you guess at an answer and it turns out to be totally wrong. You have not lost anything by trying.

Some students fear that their instructor will laugh at their answers, particularly if they are totally wrong. Moreover, they cannot imagine that their chemistry instructor ever wrote an answer that had nothing whatsoever to do with the question that was asked. In truth, no responsible teacher belittles a student's efforts, and yes, every chemist has been wrong many times. We survived our goofs, and so will you. When you risk being wrong, you may be surprised at how often you turn out to be right.

Be Willing to Give Up Unproductive Approaches

Don't insist that every problem must be related to a generic problem. If you try to draw the analogy between a hard problem and a generic problem but are unable to do so, start over and assume that you must construct a totally new solution. You may find that taking a break from the problem helps by letting you forget some of those unproductive paths. The willingness to try something new is a prerequisite for dealing with novel problems.

Value Partial Solutions

Some chemistry courses require advanced problem-solving skills from the very beginning of the course. If your skills are initially weak, it will take time to improve them. Thus, you may find that you can only partially solve some of the harder problems. Be realistic about your skills and value those partial solutions. Keep working for partial credit; it adds up.

One final note: If you feel that your problem-solving skills are somewhat weak and need improvement, here are two self-help books that you can try:

Arthur Whimbey and Jack Lochhead, *Problem Solving and Comprehension: A Short Course in Analytical Reasoning*, 5th Ed. (Philadelphia: Franklin Press, 1991). This book teaches skills for verbal and mathematical problems.

G. Polya, *How to Solve It*, 2nd ed. (G. Polya, Princeton, N.J.: Princeton University Press, 1973). This is a classic, stressing mathematical problem-solving techniques.

SUMMARY

In this chapter we have defined hard problems as those that:

· Combine two or more concepts, rules, or generic problems
· Extend information into new contexts

- Alter the usual steps in an algorithm
- Use complex language in the problem statement
- Contain combinations of these difficulties

We described 12 common types of hard problems, gave examples of each, and presented some strategies for coping with each. These harder problems are listed below:

Magician	What's in a Name
Red Herring	Hidden Information
Hidden Question	Deadly Duo
Yellow Brick Road	Kitchen Sink
Eeny, Meeny, Miny, Mo	Semantic Tangle
Play It Again, Sam	Pie in the Face

The following general approaches will help you develop effective problem-solving techniques:

- Ask constructive questions about problems. (Use the checklist in Figure 11–1.)
- Relate your problem to generic problems and their common variations.
- Solve problems qualitatively first.
- Follow processes systematically.
- Summarize the solution when you are finished.
- Seek help when you are stuck.
- Work slowly to maintain accuracy.
- Question assumptions.
- Relate ideas from different topics.
- Write some problems.
- Cultivate positive problem-solving attitudes. Believe you can learn to solve problems, take the risk of being wrong, and be willing to give up unproductive approaches.
- Value partial solutions.

SELF-ASSESSMENT

1. The relative number of hard problems I am expected to solve in my chemistry course is:

VERY ————————————————————————————— VERY
FEW   MANY

Hard problems can take up a large proportion of your study time in chemistry. To help you judge how much time you need to spend studying chemistry, you need to assess whether hard problems are an important part of your course.

2. My assigned problems are harder than my test problems.

MUCH ———————————————————————————————— NOT AS
HARDER   HARD

If the answer is "much harder," you should decide how much time and energy you should be spending working the very hardest assigned problems (especially if you are pressed for time).

3. My assigned problems are easier than my test problems.

MUCH ———————————————————————————————— NOT AS
EASIER   EASY

You learn to solve hard problems by working hard problems, using the techniques suggested in this chapter. If your test problems are not as easy as the practice problems, you will need to generate some more difficult chemistry problems on which to practice. Ask your instructor for help in finding more appropriate practice problems.

4. I can recognize some of my hard problems as being members of the Dirty Dozen.

TRUE ———————————————————————————————— NOT TRUE

Can you recognize the Dirty Dozen among your homework or test problems? If so, select the two or three you are weakest in solving. Review the techniques we have suggested for solving them. Plan some specific actions to work toward improved control over those problems.

TYPE OF PROBLEM

MY PLAN FOR IMPROVEMENT

TYPE OF PROBLEM

MY PLAN FOR IMPROVEMENT

TYPE OF PROBLEM

MY PLAN FOR IMPROVEMENT

5. Overall, I am pleased with my ability to handle hard chemistry problems.

THANKFULLY, ———————————————————————— UNHAPPILY,
YES   NO

If you are not totally satisfied with your problem-solving ability, make some specific plans to improve your skills (see page 252, General Problem-Solving Approaches). Write below some specific plans to improve your problem-solving strategies:

MY PLANS

ANSWER TO PROBLEM

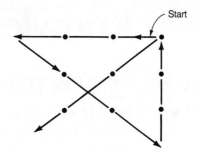

APPENDIX

Basic Chemical and Mathematical Knowledge

MATHEMATICAL PREPARATION FOR CHEMISTRY

Your chemistry instructor will probably assume that you have already learned the following mathematical processes prior to enrolling in the course:

- How to add, subtract, multiply, and divide (with and without a calculator)
- What a fraction means; what a unit fraction means
- How to work with fractions
- What a decimal means
- How to express numbers in scientific notation
- How to convert numbers written in decimal to scientific notation
- What percent means
- How to use percents
- How to solve simple linear equations
- What ratio and proportion mean

If your math skills are weak, ask your instructor for suggestions on improving your math to reach the level that is required in your course. We have also found the following book helpful to students who need to review their basic mathematics:

Edward I. Peters, *Chemical Skills* (New York: McGraw-Hill, 1983).

260

BASIC SCIENCE CONCEPTS

You have studied science in middle school and high school. Your instructor will expect you to know some science concepts when you enter your chemistry class for the first time. The following are examples of the information that you might be expected to have. Fill in the missing information to check your basic science knowledge. Answers will be found at the end of the quiz.

Basic Science Quiz

Properties of Matter

Real objects have multiple properties, including:

mass (weight)   volume
area   color
cost   length

Can you add some others? _____

_____

_____

Measurements

Measuring a property of something requires that people agree on a unit of measurement. For example, I can measure the length of a line using the unit measure of inches:

|———————————————|———————————————|———————————————|
←— 1 in. —→ ←— 1 in. —→ ←— 1 in. —→
|————————————————————— 3 in. —————————————————————|

This line is 3 inches long.

More than one measurement unit may be used for a property. The larger the unit, the fewer the number of units needed for a given measurement. For example:

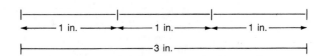

1 quart + 1 quart + 1 quart + 1 quart = 1 gallon

_____ quarts = _____ gallon

Fill in the blanks on the following table of equal measurements:

Equal Measures		Property Measured
_____ quart	= _____ gallon	_____
_____ cups	= _____ quart	_____
_____ inches	= _____ feet	_____
_____ feet	= _____ yard	_____
_____ ounces	= _____ pound	_____
_____ square inches	= _____ square feet	_____
_____ cubic inches	= _____ cubic feet	_____

Volume

1. Volume is the space taken up by something. The volume of a liquid does not change when you pour it into a different-shaped container:

Mark the approximate level of the liquid in the new container.

2. The volume of a cube is found by _____

_____.

Solutions

True or false? When you dissolve a small amount of salt in a glass of water, the salt concentrates at the bottom of the glass.

Electricity

1. True or false? A positive electrical charge will repel any other positive charge; however, negative charges attract one another.

2. True or false? When we say an object is electrically neutral, we mean that it does not have any positive or negative charges.

Density

True or false? An object that is more dense than water will float in water.

Heat and Temperature

1. True or false? Heat and temperature are different names for the same thing.

2. True or false? The direction of spontaneous heat flow is always from hot to cold.

Energy

True or false? Water always runs downhill, to get to the position of lowest energy. Likewise, all chemical and physical systems tend to go to the lowest possible energy levels.

Basic Science Quiz Answers

Properties of Matter

Other properties include boiling points, melting points, densities, temperature, and so on. Note that some of these properties can help to identify the substance involved in the measurements (i.e., if a substance boils at 100°C and has a density of 1.0 g/cm³ at 4°C, that substance is probably water). Such properties stay constant no matter what size sample of the substance is taken. A large quantity of water boils at the same temperature as a small quantity of water. Other properties vary with the size of the sample (i.e., one sample of water may weigh 15 grams while another sample of water might weigh 30 grams).

Measurements

Equal Measures				Property Measured
4	quarts	=	1 gallon	volume
4	cups	=	1 quart	volume
12	inches	=	1 foot	length
3	feet	=	1 yard	length
16	ounces	=	1 pound	weight
144	in.²	=	1 ft²	area
1722	in.³	=	1 ft³	volume

Volume

1. The level of liquid in the short, wide container would be lower than that in the taller one. But the amount of liquid in both containers is the same.

2. The volume of a cube is found by multiplying the length by the width by the height. Note that there are two different ways of measuring volume: (1) using container measurements such as quarts, gallons, and liters and (2) cubing container lengths.

Solutions

The statement is false. When you make a solution by dissolving one substance in another, the materials mix at the molecular level, and the composition of the mixture is the same throughout the solution.

Electricity

1. The statement is false. Positive charges repel one another and so do negative charges. However, negative and positive charges are attracted to one another.

2. The statement is partially true. If an object has no positive or negative charges, it will be electrically neutral. However, an object that has an equal number of both positive and negative charges will also be described as neutral. Thus, atoms that contain the same number of positive charges (protons) as negative charges (electrons) are neutral.

Density

The statement is false. If an object is *less* dense than water it will float in water.

Heat and Temperature

1. The statement is false. Heat is an amount of energy. Temperature describes the amount of heat contained in an object, considering how much of the substance is present. Heat is measured in energy units (e.g., calories, joules, ergs); temperature is measured in degrees Fahrenheit (°F), degrees Celsius (°C), or Kelvins (K).

Energy

The statement is true.

Be alert for hidden assumptions about how the world works that are not taught in your course but that are assumed to be part of your basic knowledge!

You must determine for yourself if your science background is seriously weaker than that of other students in your class. If you suspect that it is, ask your instructor to recommend a book that will improve your background. Alternatively, check for a basic physical science text at your local high school or public library.

Learning Skill Index

Chemical Content Index

About the Authors

Dr. Elizabeth Kean is associate professor of science education and multicultural education, and the director of the Center for Science, Mathematics and Computer Education at the University of Nebraska-Lincoln. She has led educational reform in the science classroom both in the public schools and at the college level. She has also co-authored educational software in chemistry and is involved in curriculum development and faculty training at several universities. She received a Bachelor of Science from Ohio University and a Ph.D. in chemistry and a Masters degree in curriculum and instruction from the University of Wisconsin-Madison.

Dr. Catherine Middlecamp is the director of the Chemistry Learning Center at the University of Wisconsin-Madison. She trains and supervises staff to work with academically and culturally diverse students, and works directly with students as well. She also teaches a graduate seminar on the teaching of chemistry and is a co-author of CHEMPROF, an artificial intelligence-based computer tutor for general chemistry. She received a Bachelor of Arts degree from Cornell University, a Ph.D. in chemistry and a M.S. in counseling from the University of Wisconsin-Madison.